Grace to Endure

Blindness and Brokeness

Marolyn Ford

Foreword

When Marolyn fell in the tub and broke her back, it was as though God spoke to me and said, "There will be rough days ahead. She's broken and you will have to take care of her. Through her brokenness, I will be glorified more than when her blind eyes were opened." However, I had no idea what that meant. Shortly after the fall, Marolyn's digestive system and bladder began giving her serious problems. When she became malnutritioned and dehydrated I visualized her being carried like a baby in the arms of Jesus.

Marolyn has tremendous difficulty just making it through the turmoil of the nights. She has an abnormal shortness of breath while sleeping. This give me great concern because it places her in great distress. Not a night goes by that I do not feel something may go wrong. I cannot understand how she goes on living with her entire digestive system not working. These are major body parts.

At times Marolyn lacks the ability to bring to mind certain words, and to focus her short term memory. Her weakness is like having the worst kind of flu. At times, she feels like she is in a fog and just wants to roll over and bury her face in the pillow. She loses focus on what is happening around her. Her body is too weak and her mind is too tired to keep up with what day of the week it is, or schedules and events. In spite of this, her intellect and photographic memory are unbelievable.

When I see Marolyn I see an angel of God. I cannot believe she is alive. To me she is more in heaven than on earth. She is a miracle! It is truly through God that we move, live and have our being. Marolyn has taken the opportunity to write about her past while extremely uncertain about her future. I always felt like she belonged more to God than she belonged to me. I love her deeply. I will gladly take care of her.

Grace to Endure

We exchanged our wedding vows in August, 1962, "For better, for worse, in sickness and in health". As Marolyn's husband and caregiver I must say, "She makes it a joy to care for her rather than a burden." I can truly say that God is being more glorified now by giving her "Grace To Endure" than when He opened her blind eyes.

Acie Ford

Acknowledgements

Grace To Endure would never have been accomplished had it not been for the strong encouragement of my husband, Acie, who has been such a sweet love and support through the hard labor it took for me to do the work during months when he truly felt I would not survive life much longer, let alone the writing of this manuscript. Without Acie by my side with his understanding love, compassion and encouragement, I would not have made it this far with my illness nor with this manuscript.

Thanks to friends like Jim Green and Billie Cash who urged me on in this endeavor at a time when I was having trouble focusing my mind, and could barely recall information regarding sequence of events that transpired after the fall into the Jacuzzi tub. My strength had bottomed out and it was very difficult to zero in on the facts. Acie, Billie and Jim were determined I should write my story. Though my notes were rough and scattered, Jim graciously took the material I gave him on "Mini-cassette tapes" and placed them on a computer disk. I am so grateful he encouraged me to write down some things because I was able to capture the intimate details that otherwise would have been forgotten because I still have difficulty concentrating.

Upon finishing that rough copy, I had to lay the work down for several months before I could get into it again. While having much difficulty coping with my illness, friends inspired me and gave me an abundant supply of fresh enthusiasm and prayer support. I picked up my writing once again feeling strongly compelled by the Lord to press on.

I want to express my thanks from a heart of gratitude to Lila Wilkinson who offered to type and became my co-worker on this manuscript. She has a full time occupation and grandchildren, so we pulled in Sheila Masterson to help with the typing, Loyce Stelling made many trips to duplicate pages for us and Gail

Nichols pulled my story from my first publication, These Blind Eyes Now See and put that on a diskette; Jennifer Edwards, who scanned notes from my second publication, Walking and Talking with Jesus, and put that on a diskette.

Lila has worked endless hours with me rearranging sentences, restructuring paragraphs, spelling and editing. She was wonderful to catch the little things that needed touching up, things that may not have sounded just right, making suggestions and using her sensitive spirit of discernment. She is good and quick with her mind and hands, chasing after loose ends and helping me to finish the work on target

David Waters, the Religion Writer for The Commercial Appeal of Memphis has taken time out of his busy schedule to read and critique the manuscript before passing it on for publication. This was really great of him to be willing to give of his time.

Linda Brigance spent a day with Acie and me at Victory Valley Bible Conference Grounds and Shelby Farms snapping a photo to use on the back cover page. That was a fun, relaxing spring day filled with joy and excitement as we praised God together for all He has done to bring about the completion of Grace To Endure.

I feel honored to have had all these sweet loving wonderful friends at my side helping me complete a task that I could not have done alone. I am deeply grateful and give praise and adoration to my Lord Jesus Christ who gives me His grace to endure!

Bellevue

BAPTIST CHURCH

2000 APPLING ROAD
CORDOVA, TENNESSEE 38018

ADRIAN ROGERS
PASTOR

March 29, 1996

Mrs. Marilyn Ford
6083 Surrey Hollow Cove
Memphis, TN   38134

Dear Marilyn:

Thank you for your note and for the materials.

I feel that I will most likely use your story in my
book. The theme is believe in miracles but trust in
Jesus.

I carry you in my heart and prayers.

In Jesus' name,

Adrian Rogers

Adrian Rogers

lg

A Testimony From A Friend

In the early 1980's a friend gave me a cassette tape entitled, *These Blind Eyes Now See.* I was deeply touched by the testimony of God's miracle in Marolyn Ford's life and her sweet spirit of sharing how God works in her daily life. No matter how difficult the circumstances became, she used the phrase "God is so good" throughout her story. The words of praise remain embedded in my mind, "God is so good" in all circumstances. I asked God to allow me the opportunity to meet Marolyn and know more about her walk with Him. I purchased several books and tapes to share with others.

In 1989, my church issued a call to an Associate Minister. When the name, Acie Ford, was first presented I did not make the connection. As God led Acie and his family to Broadmoor Baptist Church, I soon realized God was answering my prayer! It has become my family's privilege to share experiences with Marolyn, Acie and Sharon through the years. We have the privilege of praying for and with them. Their lives speak of God's constant, abiding love. Their living faith and joyful attitude in the midst of trials is something only God can do.

For some time I have been impressed to help Marolyn with the ministry God has given her, but only recently I learned how that would happen. One Sunday morning while listening to Marolyn give testimony of God's continued miracles in her life, I knew my gift could be to help with her new manuscript. Yes, God is so good and He moves in various ways to show us His handiwork and to share His love!

Lila G. Wilkinson

"Marolyn Ford, a blind woman who sees, a woman who can't eat or drink but lives, seems able to summon hope from any hopeless situation because her source of hope is infinite."

David Waters
Religion Writer of
The Commercial Appeal of Memphis

"Marolyn Ford has been used of God to bless and strengthen my own life and the lives of our people here at Bellevue Baptist Church. She dramatically shared the power of our great and gracious God. I must confess my own eyes were filled with tears as I heard of her blinded eyes so wondrously healed."

Adrian Rogers, Pastor
Bellevue Baptist Church
Memphis, Tennessee

"Marolyn is a lady possessing unswerving faith in God despite unbelievable testing. This deep faith can only come from someone who truly has a close knowledge and experience with the Lord. "

Ministries That Matter
David Sainsbury, Pastor
United Kingdom
England

"It is an honor to recommend Marolyn Ford who has ministered with such distinction throughout South Africa. Knowing her wonderful testimony and some of the difficult physical trials, she has been subjected to, she has been an outstanding witness to the Grace of God. She has a real desire to share the gospel in the lives of men and women and has a unique ability of presenting her story that is so beautiful and yet so miraculous. I heartily recommend her books as well as having her come as a speaker. She is one who oozes the love of Christ. Together with her husband, Acie, they have a great testimony in the community and the local church.

The Directive Director of Multi-ministries
Harold Peasley, Pastor
Florida, South Africa

Author's Preface

Across the years of my journey with Jesus, He has taught me many lessons about the absolute importance of walking and talking with Him. Since I first trusted Him to be my personal Savior as a young girl, He has been at work in my life, developing a lifetime of companionship and fellowship.

I often recall the scripture concerning Enoch. *"Enoch walked with God; then he was no more, because God took him away."* Genesis 5:24 (NIV). Too, I am reminded of the tremendous fellowship Adam and Eve enjoyed with God as I read, *"Then the man and his wife heard the sound of the Lord God as He was walking in the garden in the cool of the day....."* Genesis 3:8a (NIV). This precious fellowship with the Lord, walking and talking with Him, has characterized His people down through the ages.

My purpose in this book, Grace To Endure, is to share experiences with you in the hope that you will join with me in Learning how to Lean on Jesus!

> Marolyn Ford
> Memphis, Tennessee

Table of Contents

Chapter I

The Dread Of Winter

It was in the middle of a cold winter snow blizzard December 9, 1940. The wind was so strong it would nearly blow one backwards. There was no indoor plumbing so all we had was the out-door house called "the privy."

Mom (Helena Brink) was pregnant with full term twins. Feeling an urgent need she pulled on her snow boots, threw a scarf around her neck, pulled on her gloves and coat and made her way outside. Meanwhile, Dad (Henry E. Brink) was sitting in the kitchen with a neighbor who had dropped in for a visit. They had a cup of hot coffee and a snack. The visitor said, "I believe I hear something. Did you hear something?" Dad had not heard anything so the visit continued.

Mom had gone to the out-house. The wind was howling, whipping around the corners and breezy as it circled inside the four walls of the privy. She sat on the hole in the board to relieve herself but to her surprise a baby came forth and my sister Carolyn was born. Wrapping the baby up in her coat, Mom struggled to make her way back to the house. The pressure of the wind against the outside door made it impossible for her to open. She laid her body against the door with her baby in her arms, pounding, calling, but the wind carried the sound of her voice away.

After a while the man visiting said, "Henry, I believe I hear somebody calling, I believe I hear your wife calling!" There were two doors, an outside storm door leading into an area where we removed our snow covered coats, scarves, gloves and boots. From there one could either go seven steps down into the basement or three steps up, open a door and enter the kitchen. It would not have been easy to have heard her calling.

They helped her inside and onto a bed. They called for a doctor on the "crank" telephone. The snow was deep and snow drifts had closed the roads. He hitched up his horse and sleigh but he was long delayed in reaching the farm. The men made mom comfortable and warm but there was another baby coming. Thirty minutes delayed but I made my grand entry as well.

"Carolyn" was the name brother Don wanted for his baby sister, Mom laid awake three nights thinking what to name the second baby. She wasn't expecting there would be two of us. She decided to change the "i" in Marilyn and make it an "o" such as is the name Carolyn - Carolyn Jean and Marolyn Jean. We looked so much alike no one could tell us apart. She put a bracelet on us so she wouldn't get our names mixed up.

Carolyn was born with a hole in her heart. It was very serious back then and she had to take medication in pill form. The doctor told mom not to let me get a hold of those pills - they would kill me if I swallowed one of them. Carolyn wasn't even to lift a fork from the table. It would be too strenuous for her, so we grew up protecting her until she was able to outgrow the heart problem around the age of thirteen. Even though she was told that she outgrew it, her doctor found it in adulthood and now he checks on it yearly. During our childhood years my concern was always for Carolyn. Would this heart murmur affect her during her child bearing years or could it become a problem later in life? It doesn't bother her, we just know it's there. As it turned out she didn't have any problem bearing children. She has a beautiful daughter and son.

At the time of our birth, no one could have imagined the struggles life held for me. I have had five pregnancies. My first pregnancy ended in miscarriage November 22, 1965. My second pregnancy was full term and our beautiful daughter, Sharon was born February 22, 1968. My third pregnancy miscarried February 19, 1969. I had thyroid problems and on April 11, 1969 the doctor had to remove three-fourths of a goiter. I miscarried again December 18, 1971 and the fifth was a ruptured tubule pregnancy February 14, 1975. I suffered with endometriosis for ten years which resulted in the need to have a hysterectomy November 23, 1975. We are blessed with one daughter and are so thankful God allowed us to keep one baby.

The doctor's blunt announcement in 1958 shattered my world. "You are blind! The damage in both eyes is permanent, there is no surgery or medication we can give you. Go home and learn to live with it." "Learn to live with it?" My heart and soul cried out. I was not prepared for the total blindness that progressively was coming upon me. Neither was I prepared for the critical set of circumstances that have enveloped my life beginning with an injury at the age of forty-nine in 1990 which made it impossible for me to eat or drink. My digestive system malfunctioned and I became so acutely malnourished I could no longer open doors, so dehydrated my lips stuck to my teeth. After five years of near constant care, my medical condition was getting worse. I was worn out with groaning like David in Psalms 6, *"All night long I flood my bed with weeping."*

Life On The Farm

There were seven of us children growing up together. Four boys were born first - Donald, Richard, Victor, and Roger. Then my identical twin, Carolyn and I were born, followed by our sister, Virginia five years later. We were reared in a Christian home. (When I say Christian home, I don't mean just the normal typical Christian home.) Dad got up at 5:00 a.m. and went out to call the cows home and get started with the chores. In the barn, he turned on the Christian radio station and started milking the cows. At 6:00 a.m. he came into the house for breakfast and awakened everyone in the household. When he turned on the Christian radio station we were not to change the radio dial.

We kids knew we had five minutes to get dressed and be seated at the breakfast table. He didn't want the food to get cold. Family devotions were held at each meal. Prayer was said before meals three times daily and never until all nine of us were around the table. We were taught to read the Bible and pray around the table. An entire chapter of the Bible was read after every meal and another prayer followed that. We children were all called upon to be the reader or to say the prayer, but Dad or Mom always prayed one of the prayers. We took turns until the day we married and learned to pray publicly by doing this. I believe the dominant factor in forming my faith during my younger years was this practice of my parents having family devotions. Though this time was short and to the point, each of us children learned the importance of the Word of God and prayer through our participation in reading and praying. The family altar can be a time to teach children to build the qualities of "Gold, silver and precious stones" into their lives. It teaches them to worship and honor the Lord as King of Kings; to depend upon the Lord for emotional, physical, spiritual and practical needs. It can also be a time for singing and praising the Lord.

In modern day we'd rather tell the kids to hurry and eat, your food has been blessed. We fail to teach our children that there's power in prayer. We forget to teach our children to reverence God. Besides this prayer and Bible reading before and after every meal we also had our own private individual devotions with God before bedtime. Whether we were in the house or working in the barn yard, God's music flooded the atmosphere. Without even realizing it, when you hear God's music, your heart and mind are lifted before the throne of God. You find yourself drawn to God and praying in your spirit. You can spend time listening to secular music, but it doesn't edify or build up your spirit. When you get in your car, or are at home, listen to Christian music. Everywhere we turned we heard music that taught us about God's love, grace, mercy, long-suffering, salvation and forgiveness.

Mother and Dad were wonderful parents. They loved us all deeply and equally. Mom was one of the most loving mothers in the world. She worked hard to have things nice for us. We always came first, often to the extent that she would do without things she needed or wanted. We never had the slightest question in our minds about her love for us. By her example of love and affection, along with firm discipline, she greatly influenced our development and love for each other.

Dad showed his love for us in little ways. Often when we would come in hot and sweaty from hoeing the garden or working all day in the hot blistering fields, Dad would have ready a long slice of juicy, cool watermelon for us to eat out on the lawn. His smile would stretch from ear to ear as he watched us all come to get a slice. Dad's life centered around the Scriptures and his desire for people to be saved. Often as he talked with friends, he quoted verses about heaven and salvation. Before we left for school each morning, he would remind us to let others see Jesus in our lives. Before each service held in our church, he would join some other men in kneeling before God in prayer, giving that service to the Lord. Dad could be counted on to put God first. His inspiration was implanted in the heart of each of us, which blossomed into love and dedication to the Lord.

Going to kindergarten was a frightening experience for me. With nine in the family we never had need of a baby-sitter. The nearest neighbor lived three-fourth mile up the road so it was just the family mostly. When school started we had to walk one and one-half miles to school. I didn't dare talk with the other children, let alone the teacher. I was so shy that at recess time I would find one of my brothers (this was a two room, red brick school house with sixty to eighty students between the ages of kindergarten and eighth grade. My twin sister and I were in a class with two boys and one other girl). It wasn't difficult to catch one of my brothers. They were on their way out the door to play ball with the other children. When I reached one of them I threw my arms around his legs, sat on his toes, wrapped my legs around his ankles and said, "Don't leave me, please, don't leave me".

When school was dismissed we would walk the one and one-half miles home. I couldn't wait to get home. My brothers and sisters would go straight to the kitchen for some refreshment. I rushed up to my room, fell down on my knees at my bedside daily and talked to God. I could hardly wait to get there. It was such a special time alone with God as His invisible presence penetrated my heart. I stayed until I felt the presence of the Lord. Just to know that God was there for me after what I thought was a horrible day at school. I stayed on my knees until I felt God's arms of love wrapped around me. Since I had chores to do, my time in the prayer chamber couldn't be long. (If I heard someone coming up the stairs, I would immediately stop what I was doing. It would have been embarrassing to me for someone to find me in prayer). As soon as I felt the presence of the Lord I was satisfied. Oh how I needed that touch with God. I then went downstairs and joined my sisters in the kitchen.

When it came time for fun and games, we always had enough team members! Carolyn, Virginia and I played dolls every day of the week, but when we played as a family, it had to be games the boys liked best, because they were older. Baseball, football, and basketball were at the top of their list, along with one other game we all loved to play in the winter, "Tick in the Tunnels." We made long tunnels with many different openings all through the hay bales in the barn, ran across the beams, jumped from the scaffold to a bag swing hanging in the center of the hay barn twelve feet off the ground, swung to the other side, and jumped into the bales. In the spring we played "Gray Wolf" or "Seven

Steps around the House," and took turns swinging on our bag-swing hanging across the creek in the woods near our home. There was also a bag-swing hanging from the big tree in the barnyard that swung far and high. We jumped on it from standing on barrels stacked two barrels high. We used hay bales as steps to get up that high. When the swing came back a second, third and fourth person would jump on. As most children, we lived dangerously.

I was never allowed to start a job without carrying it through to completion. Whether it was gathering eggs or planting a field, I finished the job with no thought about quitting. Even as a small child coloring in a coloring book, my mother would not allow me to leave one page unfinished to go to another. I learned responsibility and "stick-to-it-ivness" by practicing what was right.

I was nine years old when I began thinking seriously about accepting the Lord as my Savior. I had never made that decision; I knew Jesus was coming back and I did not want to be left behind. I finally got enough courage to speak to my mother about it. After our meal, we were doing the dishes. Mother was washing the dishes, as she always did and it was my week to dry the dishes. Carolyn and I took turns drying dishes and/or clearing the table and sweeping the kitchen floor. After we finished, I asked Mother if she would go into the living room and pray with me so I could ask Jesus to come into my heart. She read from the Bible John 3:16 (KJV), "For God so loved the world, that He gave His only begotten Son, That whosoever believeth in Him should not perish, but have everlasting life"; and Romans 3:23 (KJV), "For all have sinned and come short of the glory of God." Then she asked me to put my name in the "whosoever" and read John 3:16 again. As we prayed, I asked Jesus to come into my life. He forgave my sins, and made me one of His children. I was thrilled and happy!

It was a beautiful spring evening and my brothers were outside. Mother informed me that I should go and tell them the decision I had just made. I rode my bike around and around in the big barn yard trying to work up courage to tell my four big brothers that I had just accepted Jesus as my personal Savior. Just before dark, I quickly told them and then ran off, not waiting to hear what they might say! That was my first time to be a witness, to tell someone what Jesus did for me.

One evening, it was my turn to read the Bible after supper. The passage was John 3:1-36 (KJV). As I read verses 16-18, *"For God so loved the world that He gave His only begotten Son, that whosoever believeth in Him should not perish, but have everlasting life. For God sent not His Son into the world to condemn the world, but that the world through Him might be saved. He that believeth on Him is not condemned; but he that believeth not is condemned already, because he hath not believed in the name of the only begotten Son of God,"* my Dad began asking me thought provoking questions, difficult for a little girl to answer.

One question was, "According to what you've just read, are you condemned or are you not condemned?" I wanted to answer correctly because my older brothers were sitting there listening. I reread it twice so I could comprehend it. I did want my answer to please my brothers and my Dad. I proudly answered, "I am not condemned." "How do you know?" Dad asked. I said, "Because it said that if I believe Jesus died and rose again from the dead for me, then I am not condemned because I asked Jesus into my heart." Dad was proud of my answer.

When I was very young, my oldest brother, Don, was drafted into the US Army. While he was stationed in Colorado, Mom and Dad visited him several days. With Don gone, Richard was the oldest, so it became his duty to watch over us in Mom and Dad's absence. Even then Richard was handy in practical matters, and had a lot of common sense. He took good care of us, and managed the farm with ease. Later Don was sent overseas, and there were times when we feared we would never see him again. When he was fighting in the Korean War there was no word from him for weeks, and no way that we could contact him. It seemed as though months had passed when we learned that his battalion had been surrounded by the enemy, and there had been no way they could get in or out. Don had been hit several times, but had not been seriously injured except that the noise from the large machine guns affected his hearing in both ears. He said that often the large guns had such an impact that the candlelight by which he wrote letters would blow out several times before he could finish.

We prayed for him day after day, trusting the Lord to keep him safe and alive. The Lord answered our prayers and Don returned home in 1952. His wife, Clara, drove him home from Battle Creek, Michigan. When he reached home, sooner than we had expected, Carolyn and I excitedly met him at the door. Mother was taking a bath. Don wouldn't allow us to tell her he was home; he wanted to surprise her himself! Oh, she was so happy to see her son and know that he was safe and all right.

Victor, a very quiet, loving, compassionate person, always loved to go to church, but it seemed the devil did his best to try and discourage him. Often on Sunday morning he took a terrible migraine headache and had to stay home while we went to church. We loved being with all the youth at the church. I felt sorry for Vic because he missed a lot of the fun.

During our younger years, Carolyn and I looked just alike; even Dad couldn't tell us apart. Because Carolyn was born with a hole in her heart, I was very protective of her. If just one of us needed to go out to the field to help with the work I would go so that she could stay and work in the house.

Grace to Endure

On the farm where one could see for miles across the flatlands of Michigan, it was exciting to watch the sky! Many times we saw thunder clouds rolling in, and we would rush about to get the wagon loads of hay bales and farm equipment into the barn and securely fasten the barn doors before the storm came in. Tornadoes were often sighted in the area. Word would come to the little red-brick, two-room Sunny Side School, that we were to go home immediately. With eyes wide with fright, we would run all the way home as fast as our little legs could carry us, praying all the way that the tornado would not hit home before we did.

One day a tornado did hit our farm. Dad and the boys had secured the doors and windows and made sure the machinery was in the barn. Meanwhile, the disastrous winds were building in strength and speed. My brother Victor was tightening the front barn door where the cows were in their stalls. Roger and I were in the next section of the barn where the hay loft was. Between the cows and the hayloft was an area where the hay wagons and tractors would enter. The middle front barn door rolled open and shut. The severe fierce wind was blowing it inward. Roger backed the tractor against it for support. Then together, Roger and Victor tried to open the door between the cow stalls and the hay loft. Roger pulled on one side and Victor pushed on the other, but the wind was so fierce that the door would not budge. While they struggled in the barn, pushing and pulling, the tornado hit and split the 80-foot barn roof right down the middle. The tornado not only broke every window in our house, but covered our living room floor with hail stones and debris, and shattered every window in the barn, chicken houses and granary, a total of fifty windows. The storm could have done much more damage, but the Lord protected us, and not one of the nine members of our family was hurt.

In winter, blizzard winds would blow so hard that at times we hardly made the mile-and-one-half walk home from school. Our noses would water as two icicles formed on our upper lip and turn icy-red from the cold, and the whirling snowflakes would catch and freeze in our hair and eyebrows. Many times the snow was so deep that snowplows couldn't get through to keep the secondary roads open and people could no longer shovel their way through the roads. If northern people like us became snow-bound, that meant it was a deep snowfall! Sometimes the snow was up to the door knob when we'd open the front door to go out of the house. The wind blew, stacking the snow into huge snowdrifts. The greater winter outdoor fun was tobogganing, sledding down the hillside, skiing across the land behind the pickup truck and ice-skating on the ponds.

During the summer months, my twin sister, Carolyn, and I earned spending money by picking blueberries on a farm two miles from ours. We rode our bikes there and picked berries from 8:00 a.m. to 5:00 p.m. daily. When the blueberries weren't in season, there was plenty of work to be done on our farm.

During our elementary school years we all enjoyed attending our little country Sunny Side School together. As with all chil-dren, we each looked forward to growing older and attending high school in the big city. Graduation from the eighth grade was a thrilling, but frightening event for Carolyn and me. We were proud that neither of us had failed along the way and now we were graduating together. It meant so much to us to come to this big day, side by side. We had never been separated, not even in the playground at school during recess. It was frightening to realize that next fall we would be attending a big city high school. We would no longer have just five pupils in our class with only one teacher. We would be among hundreds of kids with a different teacher for each class and I just knew I would get lost in the halls. It was frightening, too, that we would have to ride a school bus into the city each day, and then catch the right bus to get home.

That summer passed quickly into fall, and the anticipation of high school turned into reality. One of our concerns was for our sister, Virginia. When Carolyn and I attended school in the city, she was left to walk the mile and a half to the country school by herself. She often must have felt alone, especially when Carolyn and I would take the car and go to attend a youth meeting without her. It's just one of those things that happens when your sister is still in elementary school and you are in high school "checking out the boys". She soon found close friends at the church and really enjoyed her teenage years. After high school, Virginia attended "Infant Nursing Training" in Chicago, graduated and got married. We three sisters grew closer in much love and respect for one another.

One of our traumatic experiences was at the beginning of high school. The principal felt it best to separate all twins; therefore, for the first time Carolyn and I were assigned different classes and lunch periods. This decision was not wise. It was too abrupt. We had always been together. We were not emotionally prepared for this separation. It was not healthy for us to be separated all day everyday. Identical twins are together in the womb. Due to this intimate sharing before birth, they are one with each other. It is a oneness that no one can comprehend, neither can it be communicated. There is sense of belonging to another human being who is as much a part of you as you are yourself. A feeling that if one dies, the other half would never be complete. A great part of oneself would be missing.

We also learned how the bus ride worked. We were nearly the first to be picked up by the bus (6:30 a.m.) and nearly the last to be dropped off (5:30 p.m.) after dark during winter months. However, in time, we found ourselves adjusting to the new environment. Coming from a little country school, we found our city-reared classmates more advanced in their studies. We worked hard, however, and were able to keep up with our class.

Carolyn and I still looked enough alike that we could exchange classes, and neither the teacher nor our classmates would know the difference. Sometimes we even confused our boyfriends. Carolyn had been going with this particular boy for some time, so we took it for granted that he could tell us apart. One evening when he came to pick up Carolyn, I answered the door. Neither of us realized he was holding a box of valentine candy behind his back. He stood there looking at both of us, and exclaimed, "Well, which one is it?"

In 1959 we graduated from high school and that summer Carolyn decided she would attend Tennessee Temple College the following September. Even though our pathways parted, we still often thought alike. After we were married and living in different states, we found that we would do some of the same things at the same time. Perhaps styling our hair alike, or sewing a dress in the same pattern and/or color. Nothing could break the strong bond and love that was between us.

I loved nature, the smell of fresh cut hay and fresh worked soil was invigorating. When I worked in the fields, I felt close to the Lord. As I drove the John Deere Tractor across the acres of land cultivating the rolls of young corn, I prayed with my heart full of praise and adoration for the Lord. Since I was alone on the tractor, I would lift my voice and sing God's praises as loud as I could. When I was young, we worked with the thrasher, binder, siderake and bundled hay (Joseph in the Bible called them shieves). After farm equipment progressed and Dad purchased a Hay baler, I loved hauling in the bales of hay. The twine that held the bales together would break frequently so Dad purchased a baler that tied bales together with wire. We had a self-propelled combine as well. I loved getting the hay out of the fields and into the barns. The wheat was put into the granary bends. I enjoyed working in the fields, especially at haying time, with our brother Roger, who was a year and one half older than

Carolyn and I. During haying times we would go out early in the morning with the hay baler, tractor and trailer, and work until dark. We had the large farm equipment therefore we did what was called custom work, going to the fields of other farmers and cutting their wheat and hay. I loved every minute of it, work and all.

Living and working on a farm taught me a great deal about responsibility. Looking back, it was my preparation time for the tragedy of thirteen years of blindness which would come into my life when I became a young woman.

Although my brother Roger was a year and a half older, we were very close. As we baled hay in the fields we talked about the things on our hearts and minds. He was thoughtful and would have done almost anything for me. Roger often said, "If you can't get Dad's car tonight, Marolyn, and you want to go somewhere, take mine. I won't be using it."

Roger lived by his strong convictions and was concerned that he marry the right girl. During my last year in high school, he and Alma were the first couple to be married in the newly-built Rose Park Baptist Church. Almost a year later, their son, Linn, was born, making their life together a happy family of three. Even after Roger's marriage, we continued to work together in the fields day after day. Roger loved to sing while he worked and he often sang sacred tunes. Every other day or so, out of a clear blue sky, he would sing, "Oh, that'll be the day, when I die!" I often wondered why he sang the words as he did.

In June 1961, five months after I left for Tennessee Temple College, Roger was killed in a traffic accident. Alma was expecting their second child at the time. Two weeks before his death, he had told Alma that they needed to increase their life insurance policy. As he signed the papers, he had remarked that those might be the last papers he would ever sign. Roger and Alma's wedding had been the first wedding in Rose Park Baptist Church and his funeral was the first funeral held there. The Lord spoke to me through Psalm 116:15 at the time of Roger's death: *"Precious in the sight of the Lord is the death of His saints."* Roger's death was a great loss, but just knowing our brother's death was precious to the Lord made the burden easier to bear.

Having been active daily in personal and family devotions to God, I learned to feel an extreme God consciousness, and developed a keen desire to walk with the Lord. His presence overshadowed me. My spirit became sensitive about not grieving the Holy Spirit or walking in any form of disobedience. The questionable pleasures many teenagers enjoyed were not a part of my life. Places where most teenagers felt comfortable, I was not. I was constrained to draw back from anything that was worldly or impure.

As an example, I remember so vividly a particular restaurant where many of my schoolmates went daily for lunch. My twin sister, Carolyn, and I went in one day at lunch time. The music was loud and the decor was dark (not that there is anything wrong with loud music or dark decor). Somehow, the presence of evil surrounded us. We could not stay for lunch in a place where I knew God was uncomfortable. It was "off limits" for us. The Holy Spirit would not allow us to eat there. I diligently practiced keeping my mind on God, His thoughts, His will and way. When something was not pleasing to God, I knew it.

I remember when I learned the power of praying in my spirit. No one was there but the Lord and me. I was sick and had not gone to school that day. I gathered a pillow and blanket and made a bed under a "blanket tent" over the top of the dining chairs. Mom was working outside the house. I stayed in my tent most of the day with a song book in hand. There were several songs that I sang but when I came upon the song, _Cleanse Me_, I couldn't put it down. I sang each verse prayerfully, allowing the words to sink deeply into my spirit. I've included the words here so you can think and meditate on them. Allow the Holy Spirit to grip your spirit through them as He did mine.

Search me, O God, and <u>know my heart</u> today;
Try me, O Savior, <u>know my thoughts,</u> I pray
<u>See if there be</u> some wicked way in me;
<u>Cleanse me from every sin</u>, and <u>set me free</u>.

I praise Thee, Lord, for cleansing me from sin;
<u>Fulfill Thy Word</u> and <u>make me pure within.</u>
<u>Fill me with fire</u>, where once I burned with shame;
<u>Grant my desire to magnify Thy name</u>.

Lord, <u>take my life</u>, and make it <u>wholly Thine</u>;
Fill my poor heart with Thy great love divine.
Search me, O God, and <u>know my heart</u> today;
<u>Take all my will</u>, my passion, self and pride;
O now surrender, <u>Lord - in me abide</u>.

O Holy Ghost, revival comes from Thee;
Send a revival, <u>start the work in me</u>.
Thy Word declares Thou wilt supply our need;
<u>For blessing now</u>, O Lord, I humbly plead.

As I meditated on the words, I gave them back to God in prayer. Unaware to me at the time, the anointing of the Holy Ghost fell upon me, empowering me for the ministry God has given me today. (God's call upon my life came later.) I did not realize until years later just how much of an impact God made upon my life that day.

I must have sung "Cleanse Me, Lord" more than fifty times. Each time, I realized a little bit more how I could not face God with any sin in my life. Sin must be dealt with immediately, not later. Short accounts must be kept with God. Failure to confess sin would bring the loss of confidence gained when talking with Him. With unconfessed sin in our lives, we cannot come into His presence with boldness and expect to receive anything. Why choose to be powerless when we can be so powerful?

My heart was deeply touched by the soul-searching words of this song. In the stillness of the hour, I was brought before God. With these words burning in my heart, I learned to walk the road of total commitment. More than anything, I wanted my life to count for Jesus Christ. Years later, the words of this song still penetrate my very soul.

We read in I John 2:15-17, *"Stop loving this evil world and all that it offers you, for when you love these things you show that you do not really love God; For all these worldly things, these evil desires - the craze for sex, the ambition to buy everything that appeals to you, and the pride that comes from wealth and importance - these are not from God. They are from this evil world itself. And this world is fading away, and these evil, forbidden things will go with it, but whoever keeps doing the will of God will live forever."*

<u>O For A Thousand Tongues</u>
He breaks the pow'r of canceled sin,
He sets the pris'ner free;
His blood can make the foulest clean—
His blood availed for me.

by Charles Wesley

It is only the blood of Jesus Christ that can break the power of sin. Sin holds us captive, but the blood of Christ sets us free. Praise God!

Control of the Holy Spirit

The outflowing of the Holy Spirit is different from the receiving of the person of the Holy Spirit when one is born again into the body of Christ. Upon Salvation, the Holy Spirit comes into our lives. He baptizes us into Christ. After having been born into the family of God, the early Apostles were filled and controlled by the Holy Spirit for special ministries. The filling and outflowing of the Holy Spirit is for all who are in Christ. It is part of our inheritance.

Have you ever felt starved and hungry spiritually, wondering where the joy was to come from in your life in Christ? The reason believers are so miserable and why we see so little power in our churches today is because we have grieved the Holy Spirit and neglected His power. We will not let the power of God flow through us for fear we might offend. As God said, *"The fear of man bringeth a snare"* (Proverbs 29:25a/KJV). Upon salvation you received the Holy Spirit. Now you need to let the Holy Spirit come alive. He is bound in these bodies of ours. We need to release Him and let His power be seen or felt. We must let joy surface and flow out like a river from our innermost being. People will see it and want what we have. Jesus said, *"If I be lifted up I will draw all men unto myself"* (John 12:32/KJV).

You cannot teach another person how to experience the power of the Holy Spirit. It must be encountered, one on one, by going the way of the cross. Learn to flow with Him. It's the only way the Spirit can operate through us. He will not force His power upon us. We must open ourselves up to Him and allow Him to work His power through us. We can gain much power by praising God that we are redeemed and that we have victory over the works of the devil through the promises He gives us in His Word.

A beautiful quote I have heard is, "The person God will choose to use will be the one who has faith and expects results." If all we ask Him to bless is our food, that is all He will bless. Is His blessing on your food the only request you take into His presence?

Proverbs says, *"Everyone who is proud in heart is an abomination to the Lord"* (Proverbs 16:5). The Spirit of God can not flow through a personality that's proud, sophisticated and stiff. We must deal with our sin before we can expect God to hear and answer our prayers. Every minute detail of our lives must be examined in the light of the Word of God.

The words of the hymn Rock of Ages really speak to me. I trust that they will speak to you also.

> *Rock of Ages, cleft for me,*
> *Let me hide myself in Thee*
> *Let the water and the blood,*
> *From Thy wounded side which flowed,*
> *Be of sin the double cure:*
> *Save from wrath and make me pure.*
>
> *Could my zeal no languor know,*
> *Could my tears forever flow,*
> *This for sin could not atone -*
> *Thou must save, and Thou alone:*
> *In my hand no price I bring,*
> *Simply to Thy cross I cling.*
>
> *When I draw my final breath,*
> *When my eyes shall close in death,*
> *When I rise to worlds unknown'*
> *And behold Thee on Thy throne,*
> *Rock of Ages, cleft for me,*
> *Let me hide myself in Thee.*
>
> A. M. Toplady

We need to learn what it is to hide ourselves in Jesus Christ and rest in Him as the firm foundation of our faith. The grand hymn from the 1700s, How Firm a Foundation, whose author is unknown, is one of my favorites. Read it carefully. Meditate upon its words.

> *How firm a foundation, ye saints of the Lord,*
> *Is laid for your faith in His excellent Word!*
> *What more can He say than to you He hath said*
> *To you, who for refuge to Jesus have fled?*

Fear not, I am with thee - 0 be not dismayed,
For I am thy God, I will still give thee aid;
I'll strengthen thee, help thee, and cause thee to stand,
Upheld by my gracious, omnipotent hand.

When thru the deep waters I call thee to go,
The rivers of woe shall not thee overflow;
For I will be with thee thy troubles to bless,
And sanctify to thee thy deepest distress.

When thru fiery trials thy pathway shall lie,
My grace, all sufficient, shall be thy supply;
The flame shall not hurt thee - I only design
Thy dross to consume and thy gold to refine.

The soul that on Jesus hath leaned for repose,
I will not, I will not desert to his foes;
That soul, tho all hell should endeavor to shake,
I'll never - no never - no never forsake!

These words really say it all. Our God is with us and will never forsake us. Praise the Lord! May we never allow sin to hinder our prayers to God. A saying quoted earlier needs to be kept in mind when we submit to self-examination: "If you feel far from God, guess who moved." We must go to our knees in prayer, confess our sins, draw near to God and feel His loving arms embrace us.

God does delight in answering the prayers of His children. The big problem is that there are not too many Christians who are willing to accept His answers and *carry out His orders*. However, His blessings in our lives will be in *direct proportion to our obedience* to Him. Since we know that God does delight in answering our prayers, we must dare to believe Him for answers and then exercise the faith to carry out His will.

We believers have failed to teach and *understand what all is included* in the inheritance that is ours, that has been *bought for us at Calvary*. In Galatians we read, *"And if ye be Christ's, then are ye Abraham's seed and heirs according to the promise."* Galatians 3:29 (KJV). What promise are we heirs to? All of God's promises. We're not just heirs of salvation. There is so much more. The key is that we need to have confident assurance, being fully persuaded that whatever we ask the Father in Jesus' Name, according to the will of God, He will do.

I know there are many to whom God's Word is dead. Though they read it, the Holy Spirit has not quickened it (made it alive) to them. They are just dead words. But to me, it has always been alive and living within me. Since my coming to Christ for salvation, I ever thirst for more and more of Him and His Word.

Paul instructed Timothy that all Christians will be filled with love that comes from pure hearts, and that their minds will be clean and their faith strong. Service to God is to be from a pure heart, a clean mind and a strong faith. Having a tender conscience, I always sensed a God-given restraint to keep me from sin. I knew what pleased the Lord and what did not please Him and that had a strong effect upon what I did and where I went.

Youth prayer meetings on Saturday mornings and singspirations with the church youth group on Sunday night after church were my joy and delight. Some fifty to sixty young people would gather at someone's house and we would sing for an hour or more. Then the host served cokes and brownies or some kind of snack. There was a chorus we always sang at these "Singspirations" youth fellowships that I sang as a prayer to God. The words are:

> *Only to be what He wants me to be,*
> *Every moment of everyday.*
> *Yielded completely to Jesus alone,*
> *Every step of this pilgrim way.*
> *Just to be clay in the potter's hand,*
> *Ready to do what His will commands.*

Only to be what He wants me to be,
Every moment of everyday.
- Norman J. Clayton

I felt and understood the presence of God in my life. Learning about His power was a growing experience. I knew forgiveness and obedient living. Obedience to the prompting of the Spirit is essential to having the blessing of God. I knew that I could not approach the presence of God while living in disobedience to the Holy Spirit because God cannot look upon sin. I found the closer I came to God the more terrible the least of my sins became. The Spirit of God, His presence and the manifestation of His divine power held me close to the Lord and still does today.

Our family days were happy ones and God honored Mom and Dad's prayers and faithfulness to Him. They saw each one of their children accept the Lord as Savior, and then go forward to follow and serve God in their daily lives. Donald, Richard, Victor, Carolyn and Virginia all remained active church members in the years that followed.

When you come before the Lord and you begin to feel his presence, stay with it. That is God revealing himself to you and listening to your request. Some say, "I go to God in prayer and it is cold and empty. There's nothing there. God doesn't hear my prayer." If you are a born again child of God, washed in the blood of Jesus Christ, and you come before the Lord in prayer and it's cold, your prayers are going to the ceiling, God is letting you know something is wrong. The Holy Spirit is showing you there's sin dividing you and God. It's not that you're a great bad sinner; it may be that you had a bad attitude this morning and you need to confess that attitude to God. It has broken your communication with God. God has to reveal that to you. Therefore, when your prayer life is cold and indifferent you need to stay on your knees until light breaks through. Stay on you knees until you know God is there and He hears your prayer. Stay until you have confessed and turned from every sin with genuine repentance. Then all of a sudden the portals of Heaven just open up. You feel the presence of the Lord and you can talk to him about everything. At those times you want to pray for your partner, your children and parents, the church and pastor. Pray-walk them through each day.

God's Call Upon My Life

As I grew older I still loved to cultivate the corn, hall in the hay-bales and work in the fields with the farm equipment. I enjoyed getting on the John Deere tractor and working back and forth across those acres of land. Out there in the fields I could pray and sing to the glory of God. No one was there except the Lord and me. I could sing at the top of my voice. We girls sang every where we went. We sang ourselves to sleep at night.

Sitting on the green lawn at the end of the day, looking across the acres of land, crops ripe unto harvest, green trees and blue skies, my heart welled up within me in adoration and praise to my Lord and Savior. Those were the days of the old wringer clothes washers and drying clothes in fresh air on the clothes line. I loved to sit under the clothes line and marvel at the hand-iwork of God. As I lingered there in the spirit of prayer, I said so often, "Lord, I'm just a little country girl but somehow I pray that you will take my life and use it to point souls to the Lord Jesus Christ". I loved to get alone with the Lord and sense His presence near me.

One day it was as though God spoke directly to me, "Marolyn, I want you to be a minister's wife." My heart began beating hard and going pitter patter. I said, "Lord, there's no way. I can't be a preacher's wife, I'm this shy little country kid." Then I began to hash this out further with God. I said, "Lord, my pastor's wife speaks at banquets and she teaches the adult ladies Sunday school class." I was afraid. I literally ran from my prayer spot and never went back to pray under the clothes-lines ever again. From that time on I'd pray under the big tree located on the other side of the house. I hoped maybe the Lord wouldn't bring it up again.

As a young girl I didn't know that when the Lord calls you to do something, He places within you the desire and the ability. He will never ask you to do something that He doesn't give you the ability to do. I learned that I couldn't argue with the Lord very long. One day I said, "All right Lord, I'll be a pastor's wife and I'll be the best little pastor's wife I can be, but you just give that public speaking to somebody else." I prayed differently after that. Little did I realize my life would one day consist of doing public speaking in a world-wide ministry, sharing with people what a great God we have. You see, God knew I would be a public speaker. He knows our lives from beginning to the end. He is the "author and finisher of our faith."

Since the age of twelve I began praying for my husband-to-be, whoever and wherever he was. One night as my family and I were driving the seven miles home from church, I heard Billy Graham say in a radio sermon: "Young person, you may be only thirteen years of age, but now is the time to begin praying for your life partner." Every day after that, I prayed for my future husband. As I worked in the hay fields on our farm, I prayed that the Lord would make him a man of God, a man of prayer, and that He would keep him pure and holy during his teenage life. Then I prayed for his character, as his personality developed that he would be kind, compassionate, loving and understanding. Since my character and personality were also being developed, I prayed that God would develop within both of us just the right characteristics. I prayed that our lives would be so interwoven that when the Lord led us together, we would be able to do a wonderful work for Him. I also knew the Lord had called me to be a pastor's wife.

People said, "You don't bother the Lord about all the practical things of life, do you? God is too big a God to be concerned about the little things." Listen, if God is not too big of a God to keep track of the hair count on one's head then surely he is concerned about the tires on your car, or the lawn mower when it breaks down. Those things are never in the budget. They need to be prayed over. Ask God for the $60.00 you need to get it repaired. See the Lord give that which you have need of. He's a great God! You can pray about these things because God delights in answering the prayers of His children, not that all prayers will be answered instantly. Some prayers take 25-30 years to be answered, but that doesn't matter, that's God's timing. Noah waited twelve years for His prayer to be answered, Abraham waited a lifetime, Moses waited eighty years, (Hebrews 11/KJV). Joseph waited 30 years, Jeremiah waited 70 years (I Kings 18/KJV), and Daniel waited 21 days before his answer came (II Kings 16/KJV). Elijah prayed 7 times before the rains came (I Kings 18:41-46/RSV). God's ways are not our ways, our ways are not His ways. In His time He answers prayer, but surely you will experience answers to your prayers over the little things all along the way. If you go two weeks without an answer to prayer, find out why, something is wrong somewhere. Jesus is seated at the right hand of His Father waiting to answer prayers on earth, to intercede for us and to bless us.

The Psalmist said, "....*No good thing will He withhold from those who walk along His paths.*" Psalm 84:11b. David also wrote, "*But O my soul, don't be discouraged. Don't be upset. Expect God to act! For I know that I shall again have plenty of reason to praise Him for all that He will do. He is my help! He is my God!*" (Psalm 42:11).

Through daily confession of our sins, we will receive daily cleansing and we will conquer the sin of prayerlessness. In this way, our fellowship with the Lord will be kept constant.

Grace to Endure

The power of the flesh is insufficient to develop our prayer life. It seems we always accept God's grace for forgiveness, but many times we neglect to accept His grace for deliverance. When we fail to appropriate His grace for deliverance, we will have a struggle with sin. We must learn to confess our sins, to accept His forgiveness, and then to claim His deliverance.

Chapter II

Grace To Endure Blindness

It was 1959 and I had graduated from Holland High School in Holland, Michigan and had accepted a job working as a secretary. Since Mother and I both worked in town, she would pick me up after work each day, and I would drive home. Life was good; I was young and excited about the future.

Knowing how much I enjoyed driving, Mother wondered if something was wrong when day after day I excused myself from driving. Not wanting to worry her, I had not shared with her that I was having trouble seeing. I thought maybe I had an infection that would soon clear up. I hoped my eyesight would improve, but was greatly concerned after I saw a doctor in Holland and he did not know what was wrong with my eyes. Since my vision continued to fail, I told mother about it and she arranged for me to see other doctors and eye specialists. No one seemed to know the cause of my failing eyesight.

After three months on my secretarial job, I could no longer see to do my work. When I asked another secretary to do my part, she asked, "Why?" I was so deeply concerned over my failing eyesight, that I couldn't find words to explain my difficulty seeing. When I was finally able to tell her how poor my vision was, she pointed to a woman who had just entered the room. "Can you see her?" she asked. Struggling to get the words out, I replied, "No, I can't see that far." Upon sharing this with the secretary, I quit my job.

After a thorough examination at the Mayo Brothers Medical Center in Rochester, Minnesota, the doctor diagnosed my problem as "Juvenile Macular Degeneration", a hereditary loss of central vision. "Macular Degeneration" was a rare disease in those days and usually affected adults around age sixty-five. Since people often died in their sixties, there wasn't much research. "Macular Degeneration" is sweeping the country now and doctors are very familiar with the disease.

Eighteen years of age and I had become legally blind. This was very serious; we knew it wasn't an infection and it wasn't going to clear up. It sounded so awful when they told me it was a disease. I was scared and began to cry when they told me the damage in my eyes was permanent. There was no medication or surgery available. I was told to go home and learn to live with blindness.

For me Macular Degeneration meant I could see only the fuzzy shapes of people and tell their height and build, but I could not distinguish faces, eyes, or expressions. By straining to see the outlines of furniture and doors, with much difficulty I could move about trying not to bump into things. Life crumbled at my feet. Before me had been a promising future, college, a career and marriage. Blindness was the last thing I needed. Nobody would marry a blind girl. What would I do with my life? How would I handle this insurmountable obstacle? I was devastated.

For three weeks after I had become blind I sat in my Dad's easy chair and listened to sacred gospel records. That chair became my security pad. I am so glad my dad did not allow us to buy secular records. Had the first record I picked up been a song about love, sex, romance and marriage, I would have gone down in despair. I couldn't have handled that - not at that time in my life. I needed something I could hold onto. Sitting in that chair day after day with tears streaming down my face, I grieved over the life I had lost. I was no longer the same; I thought differently, talked differently, walked and acted differently. I didn't know myself anymore. I had become a blind personality. I couldn't continue to jump into my dad's car and go roller skating every Friday night as I did before. Life crushed within me as my sorrow grew. I went through a time of sorrow and bereavement. It was good for me to cry because tears cleanse the soul.

The first record I picked up was Ethel Waters', *"His Eye Is On The Sparrow and I know He Watches Over Me."* I needed to hear those words and I listened to them over and over as the words burned into my spirit. This was God's music. I sank my soul into the music as it lifted my thoughts Heavenward. It edified my spirit and I felt the comforting presence of the Holy Spirit surrounding me. The words of that song lifted my thoughts in prayer and praise to the Lord Jesus. In this way, I kept my mind off myself and my insurmountable blindness and had an inner strength, something I could hold onto during my darkest hours of anxiety and despair. I knew I needed Jesus, His touch, His presence, His hand to help me, and I reached out to Him. He was by my side through every hour of crisis.

As I continued listening to this song, *"His Eye Is On The Sparrow"*, I said, "Oh God, you care so much for those little birds. Lord, they fly through the sky and you feather them, clothe them and feed them. One sparrow falls to the ground and you know about it. Lord, if you care that much about the little sparrow then surely you are going to take care of me". God says, *"Put me in remembrance of your word."* I put Him in remembrance of His word as I said, "God I'm your child, I'm your child." As I listened to Jack Holcomb sing, *"Until Then"* I became deeply convicted. The song says, *"Until then my heart will go on singing. Until then with joy I'll carry on. Until the day God calls me home."* As kids growing up, we sang everywhere we went. Now my mom and sisters were all singing, but not me. I had lost my song and my joy. However, I began to feel convicted about not singing praises to my Lord. Have you ever been under conviction about something and that which brought you under conviction just keeps pulling you back? This song just kept compelling me with conviction. I prayed, "Lord, I want to sing, but my heart is crushed." I prayed, "Oh Lord, give me a song upon my lips so that I can sing with joy once again."

The song says, "My heart can sing as I pause to remember, a heartache here is but a stepping stone along the trail that's winding always upward. This troubled world is not my final home. (verse 2) The things of earth (that pertained to my eye) will dim and lose their value, if we recall their borrowed for a while. The things on earth that cause the heart to tremble, in heaven will only bring a smile. (verse 3) This weary world, with all it's toil and struggle may take it's toll of misery and woe." My blindness had taken it's toll of misery and woe. Tears still streaming down my face, the song goes on. (verse 4) "The soul of man is like a waiting falcon. When it is released, it's destined for the sky." The soul is our mind and emotions. That's what I was dealing with, my soul needed to be released. God was trying to get me to sing the words to this song so I would learn to release my burden.

When Paul and Silas were in jail they didn't feel like singing, but they sang anyway. God wanted me to sing even if I didn't feel like it because when we sing praises to the Lord the words sink into our spirit. *"Faith cometh by hearing, hearing by the word of God."* Don't just sing to yourself quietly, sing out loud. God says, *"Make a joyful noise unto the Lord."* Paul and Silas didn't feel like singing when they were in prison. Their wrist and ankles were probably bleeding from the chains and they were tired of sitting on the hard floor in that jail, yet they lifted their voices in praise to the Lord. This is how victory and joy come into a one's life. If you let the devil steal your joy, he gets the victory. This song says, " With joy I will carry on." Instead of singing, I was crying in my grief and sorrow. As I meditated on the words of that song and other songs, God ministered to my spirit. All of the old songs of faith were very precious to me. I can never express how deeply my soul was touched.

Show Me How To Go On, Lord

After about three weeks, I began to realize that "Life" is God's gift to us and what we do with our life is our gift to God. (Author Unknown) Right then, it wasn't a matter of whether I was blind or whether I could see. It was my life and I wanted to be able to lay down a life at the feet of Jesus which was worthy of His death on Calvary. Sitting in my dad's easy chair for the rest of my life wouldn't accomplish that. It was up to me to pick up the broken pieces and somehow pull my life together again. As frightening as it seemed, I knew I had to try. In order to do this, I needed to get alone with God, where I could cry it out, shout it out, pray it out and not be heard by anyone else. This was a private and personal time between me and God. With nine in the family there was no privacy at home. I knew I had to find a place to spend the night in prayer. At my request, my Dad drove me to Pastor and Mrs. Garland Cofield's house. I expressed my need to spend the night in prayer and they allowed me the privilege of using his office in their home. During that night I couldn't open God's word and read it, but I had memorized a scripture verse every week of my life from the time I was able to talk. God's word was hidden in my heart. I couldn't open up the song book and read the words but I knew the songs. All through the night with Bible and song book in hand I sang every song that came to mind and I reminded the Lord of those little sparrows over there in the book of Matthew. I gave every verse I could think of back to God in prayer that night.

What about praying in our inner spirit? We must be alone in a place closed off from everything and everybody, a place free from all distractions. Jesus teaches us in His Sermon on the Mount, *"But when you pray, go away by yourself, all alone, and shut the door behind you and pray to your Father secretly, and your Father, who know your secrets, will reward you."* Matthew 6:6. We need to close out everything from the outside world. God's Spirit will relate Himself with our spirit as to what to pray. It is the "Spirit connection" that is so important.

The greatest book known to man is the Bible, the written revelation of God. But greater still is Jesus Christ, the living revelation of God. He will reveal Himself to any person who wants Him to do so, whether or not they can read the Bible. Jesus tells us, "....for the Kingdom of God is within you." Luke 17:21b. Our fullest attention must be given to the deep, innermost part of our being. God, in the person of the Holy Spirit, lives within us and His presence is with us at all times. In Psalms we read, "Stand silent! Know that I am God."

When you don't know how to pray, when your heart is breaking and you are going down in despair, you pray-read the word of God. There's power in doing that. It's the only way you can break through. All night long was spent singing, praying and crying before the Lord. Toward morning with tears flowing down my face I said, "Lord, I am over here in I Peter 5:7." I may have been in the book of Psalms or Revelation but as far as I was concerned, I was in I Peter 5:7. I prayed, "God, I don't know how to deal with this. I don't know how to pick up the broken pieces. I don't know how to rehabilitate, but Lord you are telling me that I can cast all my care on you and you will care for me. Tonight I am laying it down at your feet." I took my Bible and as an act of my will I laid it down at the feet of Jesus. I found rest unto my soul, my will , my emotions, anxieties and fears. I learned what it meant to take your burdens to the Lord and leave them there.

As I stayed on my knees that night, I reminded God of all that he said in his word. Then again I sang "Why should I be discouraged, why should the shadows come, why should my heart feel lonely and long for heaven and home. When Jesus is my portion, my constant friend is he. His eye is on the sparrow and I know he watches me." I pondered those words, " His eye is on the sparrow". My eyes filled up with tears of joy for I knew God was watching me. My God, the God that created the universe, was watching over me. Oh it was so exciting, so thrilling! I began to let the joy of the Lord spring up within my soul as I continued to sing some more. "*I sing because I'm happy, I sing because I'm free, for his eye is on the sparrow and I know he watches me.*" It was wonderful! I could break through in song and let God's joy become my strength. One must stay in prayer until victory is won, until your heart is lifted with songs of praise and worship. Only then can God begin to help you with your troubles.

People said, "Didn't you hate God for making you blind at the age of eighteen? Your whole life is before you." No, I didn't hate God. He had walked with me and He had talked with me all the way from kindergarten. At this time of my life I needed him more desperately than I ever needed him before. He was there for me, loving and overshadowing me. Like a hen gathers her chicks under her wings, God had gathered me under his wings.

As morning dawned I said, "Lord you told us to be filled with the knowledge of your will. If you want me to be filled with the knowledge of your will, then that means you will reveal your will to me." I didn't know as I said before how to pick up the broken pieces, but it was as though God was saying to me, "Marolyn, you can go off to Tennessee Temple and further your education , you can go with the use of a tape recorder." (all we had back in the 50's were reel to reel recorders, no cassettes) I could study from the tape recordings of the class lectures and take my test orally. I was so happy. I knew this was God giving me guidance.

The State of Michigan wanted me to go to a school for the adult blind but I had just gone blind and was told that this was permanent damage to my eyes. It was too soon for me to dive into training as a blind person. I wasn't ready to handle walking with a white cane, reading Braille and learning all that the blind need to learn.

More than anything I wanted to attend Tennessee Temple College in Chattanooga, Tennessee where my twin sister, Carolyn, was studying. I sent my application to Dr. Lee Roberson, president of the school, asking if I could enroll. I explained that though I could not see to read textbooks or write exams, I would be able to do my work by recording class lectures on tapes and studying them. With hope in my heart, I mailed the letter, and then prayed every day that I would be accepted.

In a few weeks the answer came. I had been accepted and could attend Tennessee Temple, but on one condition; before enrolling I would have to ask each teacher if he or she would be willing to work with me independently. This meant additional responsibility for the instructors; they would have to cover the material in the classroom discussions verbally since I could not read the books, and ask me the test questions after class. In November 1960, I visited Tennessee Temple's campus and my sister Carolyn. I was to enroll in January 1961, and because I was positive this was the Lord's will, I knew everything would work out.

Going On In Blindness

There wasn't time for me to adjust to life as a blind person before I had to leave for college. I was unwilling to believe this blindness had really happened to me. I felt like a cripple, strange and helpless, my body had become imperfect. I really needed time for adjustment, time to come to grips with my feelings. The importance of physical perfection emphasized by the world now made me feel insecure. Blindness was more than a loss of vision; it was an attack on my self-image. It meant more than losing my eyesight, it meant dying to the only way of life I had ever known. Some things were just too painful to talk about; the inability to see my mother's smile, a child's face, another human being, or even myself, made acceptance very difficult. I could no longer watch television, catch the writings on billboards and signs, find a phone number in the telephone directory, or read books of any kind - it was a grievous adjustment. I could no longer stay alert to the changing times, new hair styles, fashions, and makeup trends. Changes in landscaping and buildings went unnoticed. Friends and relatives tried to keep me aware of changes, but I could not visualize them. It was difficult to visualize from other people's descriptions, no matter how expertly given, just what they were trying to describe. I could not see their gestures, the nodding of their heads, the shrugging of their shoulders, their posture, or their facial expressions. I felt as though I was missing half of every conversation. I was standing still while around me the whole world was moving ahead.

The first struggle to rehabilitate myself was to learn a new way of recognizing people, for I could no longer see clearly enough to recognize faces. I had to start noticing forms and outlines, and learn to distinguish one from the other. I had to find new ways of doing everything. It was a very difficult time of adjustment. To bury myself in my studies was a healthy escape. It kept my mind busy, off of self and the loss of sight. I spent much time in the prayer tower and other rooms on campus where I could be alone with the Lord. I needed God to give me His peace in the midst of my storm and an understanding to know how to make this awesome adjustment in life. It was terribly difficult to pick up the broken pieces. I was God's child. He had delivered me from hell unto salvation. He adopted me as His child and therefore would surely care for me.

Love Isn't Blind

Carolyn was dating a young man on campus by the name of Hersholt Ford, so it was natural that I should meet him and his brother, Acie. What I hadn't expected was this deep-down feeling, Acie was the answer to my prayer. He was the young man I had been praying for since I was twelve years old.

On that first meeting, of course, I did not tell Acie that the Lord seemed to say, "Marolyn, this is the one you have been praying for all these years." I didn't know him, and besides, he was dating Carolyn's roommate (who later became my roommate). Yet there seemed to be a bond of understanding and closeness between us. We were drawn to one another by a mutual feeling of deep respect. God was drawing us together.

I was unable to see Acie's features, He only knew I was legally blind, that I could not see to read and write. Like others, he didn't know the extent of my blindness because I worked so hard to cover it up. I wore glasses then, and most people assumed that the glasses helped my vision. They didn't improve my vision, they only gave me something to hide behind. Having been born with blond hair I needed to darken my eyebrows a little. Since I could not see my face, I was never sure I had my eyebrows marked right. The frames of the glasses covered up any errors I may have made in applying makeup.

On the first evening of my visit to Tennessee Temple, My sister Carolyn, Acie, his brother Hersholt, his sister Hazel (who were students there also) and I went to the dating parlor. We all had a wonderful time getting acquainted with one another, especially Acie and I, as we talked and shared together.

The next morning after breakfast, Acie asked me for our first date. He said he would pick me up at 7:00 p.m. that evening. I was thrilled about having a date with this wonderful and handsome (so I had been told) man I had just met. At lunch I found a seat at a table, and suddenly Acie was sitting beside me. We dated every night that week. The more we learned about each other, the sweeter our friendship became. Acie seemed to possess those qualities I had prayed for in the man God had for me.

He was kind, tender, compassionate, understanding, sincere, and most important, he loved the Lord dearly.

All too soon the week ended. I went back to Michigan to wait until the January semester when I was to enroll in school. Acie and I corresponded during the month of December (I typed my letters to him as I couldn't see to write). When I returned in January, I had a small gift for him - a tie clasp. We were sitting in the dating parlor again, only this time he was telling me that he had his eye on a girl he wanted to ask out. Just as he spoke the girl's name, she appeared in the parlor. "There she is now," he said. My heart was crushed, but still I knew inside that someday we would be married. Therefore I encouraged him to date her. He had to find out she wasn't the right girl for him. He had to get to know her before he could know that.

My studies consumed most of my time. Studying by tape recorder was difficult, and for every hour I spent in class, I would have to spend at least two hours listening again and again to the tapes, trying to learn the material just from hearing it spoken. The instructors were most kind and understanding. They allowed me to leave the room during oral tests, and after class they would ask me the same test questions. During this time, students who needed to talk with the professor waited around and listened to me give answers. Because I had to answer test questions orally I was at first intimidated by this. Therefore, I studied harder for these test because I didn't want to be embarrassed by not knowing the answers. My diligence resulted in very good grades (3.8). Yet I couldn't have done it without the Lord's help and encouragement.

When I was not studying Bible or music, I was studying Acie Ford. I wanted to know his strengths and weaknesses, to understand his moods and mannerisms. I wanted to know when he needed encouragement and a listening ear. Like any young woman after a man, I sought opportunities to talk with him.

God's Direction

Remember the story of Samuel as found in I Samuel 3. God called Samuel three times. Twice Samuel thought Eli had called him but was told that he had not. *"Then Eli realized it was the Lord who had spoken to the child"* (I Samuel 3:8b). As the Lord called to Samuel a third time, he responded as Eli had instructed him to do: *"And the Lord came and called as before, "Samuel! Samuel!' And Samuel replied, 'Yes, I'm listening'"* (I Samuel 3:10). Acie had answered God's call many times as a young lad. Then as he grew and matured, God's call became clearer to him.

Acie had first dedicated his life to the Lord when he was 10 years old. Even then he knew the Lord was calling him into full-time Christian service. Often as the pastor gave the invitation to come forward for those whom Christ was speaking, young Acie would respond and make his way down the church aisle. He didn't know why he went forward and didn't fully understand the prompting of God in his life. He just knew that God was calling and that his heart was sensitive to that call.

One day during the summer following his high school graduation, he was driving around with his friend, Phil Rogers. Acie had pre-registered at Northeast Louisiana State College, where Phil had attended the previous year. Thinking of the future, Acie said, "I believe God wants something different for me." Phil answered, "You need to do what He wants you to do."

That night Acie talked with Phil's father, the Rev. W. R. Rogers, who told him of Tennessee Temple College. Acie respected his opinion, for it was under his ministry that he had grown up and accepted the call to preach. So Acie enrolled at Tennessee Temple in September, not knowing how he would pay tuition and other expenses. He just knew the Lord was leading him to this Baptist College where he could prepare himself for the Lord's work. This was a real step of faith for Acie, because he knew that he was responsible to pay the school bill and had no one to help him financially. It was just Acie and the Lord. Acie only knew that, "Where God guides, He does provide." One week after school began he found work in one of the downtown clothing stores. Acie took this to be an indication of God's approval.

Acie's favorite verses are in Proverbs, "*Trust in the Lord with all your heart, And do not lean on your own understanding. In all your ways acknowledge Him. And He will make your paths straight.*" Proverbs 3:5-6(NAS). We also read in Proverbs, "Commit your work to the Lord, then it will succeed" (Proverbs 16:3).

God always draws us to Himself. Solomon said, "*The mind of man plans his way, But the Lord directs his steps.*" Proverbs 16:9 (NAS).

God made man with a body, soul and spirit. The body is external, the physical; the soul is internal, the intellect and emotions, the self-will, our thoughts, opinions, desires and feelings. The spirit of a man goes much deeper. It is the eternal, inner conscience of a man. The spirit is that inner intuition which tells the Christian whether things are right or wrong. We must learn to live according to our inner spirit and not base our decisions on our emotions. Our inward desires are what God uses to guide us into His ways, and He will never guide us in any way that is contrary to His Word.

When we read and study the Bible and find a tidbit which really means something special to us, we should write it down and memorize it. We should meditate on it throughout the day. It will be amazing what will be learned each time it is brought to mind. We should take that tidbit from God's Word and give it back to God in prayer. Mull it over in our mind. Get it into our spirit.

To have the mind of Christ does not mean that we are to stop thinking. We study and think through each situation with our own minds. Then the Spirit within us will work with our spirit to lead us and move us forward. It takes time to know the mind of Christ. We need to enter our prayer chamber and persevere with importunate prayer. We must set our hearts upon God and then He will guide us into all truth. God will give Himself to those who wholeheartedly seek after Him. He will meet us only as we give ourselves to Him. We need to let Jesus occupy our minds and enjoy His presence more than anything else.

In 1960, one day as Acie was in the prayer tower talking with the Lord and reading his Bible, his eyes fell on Matthew 5:6, *"Blessed are they which do hunger and thirst after righteousness, for they shall be filled."* Since early boyhood days, Acie had a hunger for the things of God which had drawn him to the Bible to seek after God. It was this spiritual pull which led him to the "prayer tower." This particular day was to be very special. The Holy Ghost came upon him and touched his life. He was given the gift of mercy, power and a freedom he had not possessed before.

Prior to this time he had found it difficult to witness to others because of an inhibited spirit. He now had an overwhelming desire and freedom to talk to others about Jesus' love. With no inhibitions and without intimidation he talked to others of the joy he was experiencing. His love for the Lord and his close walk with Him was felt by everyone he met or knew. Even his professors noted the change in Acie and asked about it. This change was a work of God in his life- a lifetime call of full surrender. He had no doubts now about his call to the ministry. His hunger and thirst after God has never stopped. His desire to share Jesus Christ with others has not lessened. Acie had no more doubts that he had been called to preach the Gospel and shepherd God's people.

When we abide in Christ and stay close to His Word, we have the confidence that we are moving in the Spirit because we have the mind of Christ. When He opens a door, we are to walk through it. If it is not His door, He will close it.

Meditation on the Word of God is necessary if our attitude toward sin is to be adjusted. The Psalmist teaches us, "But they delight in doing everything God wants them to, and day and night are always meditating on his laws and thinking about ways to follow him more closely." Psalm 1:2 (LB). God has given us so much in the Bible He wants us to know. And the only way we will learn these things which He has for us is through meditation.

At the time I had prayed for my future husband, whoever he would be, I had also prayed for my in-laws. I had prayed that they would love and accept me, and that we would have a sweet and lovely relationship. God answered that prayer. Even before Acie and I became serious in our love relationship, I fell in love with his parents, Virginia and Willard Ford. They came to visit him, and wanting to get better acquainted with me, they invited me to go out with them for the afternoon and evening. Should I go or shouldn't I? Acie had a date with another girl that night, and I didn't want him to think that I was chasing him by visiting with his family all evening. Mr. Ford insisted, saying that he would let Acie know I was there at his request and not for any other reason. The Fords and I had a wonderful time. It was as if we had known each other for years. Later Acie told us that the entire time he was out with his date that night, he was wishing he could be with us. That incident, along with the fact that another young man had asked me to marry him, opened Acie's eyes to his true feelings about me.

As Acie and I became more serious, we had long talks about our feelings toward each other. At first Acie thought that perhaps it wasn't love he felt for me, but pity because of my blindness. In time, we knew it was true love and it was of God that we were together.

Romance

The day came when I happily called my parents to tell them Acie and I were planning to be married in the summer. I admired their attitude; they didn't ask me, "Are you sure this is the right fellow? Can he support you?" They seemed to feel that if this was my choice, then it was all right with them. Perhaps they felt as though they already knew Acie. I had written them weekly, telling them all about him in my typewritten letters.

We were married August 14, 1962, and I was finally able to tell Acie how the Lord had seemed to say to me on the day we met, "This is the one you have been praying for all these years." Our wedding was a beautiful church ceremony with a large reception. Mother worked out most of the details, the flower and candle arrangements and the dress colors and patterns. My future mother-in-law sewed every stitch of my wedding dress, a white floor-length gown with a long train flowing behind. I often worried about the dress not fitting because she had never sewn for me before, but she assured me that it would fit because she was praying with every stitch. At the reception dinner, my brother Don, and his wife, Clara did a splendid job as master and mistress of ceremonies. Everything went beautifully.

Our plans for the honeymoon were to visit Canada. We drove from Holland, Michigan to Grand Rapids, Michigan, where at 1:00 a.m. our borrowed car refused to go any further. We walked to a nearby motel and banged on the door, trying to awaken the manager. A hippie-looking fellow heard us, and said he was about to leave, and offered us his room. We declined his offer, but asked if he would drive us into Grand Rapids to find a place to get the car repaired. He took us to an all-night wrecker service several miles from the motel. I'll never forget getting into that dirty wrecker on my honeymoon night, dressed in my "going away" outfit - a navy blue and white dress, a corsage, white gloves and a hat. Since my skirt was fitted, I could not step up into the high cab of the wrecker and Acie had to lift me up into the truck.

We were back at the motel by 2:00 a.m. to hook up our broken down car so the wrecker service could tow it. The manager was awake this time, and gave us a room. After locking me safely in our room, Acie went back with the mechanic to get the car repaired. On his way back to the motel he lost his way and couldn't locate the motel. At 4:00 a.m. he drove up with the car repaired. I had gone to bed. Acie came in, started to put on his pajamas, and found that the seamstress at the clothing store where Acie worked had sewn the arms and legs shut with fine machine stitching. We laughed and laughed as we sat and picked out the threads. I couldn't see what I was doing. Acie had a time with it.

The next day we headed for Ontario, Canada, as we had planned, but after we crossed the United States - Canadian border, we changed our minds. Heavy rains backed up traffic for miles. Everyone spoke French, but we could tell by signs along the way that gasoline and motel rates were very high. Having already spent a good bit of our money on the car, we didn't have much left. As evening came we began looking for a motel, but after talking it over, we decided to save money by going back to the States. We needed a rest room and we were hungry, but we had to stay in line to drive onto the ferry. Cars were in line four rows abreast for about a mile. It took us hours to get back on the ferry. When we were finally on the other side, we drove for miles and miles, but not a gas station, restaurant, or motel was in sight. While totally exhausted, we felt we could drive no further, we saw a sign that read "20 miles" to a motel. We made it somehow, but what a disappointment when we arrived! The "motel" was just a small roadside inn without a restaurant. It was another fifty miles to the closest restaurant. Acie summed up our feelings the next day when he suggested, "Let's go back to your mama's in the morning so we can get a good night's sleep and some good food.

We didn't let it ruin our honeymoon. Acie had been singing as we drove and he continued singing, *"Beautiful, Beautiful blue eyes. I'll never love brown eyes again"* and *"You are my sunshine, my only sunshine. You make me happy when skies are gray. You'll never know dear, how much I love you, Please don't take my sunshine away"*.

Despite the unfortunate circumstances, our marriage was off to a wonderful start. After the honeymoon, we drove back to Tennessee Temple where we moved into a second floor apartment just off campus. In June of the next year Acie graduated from Tennessee Temple with a Bachelor of Theology degree. We then moved to Grand Rapids, Michigan, where Acie enrolled in the Grand Rapids Baptist Bible College. He worked his way through school once again as a clothing salesman. Acie graduated in June, 1965.

We had been told it was best for a young minister to pastor a small church for a short time between his college and seminary education. In that way he would learn what to study in seminary, and his education would mean much more to him. Therefore, that is what we did. Two months after graduation from Grand Rapids we were called to the Bosco Baptist Church in Monroe, Louisiana, where we pastored for a year. It was at this church that Acie was ordained and licensed into the ministry, and it was here that I suffered my first miscarriage.

Trusting God For Daily Provision

In 1966, the Lord led us back to Tennessee Temple in Chattanooga, where Acie enrolled in seminary to work on a master's degree. The only thing we were sure of was that the Lord was leading us, and that where He leads, He always provides for our needs. We arrived in Chattanooga with our car pulling a small U-haul trailer holding everything we owned. We were without money and did not know where we would live or where Acie would work. We went to the home of some friends who gave us the name of a woman renting apartments near the school. We called her and found she had just built a duplex. One side had been rented to a couple who were Temple students, and the other was available for rent at a reasonable price. After we moved in Acie walked downtown everyday to look for work. The Lord was good to give him work as a salesman in one of the downtown clothing stores.

I also enrolled in Temple. The first time I had enrolled as a Bible major. This time I enrolled as a music major, and loved it! I went as far as I could go in my music training. A year before graduation I had to discontinue studies at school, but I continued to study music at home. It meant a great deal to me as a hobby, and it was always a blessing in our church work.

On February 22, 1968, during our last year at Tennessee Temple, a new Ford came into our lives. Acie chose the name "Sharon Marie" for our seven-pound, ten-ounce baby girl. Acie described her features to me, for all I could see was a little form, an outline, a bundle of flesh. Sharon added so much to our lives!

One Potato, Two Potato

We were in Chattanooga, Tennessee and it was Acie's last year in seminary. We had struggled to pay the school bill, to keep up with the house rent, utilities and groceries. Acie's mother and dad were coming to visit us from Louisiana but were not expected until around bedtime. They pulled up in our driveway just as I was boiling our one and only potato we had in the house. I said, "Acie, what are we going to do? I don't have any food for them, this is our last potato?" Mom and Dad entered the house. We embraced with much love and joyful excitement but I dreaded having to tell her about my one and only potato boiling in the little pan of water on the stove. I began saying, "I'm sorry about this little potato, I don't have..." " Oh honey," she interrupted just like she knew what I was going to say, "you wouldn't believe it, I have a bag of potatoes in the car. We backed the car out of the driveway and I told Willard I needed to go back into the house to get that bag of potatoes I intended to bring with us." She said, "I just couldn't leave without that bag of potatoes. I knew you would need it. We'll just fix some for us all." I was so relieved. She is a very Godly lady and often directed in her spirit.

God had shown us his provision more than once that year. We had been attending the Highland Park Baptist Church on campus and I had been involved in a Sunday School Class that had planned to give a "food shower" to a needy family. Everyone had been asked to bring the grocery items to the class so I gathered up my supplies and placed it on the pile for the needy family. To our surprise, two days before Thanksgiving day the food shower was delivered to us. We couldn't believe they came to our door with all these groceries. There was a big bag of sugar, a large bag of flour and rice, vegetables, soups, margarine, Crisco, canned goods and pasta. They piled my table full. We were overjoyed and giving thanks to God for supplying our need.

It is of utmost importance that we develop the habit of praying about every little detail of our lives. Paul wrote to the Philippians, *"Don't worry about anything; instead, pray about everything; tell God your needs and don't forget to thank Him for His answers. If you do this you will experience God's peace, which is far more wonderful than the human mind can understand. His peace will keep your thoughts and your hearts quiet and at rest as you trust in Christ Jesus."* (Philippians 4:6-7). What a powerful promise. Pray about everything and know His peace.

Upon rising in the morning, before or after breakfast, spend at least a half hour with the Lord in prayer and in His Word. Try to do the same in the afternoon. Feast upon the prayer promises of

God in faith throughout the day as you are occupied with multiplicity of tasks. Seek God in prayer moment by moment for His guidance. Be sensitive to the movement of the Spirit in your innermost being, then seek to follow His leading. Honor God's most holy presence by giving the Spirit complete authority over your soul, and you will have learned how to walk in the Spirit. It's a real discipline to maintain. When the end of the day comes, your heart will be at peace. You will have enjoyed sweet fellowship with the Lord all day. Before going to sleep you may only need to say, "Good night, Lord Jesus. I love you!"

This kind of praying will keep us from backsliding. Prayer only before meals and at bedtime will help us maintain a distant walk with God wherein we will experience little power with God. Continual prayer to God allows us to reach to higher levels of God-consciousness with more growth, more strength, and more of His leadership. It enables us to experience God's power and to make His blessings real in our lives. When we are drawn to prayer by God's Spirit, we must learn to receive His answer by faith. Jesus said, *"Didn't I tell you that you would see a wonderful miracle from God if you believe?"* John 11:40 (LB).

God's Call

During seminary days, Acie had many opportunities to preach each week in services at nursing homes, children's homes, jails, city missions, and detention homes for teenagers. After completing graduate work at Tennessee Temple Seminary, we began to candidate for a pastorate. Two churches called us during the same week. One was a small church in Louisiana, which could offer only a part-time position. Acie would have to take a secular job if we accepted the call to this church. The other church was a larger one in Kentucky which offered a full-time position. We prayed about the decision, and felt led to accept the pastoral position at the smaller church. We moved in September, 1968 to take up our pastorate at the Cross Roads Baptist Church in Farmerville, Louisiana, where we lived for four years.

When we know what the will of God is for us in any situation, we do not have to worry about what is going to happen. We must accept it and then do it. Paul wrote in I Thessalonians 5:24 (KJV), *"He is faithful who calleth you. He will bring it to pass."* God is in complete control. Our faith must be stable, not wavering. James says, *"But when you ask Him, be sure that you really expect Him to tell you, for a doubtful mind will be as unsettled as a wave of the sea that is driven and tossed by the wind; And every decision you then make will be uncertain, as you turn first this way, and then that. If you don't ask with faith, don't expect the Lord to give you any solid answer."* James 1:6-8.

Living with blindness wasn't easy. When I lost beyond 20/600 vision and previous methods no longer worked, I had to learn new ways of doing things. With greater loss of vision difficulties increased. My vision dropped so low I only had the ability to count how many fingers the doctor held before my nose. I became totally blind except for light-perception. The inner agony tore me apart. To keep my mind off my blindness, I began teaching a college and career age Sunday school class, led a ladies mission study group and became the church choir director.

Terribly frustrating was the fact that I could not see to recognize individuals. As music director of the church, I could seldom locate the persons with whom I needed to speak concerning special music for future services. Sometimes I heard them speaking to someone after choir practice, and if I hurried I could catch them. This manner of locating individuals caused me a great deal of stress. If I failed to catch them at the church it sometimes meant calling long-distance which over-stretched the budget. Music was an enjoyable part of my work. My choir consisted of about twenty-five people who loved the challenge of new music and it fell upon me to have a new song prepared for choir practice. Early each Monday I began preparation for the Sunday evening choir practice. From a record, I picked the song I felt led to use. If I did not have a record with a particular song on it, I would borrow it from a friend. Each year we presented a Christmas and Easter cantata. In order to be able to teach the alto, tenor and bass singers their parts I had to find the key it was written in, pick out the notes, chord and correct timing. Preparing and memorizing music for the choir weekly occupied about two hours of my time daily. By Thursday, I had the words and music memorized so that Friday and Saturday could be spent reviewing the song. By the time I met with the choir Sunday evening, I was well prepared.

I was hesitant to invite guests in for a meal because I would have to clear the dishes off the table before serving the desert. Being blind I couldn't locate the dishes without feeling around for them. It embarrassed me to clear the dishes off the table if a sighted person was nearby. I waited to do it until after even Acie left the dining area. When I did have guests over, I preferred to serve only coffee and snacks , I could manage that. Often I invited the church people over to the house following Sunday night services for a singspiration fellowship. I usually served cokes, coffee and brownies - help yourself style.

Separation

I had enrolled as a trainee at the Arkansas Enterprise For Adult Blind, Inc. in Little Rock, Arkansas. Immediately after entering the Training Center, I began attending classes. I was taught practical living courses, how to read and write Braille, walk with a white cane and how to do math on a Chinese bead-board called an "abacus." Life was hectic, there was no time for gradual adjustment. I was thrust right into activities. This constant activity was good. I didn't have time to change my mind and go home.

That first day when I was feeling so desperate and frightened, I went to a small group therapy session. Mr. Strickland, a mobility instructor, knew exactly what I was feeling inside because he himself had been blind for four years. Surgery had helped him, however, and his sight had gradually returned to normal. After that first meeting, he asked to talk with me. Going right to the point, he helped me understand that my emotional problems stemmed from the fact that I was a normal person in an abnormal situation. This was a great consolation, because I almost feared I could become emotionally unbalanced. The multiple losses of blindness had an extreme effect on how I felt about myself, yet I had to face my blindness realistically. As I became blind, I gradually lost myself in an unsighted personality; I had lost my identity. Through his help I adjusted to my new life and began to understand the reasons for my confusion.

Soon after moving to the Training Center, I added a new accessory to my everyday attire; a long, slender Hoover cane. Its purpose was not to be a crutch, but rather an extension of my sense of feel. Before receiving my own cane, I trained one week to get the feel of the cane and how to hold it. I was taught how to find doors inside the buildings and how to get to classrooms using the cane. Each building had a sidewalk around it which elevated slightly at the door, and then leveled off again. The elevation of the sidewalk established doorways for me. I learned to listen to the tapping sound of the cane. As the sidewalk elevated or declined, for example, the tap sound changed. Tapping a small cement square produced a different sound from tapping a large cement square. Tapping in front of a brick building made a sound different from that produced by tapping in front of a building with a glass front. I practiced over and over until I could distinguish the difference between these sounds.

There was a procedure for everything at the center. For example, at each mealtime we (myself and the other trainees) would go upstairs to the dining hall, which had a three-foot-wide strip of carpet all around the edge of the floor. As long as we stayed on the carpet, we knew where we were; it served as a path. Once inside the dining hall, we turned left, and followed the carpet the length of the wall. As we felt the window, we knew when to turn. The drapery established the corner for us. We would turn right and walk to the next corner. We progressed around the dining room by walking along the walls, and actually made a square before we were in line to be served.

The kitchen staff would set our plates on the counter. If they tried to hand them to us, we could either miss them completely, or bump them and cause a spill. When they set our plates on the counter, we knew exactly where to feel for them. Each blind person was assigned a particular chair at a certain table for the duration of his stay. After I received my plate, I would follow the carpet until I came to the tables. With my plate in my left hand, I would feel the tables edge with my right hand. I counted tables until I came to the third row. Unfortunately, everyone didn't use this method. Some were so afraid of spilling their food that they would clutch their plates tightly with two hands and steer themselves with the plate instead of guiding themselves with their hands. The tables were close together; therefore sometimes when I was eating, someone would crash his/her plate into the back of my head and spill food all over me. Often I felt like saying, "If you would just hold the plate with your left hand and guide yourself with your right hand, you wouldn't hit me with your plate," but I couldn't be rude to them, so I never voiced that.

Four people sat at each table which was about the size of a card table, and the table was set exactly the same way every day. The napkins were placed in the middle of the table. The salt and pepper were on the other side of the napkin holder from me. The butter was on the right of the napkins, and the sugar was on the left. My table partners were three men, one of whom annoyed me by getting his fingers in my dessert at nearly every meal. This fellow, who sat to my right, often reached into the middle of the table for sugar, licked his fingers with a smack so that I could hear it, and said, "OOPS, I'm sorry, I got in your dessert again." Had he used the correct procedure, which was not to reach, but to glide the hand across the table around the dishes to find whatever he desired. I could have enjoyed the desert. One day after he had gone, I said to the waitress, "Just on this one table, could we switch the butter and the sugar so the sugar bowl will be in front of his plate rather than over here by my dessert? This way he will be able to find it easier without reaching over my plate for it." The waitress agreed, but it didn't solve the problem, he usually forgot, and reached anyway.

When we went to the dining hall to eat, we always left our canes on a coat hook. I could find my cane after dining because each person was fitted to his or her cane, others did not feel right. Each cane also had a chain on the top with a distinctive gadget for identification. Mine was something from my key chain. I could find my cane easily enough, but sometimes someone in a hurry would make a mistake and walk off with the wrong cane. I would come from a meal, search the cane rack, and find mine was missing. I knew if I borrowed someone else's, he or she would be stranded, so I would wait at the coat rack, listening for a familiar voice. If I didn't recognize a voice, I had to ask someone who came by if she would be going to the dorm, and if I could take her arm and walk with her to get the second cane I kept in my room. Usually the person who had taken the wrong cane would discover the error and return the cane to the coat rack at the next meal.

As I began to learn my way around the Training Center, I found that the things which frightened me most were stairways. When I went up a flight of stairs I hung on to the railing. I went very slowly, and put two feet on each step before proceeding to the next step. Coming down was even worse. I felt as though I was going to fall on my face. To make a difficult situation even worse, there seemed to be stairs and steps all over the campus. I learned that with blindfolds on, most sighted people are able to go up or down steps without trouble, but the blind cannot do this without practicing and regaining their confidence in motor memory. After a couple of weeks of my slow progress, my mobility instructor asked, "Marolyn, when in the world are you going to start walking those steps like you used to do?" "What do you mean?" I asked. "You didn't put two feet on one step and pause on each one before you went blind. You put one foot on each step and kept going," he explained. I realized then how ridiculous I must have looked, and decided that no matter how unsteady I felt, I would master those steps.

Often when I went out for a walk, feelings of panic would arise because of my fear of the unknown that might be ahead. I could overcome the fear of chairs or small obstacles that might be in my path, but awnings, low-hanging signs, or tree branches that could strike me across the face were the unknown dangers and difficulties. The blind need more motivation than a sighted person would need before daring to venture out. Just because you, as a sighted person are tired of sitting, that is enough motivation for you to get up and take a walk. That may not be so with the blind.

Community travel also frightened me. Sometimes as I walked along the roadside with my mind on other things, my cane would suddenly hit a parked car, startling me. I learned that I had to think about obstacles that I might step on along the way, such as broken sidewalks, hills, or thick grass. I worried about getting lost, wandering too far, or going east when I wanted to go west. I was in constant fear of holes in the ground and pavement, rocks in my path, and toys on the floor. A barking dog became frightening when I could not see his tail wag or know he was behind a fence.

At first carrying a cane embarrassed me. It didn't bother me at the Training Center where everyone was blind and carried a cane with them, but Downtown Little Rock, in public places, was another story. I felt intimidated. Nevertheless, as my training progressed, I learned to be proud of my white cane, and to use it with dignity. My eyes didn't show blindness; therefore strangers had no way of knowing I was blind. The white cane spoke for itself. I didn't have to tell them I was blind and I didn't have to wait for people to discover my blindness through some mistake I made. They could see for themselves. Before, I tried with all my power to hide my blindness. Now I was proud that my white cane testified to that fact. It made life so much easier.

Once I got over being self-conscious about my cane, I learned what a great help it was. If I was shopping in a big department store and wanted to find the shoe department, I would tap my cane from left to right down the aisle until I touched carpet. Back in the 50's most aisles were tile and most shoe departments were carpeted. If I smelled leather, I knew I had found it. To find the cosmetic counter, I walked until I smelled powder. I found the candy counter by following the aroma of peanuts and popcorn. To find the ladies' department, I again felt for carpet with my cane. By feeling the clothes, I could tell if I was in the adult department. I would stand for a minute and listen for the cash register to ring; then make my way toward it. When the clerks were no longer busy, they would see my white cane and ask, "May I help you?" Then I would describe what I wanted to buy, suggesting color, size, style, fabric and price range.

Even though my training made shopping easier and fun, I didn't buy much while I was at the Training Center. When a sales clerk said a dress was green, I had no way of knowing if I liked that shade of green. If she said it had a nice design, I didn't know if the design was in accordance with my taste. I missed Acie's judgment, I had come to trust it so much that I didn't want to purchase any clothes without his opinion. He knew my taste in clothes and he was honest about what didn't look good and that which complimented me. I thank God I had married a man who knew the difference.

Sense of Humor

I had made many friends and we used our sense of humor once more. One day I was standing by a vending machine talking to Willard, a friend who had some vision. Another friend, Donna, who was totally blind, came down the hallway, bumped into the machine, and thinking it was a person, began apologizing in the sweetest, most humble manner. "Oh, excuse me," she said. "I didn't mean to bump into you." Willard and I both knew what had happened. There was no one else in the hall. Willard could not contain his laughter. He explained to Donna that she was apologizing to the vending machine. All three of us enjoyed a good laugh.

Another incident proved funny only after it happened. It was in downtown Little Rock in my mobility training class. I had a particular route to follow, and a friend, whom I'll call Joe, had the same route as mine, only in reverse, which meant that at some point as we walked around our block, our paths would meet. Joe never allowed himself to learn that a white cane is a delicate instrument, intended to be tapped lightly from side to side. Joe was quite robust, and would ungracefully slap his cane from left to right. I found myself in front of a bus stop on this particular day, with people on the right of me lined up against a building waiting to catch a bus. Parking meters and traffic were on the left and straight ahead I cold hear the unmistakable sound of Joe slapping his cane on the sidewalk! *Whap! Whap! Whap!* As Joe came closer and closer, I walked slower and slower. *Whap! Whap!*

Grace to Endure

Whap! Joe was whipping his cane from side to side as though he was trying to tear the sidewalk apart. There was no mistake now. He was coming straight toward me! I tried calling out to him, but my voice was lost in the sounds of the city buses as they approached the curb and the traffic flying by. We had been taught not to make a sudden move when we were uncertain of our surroundings; it was better to stand still. As I made my "uncertain stand" Joe crashed into me, cane and all. As soon as it happened, he called out, "Marolyn, is that you?" I'm sure it was amusing to the people waiting for the bus. It was funny to me only later when I mused over how we must have looked.

Every day at the Training Center we had a two-hour class in downtown mobility. I learned that when crossing a street, I should immediately start across with my cane as soon as I heard the traffic stop in one direction, and the cars accelerate headed in the other direction. I was not to pause or hesitate. Otherwise drivers would begin turning the corner because they assumed that I didn't know the light had changed; and once the cars started turning, I would have to wait until the light changed again. The whole procedure was dangerous, but my mobility instructor went with me until he was sure I could handle it alone.

Often when I was crossing a street, someone would come up to me and offer to help. I appreciated the kindness, but unless a blind person is obviously in trouble or seeking help, it is much better to let him cross the street in his own way. Sometimes a well-meaning person will take a blind person by the arm, and push him forward, without realizing that this is frustrating for the blind and may cause him to stumble.

I also had to learn how to walk a straight line; blindness had caused a loss of judgment. Veering too much to the right or left while walking could be confusing and dangerous. Holding the cane in the right position, I found out, had a lot to do with walking in a straight line. At first I learned to alternately tap the grass

56

at the edge of the sidewalk and then the cement. Later I learned to walk in a straight line without tapping the grass; there wasn't always an edge to follow.

Blindness also causes one to lose their sense of direction. I could turn around once or twice, and be completely disoriented. I learned to orient myself by the sounds about me. Sounds of busy downtown, street noises indicating which way the cars were going, and the screech of brakes were all clues to help me find my way. At home I listened for the refrigerator or the tick-tock of a clock that always stayed on the same nightstand in the bedroom. Then I would know which direction I was facing and where the door was located. If I knew that the dog was kept in a fence at a certain corner, I learned that it could help me orient myself. Certain tree branches and leaves made different sounds as the wind blew through them. Various birds singing in the trees on particular corners helped me find my way, as did the smell of roses in some yards. The warmth of the sun, coolness of the shade of a building or a tree; the way the air felt when it came through the break between two buildings helped me know how far I had progressed down the sidewalk.

My sense of smell helped me locate particular stores. A bakery smelled like dough, a pipe store - tobacco, a restaurant - food, a shoe store - leather, a dime store - peanuts, and a bank - like money. Often just when I thought I might be lost, these sounds and smells reassured me. Smelling and hearing became most important. I learned that when I put a cake into the oven, it smelled raw, but when it was ready to be taken out, it smelled fresh and well-baked. I could detect when fried chicken was well cooked and tender by listening to the sizzles to die away in the frying pan. When pouring fluids into a glass the sound changed as the liquid approached the rim of the glass.

Blindness does cause a person's other senses to become stronger and develops highly sensitive fingers and sensitive hearing.

Before losing my eyesight, I would take a dime out of my pocket, and look to be sure it was not a penny. I would hear water boiling, but look to see the bubbles. Now that I was totally blind I had to depend upon my other senses. I gained confidence in knowing I had not been totally impaired by the loss of my sight.

Developing my sense of touch was extremely important. I wanted very much to learn how to pick things up without knocking them over. I learned to move my hand lightly and let my little finger be my guide. The touch of the little finger, I was told, was so delicate that it wouldn't cause a spill. After locating an object, I could put my hand around it and not worry about tipping it over.

Business Independence

Everyone who attended the Center was required to learn to knit and crochet. This was good even for the men; it developed our sense of touch and prepared us for feeling the Braille dots. I learned that Braille was made up of six little raised dots that, when arranged in different positions, formed every word in the English language, including letters, punctuation marks, numbers, Roman numerals, fractions, and decimals.

Each day I learned lessons in Braille. In the beginning, when I was learning the alphabet, the lessons were easier, and I was able to accomplish several lessons a day. I soon found out, however, that Braille is a kind of shorthand. The dots that stood for the word "knowledge" were used in different positions and stood for many different words. Braille required much memorization.

When I reached third grade Braille it seemed at times I couldn't comprehend any more. I thought, "Oh, dear! I've come to a standstill. That's all I can learn." My fears overwhelmed me. My instructor explained that this often happened. Since I was trying to learn so quickly, I could expect this to occur at different times throughout my Braille studies. He recommended a break in the lessons. When my mind had absorbed the first and second series of lessons, I would be able to go on. I took his advice, and found that after a few days I was able to continue Braille lessons.

Most of the trainees did not rush through several lessons daily, but I wanted to complete my training in three months. I wanted to get back to my husband and daughter, my church work, and all the things that were waiting for me. I worked desperately every day to comprehend everything I needed to learn. As I progressed further into the lessons, I came to another standstill. My Braille Instructor said I could go ahead two or three lessons, and gradually the previous lessons would fall into place.

I learned Braille in two months, and spent the third month reviewing it and putting it into practice. I could not have learned so quickly without the Lord's help. Jesus said, *"The effectual fervent prayer of a righteous man availeth much"* (James 5:16 KJV). I prayed every day that the Lord would be with me, to help and strengthen me. I prayed that I would be able to comprehend Braille, and develop my other senses and rehabilitate myself quickly. Philippians 4:13 meant so much to me: "I can do all things through Christ which strengtheneth me."

An instructor showed me how I could take care of my own business affairs by using an abacus for adding, subtracting, multiplying and working with fractions and decimals. In addition to learning Braille, typing, mobility, sewing, crocheting, knitting, wood crafts, abacus etc., classes at the Training Center also involved kinetics, the science of dealing with the motion of masses in relation to the forces acting on them. I learned that if I held the edge of a book toward my face, then turned the book so that the face of it was in front of my face I could feel the pressure on my cheek or forehead. I learned to detect a wall or chair as I approached it. Some people can only feel an object when it is within inches in front of them; others notice it a few feet away.

Those blind from birth have a greater capacity for kinetic perception because they developed it from youth.

After three months, I completed my training at the Arkansas Enterprise for Adult Blind, Inc. and was ready to go home. It was time to live the lessons I learned in Braille, typing, abacus, cooking, practical living, and mobility. Since I was married to a very special guy, had a darling little girl and a full active life of ministry work at the church I could hardly wait to get home with my family.

Together Again

The time we spent apart was difficult for all three of us. Sharon had stayed at Grandma Ford's house while I was in training. Acie had a bi-vocational church; therefore, he worked in a men's clothing store selling suits all day and pastoring the church during the evenings and on weekends. We were so glad to be back together.

As a blind person, I did not want to appear awkward to others. Not knowing how I looked, I depended on others to tell me if I did something incorrectly. Friends assured me that I handled myself with dignity and used my cane gracefully. Their words gave me the confidence I needed. As a minister's wife, I went to many church meetings and into many homes for visitation and it was important that I handled myself well.

Acie was a tremendous help. Being a meticulous man, he was quick to tell me if anything was wrong with my appearance, whether it was my slip showing or a run in my hosiery, my hair style or make-up. He assured me that all was well or not well. I felt confident when I was with him, for I could depend on him to keep an eye on these things. He always did it in love because he knew I wanted to know. I looked my best for Acie's sake as well as my own. This lack of self-sufficiency and personal independence made me feel my losses from the first day I lost my sight at age eighteen. I prayed that the Lord would help me to have a healthy emotional attitude as I learned to depend on others.

However, I was able to be independent in many things, teaching my college and career Sunday School class, directing the church choir and organizing the ladies missionary group at the church. Most importantly, I was able to take care of my family and my house.

Although I was taught how to hand write at the Training Center, it was never easy to do. I usually made the letters too narrow, on top of each other, or I drew them out too far. Everyone at the Center had to learn to type. I just had to increase my speed and accuracy in typing.

By not being able to see facial expressions and hand gestures, I found I missed much in conversation. For example, a grin on the face, a shrug of the shoulder, or a look in the eye indicates a person's attitude about what was said. Often my sighted friends would forget that I could not catch this unspoken part of the conversation, and I would wonder, "Did they like the idea? Did they accept what I said? Did they agree or disagree?" It was difficult to judge people's reactions without seeing their expressions. I listened for different tones in the voices, for feet beginning to shuffle from uneasiness, for anything that would help me understand the mood of the conversation. If there was a lengthy pause in the conversation, I wondered if the person I had been talking with had left the room, or perhaps they were still there and expecting me to say something. I was never sure whether to speak or keep silent. It's uncomfortable to find your friend had left your side and your words were just spoken into open air. Then you wonder if anyone saw you do that. I appreciated those friends who told me when someone new came into the group or when someone left. Thick carpet prevented me from hearing approaching or receding footsteps, and I had no way of knowing unless someone told me.

I had to consciously avoid picking up blindisms, those habits or peculiarities unconsciously practiced by the blind that draw attention. Some persons display blindness by shuffling their feet, standing or sitting crooked, rolling their eyes, or showing no facial expressions or hand gestures. These blindisms interfere with conversations, and set up barriers. Knowing that, I tried to look as natural as possible. I practiced using expressions and hand gestures, and responding to noises or my surroundings. If a door slammed, I looked in that direction; if something dropped, I looked down. I also practiced scribbling with a pencil or looking out of the window as though I could see. I didn't want to stand out like a sore thumb.

Show Respect

I hadn't seen my face since I was a teenager. Having been unable to see other people's expressions, I wasn't sure my expressions were always correct. Usually I would show no reaction at all until I was sure of the mood of conversation. I asked Acie to tell me if I did something strange or peculiar. I knew that by appearing as normal as possible, my sighted friends would feel more comfortable around me. Sighted people are often afraid they might say the wrong thing to the blind, or use words like "look" and "see." Those words were part of my vocabulary, feeling free to use words like "look" and "see" seemed to remove awkwardness from the conversation. I never wanted sighted people to feel that they had to apologize for using these words in my presence.

Sometimes a person can be blind, yet able to see outlines and shadows which helps them not to bump into people and things as they move. The brightness or dullness of the sun and/or physical and emotional health are other factors. One day a blind person may feel excellent and be able to read a little by holding the printed page close to his nose. The next day he may feel tired, and not be able to read at all.

My eyes did not show blindness. I tried to look into the face of people when they spoke to me. By listening to where their voice came from, I could tell if they were taller or shorter than I was. If they were taller, I would look up slightly. If they were shorter, I would lower my eyes hoping to catch their level and make eye contact with them. My eye muscles worked well because I exercised them every day. I knew that the ability to look toward the person speaking made them feel that I was interested in what they were saying. Before I became blind, I had talked to blind people who looked in another direction when I was speaking to them. It was so distracting to me. Therefore, I knew that looking directly into the face of the one with whom I was communicating was important. I stayed involved and interested in what a person was saying to me.

People sometimes speak to the blind through a third party rather than speaking to them directly. For example, instead of asking me if I wanted sugar in my coffee, they would ask a friend I was with, "Would Marolyn like sugar in her coffee?" The blind should not be deprived of the opportunity to answer for themselves, and do not want to be referred to as "That blind person who lives down the street." It seems hard for some people to realize that blind people aren't helpless beggars sitting in a rocking chair. A blind person wants to retain his identity. Also people will often speak very loudly when talking directly to a blind person. Once a group from the blind center went on a tour of some old homesteads. The guide was standing only four feet in front of us, but he shouted at the top of his voice. I guess he thought since we couldn't see, we couldn't hear a word he said. Most of us were quite upset, but out of politeness we heard him out trying to be kind about it.

Grace to Endure

It helped me greatly when sighted people called my name when asking a question or addressing me directly. "Marolyn, how are you today?" That made me much more comfortable than when someone simply asks, "How are you?" which left me wondering if the speaker was addressing me or someone else. I also appreciated the people who announced who they were. I didn't like the guessing games. Once I felt secure in my abilities and had accepted my blindness, I was no longer embarrassed to say, "Were you speaking to me?" or, "I didn't catch your name".

I found that attitudes of the sighted and the blind go together. If the blind feel inadequate, have resentment, and do not handle themselves well, sighted people will recognize these attitudes. The blind who work at developing their lives find they are not misfits in society. Some things cannot be overcome, but acceptance of others depends on the individual. Blind people need to understand difficulties that sighted people have in meeting and talking with them. Even though a sighted person cannot know a fraction of what a blind person has to cope with, a good relationship can be established.

When a blind person has a good attitude about himself, he is not concerned about making a mistake in front of others. He does not depend on others to do everything for him and he accepts help only when needed. A well adjusted independent blind person can appear to have a strong personality. Indeed, he has, for he has overcome blindness.

Acie was good at handling the fact of my blindness. He often told people, upon meeting them, that I was blind; therefore I felt more at ease, as did our guest. If I goofed, they would understand, so I could relax. Still I did my best to be graceful and poised. Friends accepted my blindness in a wonderful way. Some of them would joke about my cane in such a way that I knew they accepted me. My blindness had nothing to do with our friendship.

To recognize people I learned to listen to the way people walked. Some people shuffled their feet, some people walked on their heels, others on their toes, some people walked with a limp. I also recognized people by the way they smelled. Some used the same powders or after-shave lotions week after week. Some breathed heavy, some had a nagging cough, others rattled keys in their pocket while they talked. I listened for anything that would help me identify people. One of the men at the church made a game of standing close to me to see how long it would take me to know he was there. It was easy, really, because he usually unconsciously rattled change in his pocket.

On Sunday mornings before the service, I would direct the choir in a brief rehearsal, leaving my cane against the wall. One man moved my cane to see what I would do when I found it was no longer there. I felt a little embarrassed reaching for it and being unable to find it, but I laughed and said, "Someone has moved my cane." He gave it to me. Even though I felt a little sensitive about feeling for a cane that wasn't there, I enjoyed it because they did it in love, and I felt that love.

House To House

I could take my cane and find my way to the community grocery store by locating the church, which was next door to the parsonage. I tapped my cane till I came to the side of the church, followed the church building till I came to the front, and walked down toward the church sign. That sign was one of my landmarks. From there, I walked to the corner where two highways intersected each other. I could judge how far I was from the corner by listening to traffic noises. Once there, I listened till I was sure no cars were coming from any of the three directions before I crossed. The blind do not cross a highway when hearing a noisy truck coming way up the road. A more quiet running car may be in front of that truck and coming close. When I knew it was safe I'd have Sharon take my hand and we'd cross the highway. I tapped my cane till I detected a place where the cement had been torn up to lay a pipe line. The strip of gravel laid across the store parking lot, which was another landmark.

If I wanted to go on to visit a friend, or those who had missed church on Sunday, I tapped alternately the side of the road (which was blacktop in the country) and the grass. When my cane hit gravel, I knew I had approached the desired driveway. I continued till I had gone as far as I needed to go. It was wonderful to be able to visit friends again. Acie began to see how much more meaningful my life had become.

I found it was a great help for Acie to think of my plate in terms of a clock. The top was twelve o'clock; the bottom, six o'clock. When at banquets and restaurants, Acie would quietly say, "Marolyn, your creamed potatoes are at two o'clock, and green beans are at four o'clock." He would tell me everything I had on my plate, and where it was located. This saved me from the embarrassment of fingering my food as I tried to find it, or putting my fork in my plate and having it come up empty.

Some foods gave me a good deal of trouble. Jell-O, for example, was so light I could never tell if it was on the fork or not. Still more embarrassing was to think I had small pieces of meat on my fork, and then find out the hard way that it was a big piece of meat and I had to go back to the plate with it. Usually when in public, I ordered fish because it separated easily, and was not as awkward as steak, which needed cutting.

Buttering bread was quite a task, especially if the butter was at room temperature. I would reach for the butter with my knife, and because the butter was soft, the knife would go right through it. First thing I knew, my knuckles were in it rather than the knife. I wanted to give up on butter, but I liked it, so I kept trying. There is always something that keeps one trying.

When Acie and I walked together, I took his arm a little above the elbow and walked a half step behind him. Whether he went upstairs or down, to the right or left, he never had to speak a word; I could follow beautifully. My eyes didn't look sightless and unless I carried my cane, bumped into the furniture or did something silly, strangers didn't realize I was blind.

Shaking hands with people can be a real problem when you can't see. I would extend my hand into the empty air, and decide that my friend wasn't going to shake hands with me. What actually happened was that as I was withdrawing my hand, my friend was just extending his. We would miss each other completely. While it must have been quite a comic scene to others; it was embarrassing to me. I learned that the matter of shaking hands could be much easier if I would first determine the height of the individual with whom I was going to shake hands. I could determine this by listening to his voice. If the sound of his voice came from someone shorter than I, I would know to lower my hand. Generally, I found that this technique worked.

When I approached a car, I felt the handle of the car door to determine the direction in which the car was facing. This way I did not find myself trying to get in the car backwards. If someone opened the door for me, I placed my hand on the door frame to determine the direction. Sharon was thoughtful even though she was very young, when we came to a car, she took my hand and placed it on the door handle. I could have found it myself, and often did, but it always touched my heart as I knew this was one of the little things she enjoyed doing for me. Before sitting in a chair in the house, I felt the chair with my hand to find out which direction the chair was facing. At home this was not a problem, except in the kitchen where chairs were often moved.

Reading With My Fingers

Sharon needed someone to read to her. Acie read to her frequently, but he wasn't home until evening. We had to make visits in the homes of church members in the evenings so he could not read to her as often as a mother would. I ordered children's books that had Braille on the left-hand pages and print and a picture on the facing pages. That way, either Acie or I could read the Braille books to her. The books helped me to gain speed in reading Braille. There were Children's Bible storybooks, fairy tales, ABC books and library adult books available in Braille.

Braille became a tremendous help in my daily living. To keep a budget, I wrote checks by using a clear piece of plastic that fit over the check, with cut-outs where the date, the amount, and the signature were to be written. I used Braille to mark my music folders for choir numbers, make notes for myself, jot down appointment dates, prescription numbers, telephone numbers, recipes. When I came home with groceries I marked all my spices, and seasoning jars with Braille but I didn't need to mark my canned goods. I could shake the green beans and hear them swish around in the can. Corn has very little water in it so it falls from one end of the can to the other, ca-plop, ca-plop. Peas roll around in the can and have a lot of liquid content. All I had to do was listen to the sound.

By purchasing appliances from the American Foundation for the Blind which had Braille markings to identify the heat settings, I could do all my cooking (you don't have to touch a burner to know it's hot - heat rises). I had cookbooks, measuring spoons, and temperature gauges marked in Braille, as well as gadgets for slicing pickles, carrots, pies, and cakes evenly. While frying chicken, it makes a lot of popping sounds, when it gets tender the popping gets quiet. When a cake is baking, it smells raw, when it is fully baked the smell changes.

I bought little Braille tags and sewed one in each garment to indicate color. This made separating colors for washing much easier. I had a wonderful little helper in Sharon, who would tell me what color the clothes were if I was in too big of a hurry to read the Braille "color tag," as I sorted the clothes before I put them in the washing machine. Whatever we did, we did together. I had learned how to sew on buttons, sew in hems and side seams. By feeling the material and the stitches, I could do whatever mending was necessary. To iron our clothes, I set the iron on the board, let the cord hang over the edge, and guided my hand across the bottom edge on the ironing board to the cord. I followed the cord with my hand up to the handle on the iron to keep from getting burned. By feeling the material I could tell whether I had ironed it smooth or if I had ironed a wrinkle in it.

I knew where everything was kept, and made sure it was always in its place. It was easy to lay something down on the piano, go about my housework, and later wonder where I put it. Even if I put something aside temporarily, I had to put it in its place or it may take me a day or two to find it.

I taught Sharon to play with her toys on the bed, chairs, table, or piano bench, anywhere but on the floor. She learned that when she took off her shoes and clothes in the evening, she was to put them in the chest or on the bed. She knew if she left them on the floor, I would have an awful time trying to find them, and of course, I might stumble over them. Sharon was always conscious of my blindness, and had a good attitude toward it. When Acie would leave his shoes on the floor she would say, "Daddy, you better pick up your shoes 'cause Mommy's going to fall over them."

I didn't have to see dirt to know it was there. Everything in the house needed cleaning weekly and some things everyday. I knew how to clean my house and to take care of my little girl. Being a blind mother I needed to know where she was at all times. If she sat on the floor and I was unaware of where she was, I could have stepped on her leg and broken it, so we play-worked (at least that's what I called it). She probably learned to walk pulling bed sheets and blankets to the front of the bed as we made the beds together. I stood her on a chair by the sink tied an apron around her neck and tied another around her waist. Then I gave her some unbreakable dishes to wash while I washed the breakable dishes, pots and pans.

When we mopped the floors I gave her a little bucket of water and a mop as well. Children's hand muscles are not developed to where they can ring water out of a mop; therefore, all the water came out of her bucket onto the floor. I mopped from the far end of the room taking a three-foot space across mopping horizontally then came back across the same three-foot strip vertically to be sure I had not missed spots. It's easy to miss spots when cleaning and mopping in a circular pattern. I mopped with bare feet so that as I progressed across the floor with the mop I would find her big water puddles and mop them dry. As I neared the finish line I said, "Sharon honey, go take care of your mop and bucket, mommy will be right there to help you." She even had her own little broom to help me sweep the floors.

After cleaning the house, Sharon and I walked down the drive-way together and crossed the highway to get the mail. At a very young age she learned to watch for cars. We didn't cross the highway, however, until I knew the way was clear. When she stayed with her grandmother for a few days, before leaving she would always say, "Momma, you be careful when you cross the highway to get the mail." When she returned, her first question would be, "Momma, were you careful crossing the highway?"

I prayed for the little things; that God would remind me to open my eyes at the close of a prayer, especially if I were in church. I did not want to be caught with my eyes closed when they should be open. When you can't see you forget to open your eyes so this had become habitual. I prayed God would help me to use small hand gestures so that I wouldn't hit someone in the face or knock over a lamp. Always standing with your hands in your pockets or arms continually folded can be distracting. I just did those things which I would normally do. I even prayed about my facial expressions. You don't have to be blind too long before you forget what facial expressions look like. I'd check with Acie to see if I was responding correctly.

I had to pray and have faith in God's direction. I found that by putting my trust in God, and depending on Him, I could *"do all things through Christ which strengtheneth me"* Philippians 4:13(KJV). When our daughter, Sharon, was very young, she was afraid to be alone in the darkness at bedtime. I had taught her that Jesus was with her and that she need not be afraid. One night she said to me, "Momma, Momma, I see the angels in my room. They're everywhere. There are so many they have to fold their wings so they can all get in." After that, every time she became afraid she would say, "God's angels have come in to watch over me." What beautiful, child-like faith. It is this kind of faith, knowing that God hears and will answer, that gives power to our prayers.

We prayed and prayed that God would restore my sight like He did for the blind when He walked on earth. Jesus came to do the Father's will. If that was the Father's will then, it is God's will today. He is the same yesterday, today and forever. He heals us of our sore throats and broken bones, so why not my blind eyes? This was before we knew anything about the healing ministries of today. We were simply trusting God that one day I would be able to see. I thought it would come through an eye transplant, or medical science would come up with something to give me a way to see again.

Prayer Moves The Hand of God

I had a good life but I prayed, "Lord, if I have to be blind, please God, may it be for a reason, may it not be in vain. Take my life and use it for your glory." I had been blind for thirteen years. There was so much work to be done. Whether it was ironing a shirt, preparing sandwiches or cooking a meal, everything took me double time. It seemed I could do so much more for the Lord if He would give me back my sight.

On the evening of August 25, 1972, Acie, Sharon and I went to Bastrop, Louisiana, to visit one of our church members who had a heart attack and was recovering at his mother's home. We also were in Bastrop to see Acie's parents. His mother had baked a birthday cake for Acie's birthday which was the next day, August 26th. When it was time to leave, Sharon begged to spend the night with her grandparents, so Acie and I returned to Farmerville alone.

As we drove we had a long talk about my blindness, sharing together our deepest feelings. We had accepted my blindness, and Jesus had helped us live with it, but sometimes it had become a real burden. Being a minister's wife, and involved in the church work and daily afternoon visitation, I was overwhelmed with the work and Acie had more than he could do trying to hold down the full-time job and full-time church work. We had prayed many times during the thirteen years of my blindness that God would restore my sight. Acie would pray, "God, I know you have healing power and can do all things. Nothing is impossible to You. You can do it, if it is Your will." Each time we prayed I was reminded of the Apostle Paul, who also prayed that the Lord would take away his affliction. But the Lord said, "No, Paul." 'My grace is sufficient for thee,'" (2 Corinthians. 12:9 KJV). Each time I prayed, it was as if the Lord was saying to me, "Marolyn, I have a reason for you to be blind."

It was after midnight, August 26th (Acie's birthday) when we reached our home in Farmerville. Both of us were exhausted. Acie picked up a religious periodical, and I climbed into bed. After reading a minute, Acie put the magazine down and got on his knees for our nightly devotion. After reading the Bible to me, he began praying as he had prayed many times before with great feeling and boldness, "Oh, God! You can restore Marolyn's eyesight tonight, Lord. I know You can do it! And, God, if it be Your will, I pray You will do it tonight." We both received a wonderful gift on his birthday. For on this night God answered our prayers.

After thirteen blurred and dark years, there was sharpness and light when I open my eyes at the close of his prayer. After ten years of marriage I could see my husband for the first time. I shouted "I can see, Acie I can see." "You're kidding," he answered. I repeated, "I can see! I can see the pupils in your eyes!" Acie thought that perhaps just a little vision had come back. I said, "Acie, it's 12:30 at night! You need a shave! I can see!"

Acie still couldn't believe the miracle that had really occurred. He grabbed a newspaper, pointed to the large print at the top of the page, and asked, "Can you see this?" "I can do better than that!" I exclaimed. "I can read the smaller print!" Acie got excited. "Marolyn, can you see the dresser? Sharon was at Grandma's house but her picture was on the dresser. As I held her picture I kept saying, "Oh my baby, my baby." We both cried and shouted, "Glory, Hallelujah! Praise the Lord! Thank you Jesus!" We shouted and praised the Lord for what He had done! Such a miracle was overwhelming. We were on Holy ground that night. What a night of rejoicing!

Things had been rough for Acie lately as he tried to keep up with both his church work and his sales job. He had nearly reached his limit that evening when the miracle happened. We knew that God was able, but we couldn't comprehend that something so wonderful and miraculous had happened to us.

Jumping off the bed, Acie asked the question again, "Marolyn, you can see this?" "Yes," I said. "Can you see that?" "Yes , yes!" In surprise and astonishment I could see everything. "Praise God! Praise God! Praise God! Glory, glory, glory to God! It can't be!" Acie exclaimed. I was praising God that I could see the floor, steps, doorway.   We were overwhelmed with happiness. "This is Heaven!" Acie shouted. "It has to be! Oh, God why did I doubt You?" Then he turned to me, "Why did I doubt God? I didn't believe He could do something like this! He did it!"

Psalms 116:12 came to Acie's mind, *"What shall I render unto the Lord for all His benefits toward me?"* We were jumping up and down and crying at the same time. I was getting my first look at my husband. For the first time, I could see his face, his eyes, his nose, his mouth. I could see! I ran to look in the mirror. I could hardly believe how my facial features had changed. I had become blind at 18, now I was 31. I kept taking a second look.

We reached for the phone to call our parents. When the phone rang at my parents' home in Michigan, Mother was awake. She had not been able to sleep that night. For years she had been burdened with the thought of my blindness and her own helplessness in not being able to do anything about it. How happy our news made her! She rejoiced with us over the telephone. I asked her to share the news with the others in my family who lived in Holland, Michigan and with my twin sister, who was living in New York.

Acie telephoned his parents, and his mother sleepily answered. Acie shouted, "Mother, Marolyn can see!" Mom Ford had been awakened in the middle of the night by a son too excited to speak calmly. She asked, "Is everything all right?" But Acie could only repeat over and over: "Marolyn can see! Marolyn can see! She can see!" We realized about this time that it was Acie's birthday - his thirty-third. How we praised God and thanked Him for His wonderful birthday gift!

We were so excited we could not get to sleep. Acie had to go to work the next morning yet, he was afraid to go to sleep, afraid he might wake up in the morning and find it wasn't true. Finally, we asked God to help us sleep, and He did. When we woke up at 7:00 the next morning, Acie's first words were, "Marolyn, is it true? Can you see?" It was true! I could see! Acie called his boss, and said he would be in a little late because his wife's eyesight had come back. When he got to the store, five minutes late for work, he ran in and told everybody there about the miracle. Acie couldn't sell anything that day. He'd walk up to a customer and say," You know what? My wife was blind and now she can see! It's a miracle! She can see!"

Acie called me at 2:00 that afternoon and asked, "Marolyn, can you still see?" He couldn't wait to get home. Home seemed like another world - a world of joy and freedom. When his long day ended at 6:30 p.m., he rushed to his car to hurry home. When he arrived at the house, he threw is arms around me, and asked, "Marolyn, can you still see?" Together we praised God! (Acie not only called home on the day following the miracle to ask if I could still see, he called home every day for weeks after, and asked, " Marolyn, can you still see?" I would answer, "Yes, I can see! Everything is wonderful!")

The day of the miracle was wonderful! News of the event spread quickly, and people called all day long, wanting to know if what they had heard was true. Could I *really* see? Yes, I could see, I told them as I happily recounted over and over again how the miracle had happened. The doorbell frequently rang as it seemed everyone stopped by to see for themselves if the miracle were true.

When I had a few minutes to myself, I ran to my closet to see what my clothes looked like! I went to Sharon's closet and Acie's closet to see what their clothes looked like. I looked at pictures of my family. In thirteen years they had changed. I went to the church to see what it looked like! What a glorious day of discovery I had! What a marvelous, wonderful day!

The morning after the miracle, the sun shone brightly. Words cannot express the beauty I saw. My heart was full of praise to God for His creation. Later the clouds covered up the sunshine, and poured out beautiful raindrops. How wonderful of God to let me see both the sun and the rain on that first day!

Sharon had been asleep when we called Mom and Dad Ford about the miracle that night. They didn't tell her that her Momma could see until the following morning when they were on their way to our house. Acie's sister, Hazel, began telling Sharon that Jesus had performed a miracle during the night and opened Momma's blind eyes. Her mother would be able to see her when she arrived home. Sharon expressed her joy, then thought for a moment, and said, "Oh goodie, I can put up my mop and broom 'cause I won't have to help Mommy anymore."

When Sharon arrived, I saw my child for the first time. When she was born, I had seen only an outline, a little bundle of flesh in my arms. Later I could see nothing. Now I could finally see her, my curly blond hair, blue-eyed, four and one-half year old daughter. When they arrived, Mom and Dad had to park behind the cars of church members who had come to see. As Sharon came walking up the driveway toward the house, I ran out, threw my arms around her, hugged her and said, " Sharon, I can see ! I can see! I can see what you look like! I was excited, but Sharon started to cry. I had expressed my joy to her, not realizing that she had her little heart all set on what she wanted to say when she saw me. Through her tears she said, "I wanted to say, Mommy, can you see, can you see?" She wanted the joy of asking me if I could really see, rather than having me tell her first. She made up for it because everywhere we went she shared this miracle with everybody, "My mommy was blind, but now she can see."

During the week prior to God giving sight to my blind eyes, Acie had been preparing his sermon for Sunday morning about how God sent an angel to rescue Peter from jail on the day before his execution. The church had been in prayer all night for Peter's release. Upon being freed, Peter immediately went to the home of Mary, mother of John Mark, which was where the people had gathered to pray. A girl named Rhonda answered the door and became so overjoyed at hearing Peter's voice that she left him standing at the door while she ran to tell the others he was there. They didn't believe her when she told them Peter was standing at the door (Acts 12: 6-17). Acie had certainly identified with Peter. For years we prayed to be released from the blindness which held me prisoner.

It was time for the Sunday worship service and he told the congregation how the Lord hears the cries of the righteous. I led the choir in singing "Amazing Grace" (I once was blind, but now I see). I gave my testimony, and told what great things the Lord had done for me. When I finished, I asked Acie if he would join me in singing, "He Touched Me." People wept unashamedly as they rejoiced with us!

Three days later, Acie wanted to call my eye doctor and let him look at my eyes. I said, "Acie, he's busy and booked solid for months. I'll never get in to see him." Acie was persistent and called anyway. The doctor said for me to come in the next morning at 8:30 a.m. before his first patient came. The doctor's startling report indicated that my eyes, medically speaking, were the same. The macular was still full of holes; the nerve endings were dead; the mirror in my eyes was like an old-time mirror with the silver scraped off the back. A miracle had indeed taken place. As the doctor gave the report, I realized the possibility that I could be blind again tomorrow. My vision could leave me as quickly as it had come back but I never gave that a second thought. God gave sight to my blind eyes and it's for keeps.

After receiving my sight, I went through a period of adjustment. People had accepted me as a blind person and many did not know me any other way. During the 13 years of blindness, I had lost my identity as a sighted person. When my sight returned, I had to find a new identity. I no longer was a blind person, concentrating on my every move. Suddenly, here was a new Marolyn! I could now do everything so quickly and differently. I could see anything without relying on my sense of touch to find out about it. I could accomplish so much in so little time. I could catch people's expressions in conversation. Life had wonderfully changed for me, but I felt lost in the new me. It bothered me until suddenly I realized that I had lost my identity as a blind person! I was thrilled!

Seven weeks after the miracle, we visited the Training Center for the Blind. I wanted to see where I received my training and see what the facility, friends and acquaintances whom I met while in training there looked like. We had a wonderful visit with many friends. While we were visiting we happened to see a nice looking young blind man with a brief case walk right into a wall. We could only think that except for the grace of God, seven weeks ago, it could have been me walking into the wall.

After the miracle took place, the Lord began to open opportunities for me to give my testimony, to tell what the Lord had done for me. Two weeks following the miracle, Acie and I were invited by Rev. Paul Carter, pastor of the Rocky Branch Baptist Church, to join them as they celebrated their centennial year of the church history. People came with all their relatives, pastors and their families came from far and near to share in this big day and to share potluck dinner on the grounds.   I was so very excited over the potluck dishes and that I could see to fill my own plate. I no longer had to eat what other people thought I might like and had put on my plate. I was in my glory filling my plate when the pastor (who was filling his plate across the table) said, "Marolyn, I would love for you to tell the people about your restored eyesight during the afternoon meeting. Would you mind if I call on you to share what has happened?" I replied, "Oh, I'd love to! However, I'm not sure that I'll be able to because when I get in front of a crowd of people my lips tremble and my teeth chatter so badly I can't get the words out. I'll tell you what," I said, "I'd like to try and if I can't get the words out, you'll have to come up and finish telling them what God has done for me." He agreed. I was nervous thinking about it, wondering how and what I might say. To my surprise when I approached the pulpit and began speaking, it was as though the Lord loosed my tongue and delivered me from the fear of speaking publicly. I shared with all the thrill, joy and excitement, rejoicing over the miracle God had given me, "I can see, Glory to God, I can see!"

Most of the pastors who heard my testimony that day invited me to share with their church congregations in the weeks and months that followed. Sharon was not yet in kindergarten so we traveled nightly sharing, "I once was blind, but now I can see." One speaking engagement opened up many other doors. These pastors told their ministerial friends about God's miracle, then they telephoned to ask me to share with their congregation and so on. The news of my restored vision spread all over the state of Louisiana and my ministry (which is "God's ministry") grew rapidly. I was booked with speaking engagements nightly and began receiving newspaper clippings about the miracle from unknown people in other states. Letters came from people asking for help for themselves or someone they knew who was blind and could not cope. I appreciated those letters. It thrilled me to give them words of encouragement and strength, "With God all things are possible!"

Meanwhile, Acie and I felt the Lord leading us to another church. We were not sure where we were to go. We had prayed about it for more than a year when the Lord used Rev. Michael Howard, a Baptist pastor in Felsenthal, Arkansas to show us His will. The Lord impressed Michael to give our name to the pulpit committee of the First Baptist Church of Huttig, Arkansas. Later he visited us and told us about the work of the church. We began praying about it. By the time the pulpit committee came and Acie preached his trial sermon, we knew it was the Lord's will for us to pastor at Huttig. We moved there in October, 1972, two months after the miracle had occurred.

Shortly after we moved to Huttig, the people there made it possible for me to return to Michigan to see my family. I had not seen the faces of my parents and brothers and sisters for thirteen years. I was thrilled and excited to know I was going to be able to see the face of my Mom, Dad, Brothers and Sisters. The delight of that unforgettable visit home can't be expressed in mere words. My parents and family could hardly believe I could see again. I shared my testimony in my home church in Holland, Michigan many years before telling how God helped me live with blindness. This time I spoke as a sighted Marolyn to an overflowing crowd of people saying, "These blind eyes can now see!" Many friends there had been praying for me for years, and I love them dearly. We praised the Lord as we shared God's miracle with them!   I am so very thankful we made that trip home to see everyone and share my miracle. Shortly after we returned home, November, 1973, my Dad passed away very suddenly due to a blood clot following hip surgery.

After moving from Louisiana to Arkansas, I thought I might not be giving my testimony as often, since we were not known in Arkansas. Yet the Lord continued to open opportunities weekly for me to share this testimony. Shortly thereafter, I received a phone call from the Southern Baptist Arkansas State WMU program chairman asking me if I would share my story at the state conference meeting. I accepted the invitation. Evangelist James Robinson was scheduled to preach following my testimony. After the meeting he invited me to share on his nationwide telecast and that opened the door for me as a public speaker nationwide. I have had a full-time ministry of speaking engagements since 1972.

When Jesus healed the blind man by the pool of Siloam, that man said, *"One thing I know, that, whereas I was blind, now I see"* (John 9:25). After healing the demoniac of Gadara, Jesus said to him, *"Go home to thy friends, and tell them how great things the Lord hath done for thee, and hath had compassion on thee"* (Mark 5:19). Certainly the Lord has had compassion on me; He has given Acie and me a whole new wonderful life, and we'll not stop sharing the testimony of that life with others. We will continue to praise the Lord for His loving kindness.

There is no question that God did have purpose in my being blind. So many times during those thirteen years I prayed, "Oh, God, if I must be blind, please let it be for a reason, may it not be in vain" That reason was to give me a message whereby I can glorify God everywhere I go. He has given me the opportunity to speak weekly to audiences ranging from fifty to several thousand. As a conference/crusade speaker I travel world-wide. I speak at seminars and retreats, on radio and television interviews, in churches, at associational meetings, banquets, Christian Business Men's meetings, and Lions Clubs. Through my testimony God had reached down into the hearts of many, and enriched their faith in Him. My ministry is to edify God's people, to increase faith in God's word, to give glory to God for his healing and to see the sinner come to Jesus for salvation. I have spoken to non-Christian groups where people have come in swearing and gone out crying, too broken to speak more than just to say thank-you as they grasped my hand. I am thankful for the ministry God has given me. My life is God's. I don't know what He has in store for me, but I'll praise Him everywhere I go.

After the miracle, I began reading every book I could get my hands on. Once when Acie expressed concern about the strain on my eyes - Sharon said, "Daddy, don't worry about that. Jesus healed Mommy, and He will take care of her." And yes, He does take care of me.

Chapter III
Go And Tell

Shortly after the miracle of restored sight, many people wanted me to write a book about my story so they could know the details and carry a copy with them. It was obvious that I needed some way to spread the testimony beyond my personal appearance. I wrote, *These Blind Eyes Now See*, first published in 1975 by Victor Books Publisher, Inc. The purpose of the book is to edify God's people, to increase people's faith in God's Word and to give God glory for His healing. It also presents the saving grace of Jesus to the reader.

Salvation is the grace of God to live by the power of His mighty Spirit. Healing is the grace of God to transform physical limitations into wholeness and an instrument to show forth His greatness. God always finds a way to grow great things from small seeds to use for His purpose. My book was just such a blessing to the Braille Bible Foundation in Chicago, IL. After reading my book, the President of the Foundation wrote:

Dear Marolyn,
Thank you for writing your wonderfully inspiring book, These Blind Eyes Now See. I have received such encouragement and faith while reading of your marvelous miracle. Praise God forevermore for restoring your sight. Thank you again for this uplifting book. We would like permission to publish your book in Braille for our free distribution to many thousands of our Braille readers. I am sure that a good many of them will also be inspired to fully believe and trust Jesus for salvation, as well as for their healing needs.
Yours in Christ,
Dr. Donald V. Howell, June 1997

My book, *These Blind Eyes Now See* was made available to the Foundation and is available to the blind in Braille, audio cassette and Talking Book Records. In 1978, *These Blind Eyes Now See* was named as one of the 5 finalist in the First Annual Gold Medallion

Awards Competition sponsored by the Evangelical Christian Publishers Association. It was narrowed down to one of the two final books in the Biography category. It was a special honor that God allowed my book to be listed as one of the finalist.

God has honored my ministry and has given me the strength to continue, even under heavy stressful physical illness. I like to be active and feel better when I am on the go. God has proven himself faithful to me throughout my life. The smallest thing I do in His Name is magnified to be a greater work than I could have ever imagined. *"Give and it will be given unto you; good measure, pressed down, and shaken together, and running over, shall men give into your bosom. For with the same measure that ye mete withal it shall be measured to you again."* Luke 6:38

The Ministry Is God's

It was the miracle gift of restored sight that launched my public ministry of sharing this miracle with others. It is a special calling and the joy of my life. Word of my eyesight having been restored after thirteen years of blindness began to spread far and wide. Miracles were not heard of in modern day Christianity. This was before the days of the outpouring of miracles as we know it today. Speaking engagement opportunities began pouring in. Since our daughter, Sharon was not yet in kindergarten, I could speak at meetings nightly. I was excited to tell of God's mercy and grace.

I teach seminars, speak at conferences and church meetings. Frequently, I speak at schools and do television and radio interviews. I have traveled with two crusade teams, (one for twelve years, the other for six years) crossing the country, sharing what it is like to be blind, how I lived with blindness and then the miracle of restored sight. The Lord greatly blesses my ministry. I still continue to pray, "Lord, take my life and use it to your glory."

My husband, Acie, has been the most supportive person of my ministry. It hasn't always been easy though. One could imagine the difficulty. For thirteen years of our marriage, I was blind. During these years I went with him while he tended to the pastoral duties of the church where he pastored. I was with him wherever he went. Then, after the miracle of my restored sight we both cherished the joy of sharing this blessed miracle with others. As long as the speaking engagements were close to home, there was little stress.

Following the interview with evangelist, James Robison on national television, speaking invitations came from across the USA, no longer just from the south. I had to fly to meetings. The days and nights had to be lonely for Acie. When I returned from a speaking engagement he met me at the airport, and we would hug and kiss, but I know it is always most difficult on the partner who stays behind.

As we would drive home from the airport, I would share my experiences and he would tell me of his work at the church where we pastored, his hospital visits, etc. When I got home, my life was much like that of every other married woman and mother. There would be washing and ironing of clothes, cleaning house and cooking dinner. I suppose many men would feel challenged if their wife had a worldwide ministry. Acie is very supportive of my travels. It is his ministry too. He loves our ministry.

Perhaps nothing demonstrates my husband's regard for my ministry like the time I flew into the Monroe Louisiana Airport. Acie picked up my luggage and put it in the car and we started driving home. Acie told me he had a dream while I was gone. He said, "I'll never complain about you being gone, not ever again!" I was surprised to hear him say that. I said, "Acie, you've never complained about my travels." He said, "I haven't complained to you about it but I sure let the Lord know I didn't like it." I asked, "Do you not want me to continue my ministry and traveling?" He quickly replied, "Yes, oh yes, I do!" He said, "In my dream the Lord asked me, "What would you rather have, a wife that is blind or one who can see and goes telling this wonderful story as my witness?" Acie told me, "I'll never complain again about you being gone. You go anywhere God opens a door." God's Word says in Proverbs. 16:3, *"Commit your work unto the Lord and your thoughts will be established."* Acie said, "I believe God established my thoughts through that dream."

Each time I speak about the miracle God has given me, groups want to hear more about what God is doing in my life. Therefore, my ministry enlarged as I became a seminar/conference speaker. Knowing that God will provide all our needs, I prayed for a PA system to use in my speaking engagements. I especially needed this system at camp retreats and seminars. I did not make this need known to anyone other than God. Several Christians saw my need and God laid it upon their hearts to purchase a PA system and give it to me as a surprise gift for use in my ministry. Jesus said, *"Ask, and you will be given what you ask for......"* Matthew 7:7a. Paul told the Philippians, *"And it is He who will supply all your needs from His riches in glory, because of what Christ Jesus has done for us."* Philippians 4:19 (LB). Let us not doubt His ability to supply our needs; He has promised to do so. No matter how dark your circumstances may seem, God's Word is true. Not to believe in God's Word is sin and the cause of Christians living defeated lives - living below God's place of blessing. *"Whatsoever we ask, we receive of* Him, *because we keep His commandments and do those things that are pleasing in His sight."* I John 3:22.

On Monday morning following the hectic pace of the weekend with a Friday night Banquet, Saturday 9:00 a.m. Seminar I, 10:30 a.m. Seminar II, 12:00 Lunch break, 1:00 p.m. Seminar III, 2:00 p.m. Seminar IV, 4:00 p.m. Autograph party at a bookstore and speaking at two churches on Sunday, I am worn out. Operating on the excitement and adrenaline flowing through my body, I head for the airport and home. Sometimes there are meetings on Monday, Tuesday and Thursday. People ask, "What keeps you going at such a pace?" I believe it is the excitement of the meeting and the presence of God's Spirit with His anointed power abundantly present. Every meeting and every work I undertake is for the glory of God, and it needs to be submerged in prayer.

Jesus found it necessary and of utmost importance to rise early in order to talk to His Father. Mark writes, *"The next morning He was up long before daybreak and went out alone into the wilderness to pray."* Mark 1:35. Before choosing His twelve disciples, Jesus prayed. In Luke we read, *"One day soon afterwards He went out into the mountains to pray, and prayed all night."* Luke 6:12. If prayer was this important to Jesus, surely it must be to us as well.

Each time Jesus was to do a mighty work for His Father, He prayed for strength for the task before Him. He sought His Father's face in prayer for His miracle-working power. Today we often think we are capable of singing, teaching, or preaching before people without even so much as fifteen minutes spent in prayer to receive the power necessary for the task. God's Son, Jesus, would not have done the work of His Father that carelessly. We must remember that we cannot do the work of God in our own strength. We have no power in ourselves. The power is all in the name of Jesus. However, we must ask for it.

Pastoral Moves

We always marveled at the way God moved us after six years of ministry in our beautiful pastorate at the First Baptist Church of Huttig, Arkansas to the Boulevard Baptist Church, in the south part of Memphis, Tennessee in 1978. It was strange how God directed the pulpit committee to telephone Acie one evening. He was one of the first ministers they talked with regarding their need for a new pastor. When the call came, we felt the Lord had directed them to contact us because we knew in our spirit that God would be moving us. I mentioned to Acie that it was too bad our name had been first on the list to call, because rarely does a church pulpit committee extend an invitation to the first contact they make. I had rather we had been last on their list. Nevertheless, Acie sent them his resume.

Months past and we hadn't heard any reports from them. We learned later that the committee had lost his resume, name, address and phone number. Meanwhile, they had eliminated all other pastors who were candidates on their list. One of the committee members recalled the phone call and asked, "Whatever happened to that Rev. Ford we contacted in Arkansas?" They found the misplaced resume and telephoned Acie asking if he would be willing to come in view of a call. We had been praying about this for several months. When they extended the call for Acie to be their pastor, we knew God had opened that door.

In 1981, God led Acie to make a drastic move in his ministry position. He had always been Senior Pastor with Associate Pastors working under him. God led him to accept a position as Associate Pastor at Broadmoor Baptist Church, on the north side of Memphis where we are currently serving. We knew God was leading us into this associate ministry at Broadmoor even before the church had officially invited Acie to come in view of a call. We were so sure that God wanted us to be at the Broadmoor Baptist Church, we had already scouted the area for a house to purchase.

There are often needs in our lives for which the supply simply is not available to us. We must not allow circumstances to intimidate us or cause us to come stumbling to God in unbelief and fear. Scripture says, "What is faith? It is the confident assurance that something we expect is going to happen. It is the certainty that what we hope for is waiting for us, even though we cannot see it up ahead" (Hebrews 11:1). Don't allow your faith to waver. Come boldly to God in prayer with Holy confidence and joyful assurance. God encourages us to come to Him, asking Him for those things which are in agreement with His will. Stay with it, allow faith to rise in your heart. Remember, God lays down a "condition" that must be met before we can expect to see God fulfill His promises to us. He says, *"Seek ye first the Kingdom of God and His righteousness and all these things shall be added unto you."* We have to be seeking God, delighting ourselves in Him, obeying His word and following His commands and precepts. Then we can believe that we will receive that which we are asking of Him.

We must believe in 'believing' before we can trust God for anything. If we have a legitimate need, God says, "Trust Me!" He is our God; He will hear our prayer and He will bless us. The Apostle John wrote, *"And we are sure of this, that He will listen to us whenever we ask Him for anything in line with His will. And if we really know He is listening when we talk to him to make our request, then we can be sure that He will answer us."* 1 John 5:14-15.

A Word from God must come to you first. Then put your belief in that Word and not in your feelings. Faith is how you react to what God has told you in His Word. Jesus says, *"And all things, whatsoever ye shall ask in prayer, believing, ye shall receive."* Matthew 21:22 (KJV). I can have the things God says are mine as I accept them by faith. Abraham was walking in obedience to God. He was fully persuaded and he acted upon it. He chose to believe God. He walked up that mountainside with his son, Isaac, saying, "Son, God will provide the sacrifice. God provided the lamb for Abraham and He provided a house for us. By trusting in God's Word you will find the infinite power of God manifested in your life.

By way of illustration: We had three non-budgeted bills to pay which totaled $675.00. I prayed, asking the Lord for $675.00, plus a tithe over and above the amount needed, making a total of $750.00. Three years prior we had made an overpayment to an Insurance Company. We didn't owe it, but they said we did, so we paid it. Here it was 3 years later and they located their mistake. They realized they had over-billed us and sent us a refund check. Then, two additional checks were sent to us that week. The total amount was $750.00. Isn't that just like the Lord? Praise His Holy Name!

The Bible says, *"You can never please God without faith, without depending on Him. Anyone who wants to come to God must believe there is a God and that He rewards those who sincerely look for Him."* Hebrews 11:6. It is the will of God to supply our needs.

I had been invited to do a TV interview in Florida. It was a tremendous outreach for the Lord and I was excited with God's opportunity. The flight expense was covered; the airline ticket was in hand. I was to leave on Saturday morning; this was Thursday afternoon. A phone call came and I was told that I would have to take a limo from the airport to the motel, some 22 miles from the airport, and return by limo to the airport after the interview was over. I did not have the money for the limo fare. At first, it really upset me. Then I realized I was sinning, for I was worried about how I was going to get from the airport to the interview. I confessed my sin as I prayed, "Lord, I am sorry. You are my Provider. This is Your ministry and a big opportunity to glorify Your Name and share Your wonderful work. I thank You that You are my Provider and that somehow You will give me the money that is needed to make this trip. Lord, Your Word says that You will supply all my needs according to Your riches in glory by Christ Jesus."

As I gave the problem to Him, in faith believing, He was able to provide. This was Thursday afternoon. On Friday the Lord sent me $50.00 in the mail. On Saturday I flew to Florida. The $50.00 was exactly what the trip expenses cost me. Praise the Lord! He does hear and answer prayer. God will show us, in our spirit, that everything will be all right.

God speaks to us through our desires, as well as our needs. The Psalmist says, *"Delight yourself also in the Lord and He will give you the desires of your heart."* Psalm 37:4. He enables us to desire that which He desires and then gives us "all our heart's desires." The Psalmist also instructs us, "That is why I wait expectantly, trusting God to answer."

Walking In Obedience By Faith

JESUS IS OUR EXAMPLE in learning to walk obediently by faith. 1 John 2:6 says, *"Anyone who says he is a Christian should live as Christ did."* Walk in the light of God's Word. Every word He spoke, every promise He has given is to be received by faith. We must refuse to allow our minds to wander off the course set before us. We must refuse to be overcome by doubts, frustrations, despair and anxieties. It is then we can come boldly before Almighty God with our requests.

> *Every promise in the book is mine;*
> *Every chapter, every verse, every line;*
> *All the blessings of His love divine;*
> *Every promise in the book is mine.*
> - *Pearl Spencer Smith*

It is often necessary for us to wait before the Lord. Sometimes there are long periods of time between our asking and our receiving the answer. Isaiah says, *"But they that wait upon the Lord shall renew their strength; they shall mount up with wings as eagles; they shall run, and not be weary; and they shall walk, and not faint."* Isaiah 40:31.

The path of obedience is difficult. David said, *"I am always thinking of the Lord; and because he is so near, I never need to stumble or fall"* Psalm 16:8. Paul instructs us, *"Let this mind be in you which was also in Christ Jesus"* Philippians 2:5 (KJV). It is not easy to keep our mind set on Christ. It will drift away at times. Recognize, acknowledge and confess that you have allowed your mind to wander off course and then keep on going. Don't allow the devil, to heap guilt upon you. Guilt is never of God. Confess it, make it right and go on. Accept God's forgiveness which makes for sweet, beautiful fellowship with Him. Earnestly, practice God's presence. Seek to have a heart that constantly yearns after righteousness.

James says, *"...The earnest prayer of a righteous man has great power and wonderful results."* James 5:16b(LB). Never allow the world and its responsibilities to take place over your prayer time. Guard it. Treasure it. Give yourself to it. It is not possible to go into a prayer mood of intercession quickly. It takes heart preparation: time spent with God in deep abandonment and a personal devotion to the Lord before one can move into the depths of prayer.

We belong to Christ, God chose us to be His very own. We are adopted into His family and are accepted in the Beloved One. We are Christ's gift to the Father. As His children, we are His delight. The prayer of Paul for the Ephesian Christians was, *"I pray that you will begin to understand how incredibly great His power is to help those who believe Him. It is that same mighty power that raised Christ from the dead and seated him in the place of honor at God's right hand in heaven"* (Ephesians 1:19-20). Praise God, we can appropriate this power in our lives!

Now that God is our father, we can come fearlessly into His presence, assured of His glad welcome. Out of His glorious, unlimited resources He will give us the mighty inner strength of His Holy Spirit. Plant our roots deep into the soil of God's marvelous love.

I am not suggesting sinless perfection. We will not reach sinlessness until we reach our eternal home and stand complete before Him. Yet we are to strive toward maturity. In the Sermon on the Mount Jesus said, *"But you are to be perfect, even as your Father in heaven is perfect."* (Matthew 5:48). Yet we do sin. And because we do, God has made the way available for our immediate forgiveness. 1 John 1:9 says, *"But if we confess our sins to Him, He can be depended on to forgive us and to cleanse us from every wrong."* It is perfectly proper for God to do this for us because Christ died to wash away our sins.

If God tells us to do something, we should just do it. Godliness is within our reach because we possess the life of Christ. If we are always wrapped up in thinking about our old nature and paying attention to it, it becomes more and more active. Self-discipline and self-denial are necessary to decrease our desires for sin and wrong. We must take our minds off our sins and turn them inward to focus on God's deliverance. As we turn our thoughts to the new man within in Christ, then the old man will become weaker and weaker. Fires which are not kindled will die.

In order to make the fact of our crucifixion with Christ effective in our lives, we must in faith surrender our "old self" to God. Paul wrote,

> *"Well then, shall we keep on sinning so that God can keep on showing us more and more kindness and forgiveness? Of course not! Should we keep on sinning when we don't have to? For sin's power over us was broken when we became Christians and were baptized to become a part of Jesus Christ; through His death the power of your sinful nature was shattered.*
>
> *Your old evil desires were nailed to the cross with Him; that part of you that loves to sin was crushed and fatally wounded, so that your sin-loving body is no longer under sin's control, no longer needs to be a slave to sin; for when you are deadened to sin you are freed from all its allure*

and its power over you. And since your old sin-loving nature 'died'
with Christ, we know that you will share His new life."

We will then think His thoughts, take on His desires, and strive to do those things which are pleasing in His sight. It is possible to live such a dedicated life. As we seek to live a holy life, Jesus Christ will make Himself real to us day by day. As we ask Him for His help, He will renew His character within us.

Paul continued,

"So look upon your old sin nature as dead and unresponsive to sin,
and instead be alive to God, alert to Him, through Jesus Christ our
Lord. Do not let sin control your body any longer; do not give in to its
sinful desires. Do not let any part of your bodies become tools of
wickedness, to be used for sinning; but give yourselves completely to
God - every part of you - for you are back from death and you want to
be tools in the hands of God, to be used for His good purposes."
Romans 6:11-13 (LB).

We are to declare our old desires as dead with Christ and claim our new desires in the resurrection of Christ. We are to rely upon, roll over upon, or trust God by faith to produce His life through our flesh. Remember we cannot crucify self; we are to declare it dead. We do not need to give in any longer to bad attitudes, selfishness and pride, the old sins of the flesh, or to the temptations of the devil.

We read in Romans,

"So there is now no condemnation awaiting those who belong to
Christ Jesus. For the power of the life-giving Spirit - and this power is
mine through Christ Jesus - has freed me from the vicious circle of sin
and death. We aren't saved from sin by knowing the commandments of
God, because we can't and don't keep them. But God put into effect a
different plan to save us. He sent His own Son in human body, like
ours except we are sinful, and destroyed sin's control over us by giving

Himself as a sacrifice for our sins. Therefore, we now can obey God's laws if we follow the Holy Spirit and no longer obey the old evil nature within us. Those who let themselves be controlled by their lower natures live only to please themselves, but those who follow after the Holy Spirit find themselves doing those things that please God." Romans 8:1-5 (LB). And this leads to life and peace.

God has provided a oneness in Christ for us. Our trust in God by faith is based upon our position in Christ. We can come boldly to the throne of Grace, anytime and anywhere. All who have been elected, chosen, born again, cleansed by the blood of Christ and resurrected in Him, have the right and authority to come into the presence of Almighty God fearlessly and with boldness. Always remember, a clean conscience is necessary for great faith.

The element that prepared me for life was the discipline of Bible reading and continual prayer. It is important, not only to bring our petitions to God, but also to take the time to listen to what He wants to say to us. Our needs and desires are not nearly as important as listening to Him. God speaks to us in our spirit through the written Word. It is vital that we listen to Him. Permit the Holy Spirit to take control of your life! Don't be hesitant or defeated when you don't feel God's power. It's not how you feel that counts, just believe God and accept it by faith.

We should not hesitate to believe God when His will has already been predetermined through His Word. Rather than spending precious time in prayer about something that has already been determined through His Word, we should merely remember what the Word says and thank God for its power. When we are abiding in His will and confessing our sins daily, we do not have to worry about being in God's will. We are already there. Praise God!

We Entertain Angels Unaware

God will confirm His call when we ask Him to do so. He might bring someone into our life that delivers His message. God sent someone like that to me, Samson Rajkumar, who is an evangelist from Madras, India. At the time, he was 26 years old and came to Memphis on an impression he received from God. Not knowing where to go or what to do, he felt God was leading him to come to America to preach.

Many young people in Samson's land longed to visit Orlando, Florida in the United States. There they could visit the popular Walt Disney World. Another place the young people of other countries yearned to visit is Elvis Presley's Graceland mansion in Memphis, Tennessee. While most youth dreamed of touring these American sites, Samson dreamed of preaching in America. Guided by strong faith, he bought an airline ticket to America and flew into the land of opportunity. When he arrived in Memphis he rented a van. What was his destination? He knew it was Memphis, but where in Memphis? Not planning to see Graceland, he had no other destination in mind. He just knew he had come here to preach the gospel. His American trek was indeed a mission of faith. He knew God would fill in the blanks when he arrived in Memphis.

Samson did not know that I had been praying daily for the Lord to send me someone in answer to a special prayer. I was seeking insight into understanding the meaning of Ephesians 1:3-20. I was praying desperately for God to give me a full understanding of this passage of scripture. As I read verses 17-19, I prayed, "Lord, just send someone who can help me understand. In these verses is the truth I need!" The passage reads,

"That the God of our Lord Jesus Christ, the Father of glory, may give unto you the spirit of wisdom and revelation in the knowledge of Him, the eyes of your understanding be enlightened; that ye may know what

is the hope of His calling and what the riches of the glory of His inheritance in the saints, and what is the exceeding greatness of His power to usward who believe, according to the working of His mighty power, which He wrought in Christ, when He raised Him from the dead, and set Him at His own right hand in the heavenly places."

These verses are so full and rich. I love them. The treasure in these verses is so vast it would take a lifetime to fully explore everything it says. I knew the meaning of the verse, but I was seeking more direct meaning in my own life. I knew God had a special word for me. I had set my mind to embrace the truth of the Word of God and wanted to know God's message for me. I knew God would answer my prayer, but never expected Him to send it in the way He did.

This young preacher left the Memphis airport in South Memphis and drove the rental van around Memphis looking for a sign from God as he viewed highway signs. He passed many churches until he got to North Memphis. He prayed as he passed each church asking God, "Is this the place I am supposed to stop?" He never felt the nudge of the Holy Spirit as he passed by all those churches. When he approached the intersection of I-40 and I-240 he saw a sign indicating a turn toward Nashville. As he approached the exit for Nashville he prayed, "Lord, I understood I was to come to Memphis. This road will take me to Nashville. Do I turn this way?" With no affirmation from the Spirit, he kept driving on the interstate until he saw an exit for Austin Peay Highway. "This is it!" He turned off the expressway and again passed several churches before seeing our church, Broadmoor Baptist Church. He felt impressed by God to turn into the church parking lot, wondering what God had for him here at this place.

Acie was sitting in his office where all benevolent needs come across his desk. This young man walked up to Acie's desk and introduced himself. Samson said, "I felt impressed in my spirit that this is the church I am to come to and you are the man I am to see." Acie felt this person's need was benevolence and wondered to himself, "I wonder how much money he needs?" That was not why he was there. Then in a calm and deliberate voice, Samson began speaking his heart. "The reason I came here was to preach the Word in Memphis. God has called me into a worldwide evangelistic ministry and I have been to many countries preaching, but God has burdened me for America." Acie looked at this young man. Here was a handsome, well dressed and intelligent man sitting across his desk. Acie thought to himself, "He's not asked for a dime. He's not asked for food to eat or a place to lay his head. He claims to have no money to rent a room. He states his van is nearly out of gas, but he is not asking for material goods. He wants to preach. What do I do with him?"

Acie phoned me at home. "Marolyn, I have somebody I feel led to bring home with me tonight. He needs a place to sleep and something to eat. You know this isn't like me. I never call and ask to bring a stranger home, but it is almost as though I have an angel sitting before me. He has beautiful large brown eyes and is from India. I'd like to introduce him around at church tonight at the mid-week supper/prayer service and then let him stay with us for a while." I told Acie it was fine but reminded him that we had several college friends of our daughter's staying with us for an extended period of time. All the beds were taken. Where would he sleep? Acie offered Samson a place to stay and he expressed his gratitude for our hospitality.

I believe in taking care of God's shepherds, or preachers. God reminded me of the biblical account of Elisha and the widow at Zarephath (I Kings 17:13). The prophet was commanded by God to go to the place where a widow would supply him with food. This was a time of great need in the land. Food was scarce and literally had to be rationed to meet the need of the family. Now the prophet of God was coming to dinner and all she had was flour and oil, enough for one last meal for her and her son. The widow must have asked God, "How can I feed him?" The worst thing a child of God can do in times of need is to allow fear to control the mind. It advances the very thing you are trying so desperately to avoid. God's Word says, *"Believe in the Lord your God, so shall you be established. Believe in the Prophets so shall ye prosper."* II Chronicles 20:20b

The widow trusted the man of God when he said, "Don't fear." At that moment she confronted and defeated her fear. She quickly chose the position of faith. A faith that turned the devil's attempt to destroy her into a faith that brought an abundance for her, her son and Elisha for the many months ahead.

Elisha's second word of instruction was equally important, *"Go and do as thou has said."* What had she said? She had just told Elisha that she and her boy were going to eat. If she had ignored the word of the prophet and continued to speak words of death and insufficiency, God would not have been able to work the miracle she so desperately needed. The widow had planned to eat a meal. Elisha said, *"Go ahead and do that but make me a little cake first."* One would think Elisha was thinking only of himself and that it was selfish of him to ask her to give him a cake to eat first, but Elisha knew the importance of giving. She had to give before she could receive the blessing. Giving is an essential part of effective prayer. *"Give and it shall be given unto you in good measure, pressed down shaken together and running over."* (Luke 6:38). Her negative spirit of fear was turned into faith power. She gave what she had and her action prevented the death of her and her son. God supplied her with enough to get through the days of Famine when others were dying from starvation.

God showed me Samson's faith and God answered my prayer. Samson Rajkumar came all the way from India. He knew Memphis was where God was leading him, but he allowed God to lead him one step at a time. He did not know us, but we had fellowship together while he was here. We drove him around to other churches where he secured preaching engagements and God blessed him. God blessed us too - abundantly!

Life on the Farm

My Dad lived on this farm all his life and purchased it from his father. It was a beautiful place to live and very special to me.

I loved working in the fields.

Sunny Side School House attended through the 8th grade.

Marolyn and Carolyn, it is hard to tell them apart.

Acie and Marolyn

I began to pray at the age of twelve for the young man I would marry. When I met Acie in 1959 he was 21 years of age.

Acie and I were married August 14, 1962.

Our Wedding Reception Dinner.

A new Ford in the family, Sharon Marie
Ford, born February 22, 1968.

Acie graduating from seminary.

Marolyn received training at the Arkansas Enterprises for the Blind, Little Rock , Arkansas.

Our Daughter Sharon

Sharon at age 3 years.

I saw my daughter Sharon for the first time when she was 4 years old.

Marolyn reading Braille books to Sharon.

Sharon playing with Momma's white cane.

Sharon helping Momma wash dishes.

Sharon playing.

Speaking Ministry Begins

Speaking Ministry begins following the miracle- 1975.

Autograph parties are always special, Marolyn and Betty Crocker.

Oklahoma Evangelism Conference 1977.

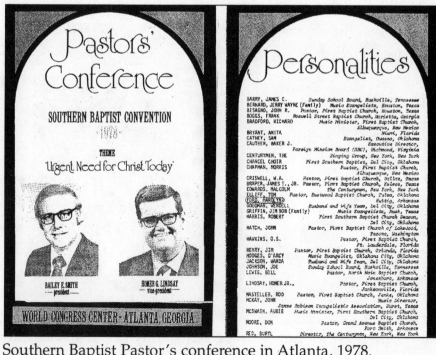

Southern Baptist Pastor's conference in Atlanta, 1978.

Sword of the Lord Conference, 1977.

The Churches

Acie is pastor of our first church Bosco Baptist Church, Monroe, LA.

Crossroads Baptist Church Famerville, LA-1968, Pastor, Acie Ford

First Baptist Church and Parsonage Hutting, AR-1972, Pastor, Acie Ford

Boulevard Baptist Church Memphis, TN-1978 Pastor, Acie Ford

Broadmoor Baptist Church, Memphis, TN. Acie, Associate Pastor since 1981.

Marolyn and Family Today

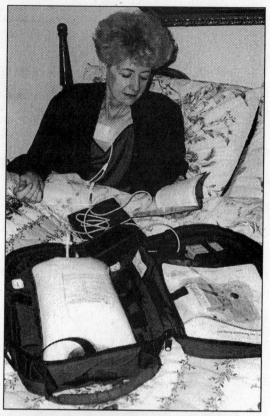

Reading God's Word as I connect to my "Nutritional Feeding" daily.

Marolyn in driveway on her scooter.

Marolyn's overseas trips of speaking engagements were booked with morning and night meetings during the two to three weeks she would be in a country.
South Africa Meetings- 1995.

Mucha Miew, Spain- 1995. They had no rain for six months. The land was so dry the river beds were parched as you see here. Yet it is surrounded by the Mediterranean Sea.

It's good therapy to be together enjoying God's countryside.

The kids moved in with us for a while.

Sharon, John & children moved to Alaska- 1998.

Chapter IV

Grace To Endure Brokenness

We were a normal family and our plans were nothing extraordinary, but after one evening in April 1990, our lives would never be the same again. I was tired and a bit shaky after a hard day's work. I relaxed in our Jacuzzi with honey bubble-bath. I felt the honey on the tub floor so I mixed it well into the water. I washed well under my feet and between my toes using a washcloth and soap. After drying my right foot and leg, I placed my foot on the marble step of the tub. As I lifted my left leg out, the right foot slipped like it was on ice and I lost my balance. I reached out to grab hold of something but found nothing. With a loud thud, my lower back hit the tub's water spout with all my weight. The sound reverberated loudly through the house. Knowing that my husband heard the thud, I called out to him, "I'm okay Acie, I'm okay." He came running to see what had happened. As he turned the corner, I quickly tried to calm his concern. I was trembling but I said, "I'm okay Acie. It's a miracle I didn't hit my head on the marble shelf." The water, still draining, cushioned my fall into the tub. I felt I had narrowly escaped a bad accident.

I was trembling and shaking when Acie draped a towel around me. My back hurt but I was standing and was alert. There was no reason to imagine anything worse than being badly bruised. I knew our plans for the evening were curtailed, but I never thought the plans for the rest of my life would be rewritten as well. Acie said, "It was as though God spoke to me right then telling me there would be rough days ahead. She's broken and you are going to take care of her. Through her brokenness I will be glorified more than when her blind eyes were opened." Acie had no idea what it meant and dared not mention it to me.

Something Is Wrong!

After my fall, I was lying in bed trying to sleep, but I could not. What started as discomfort steadily increased as pain shot through my body. I tried to turn over and realized I could not bend my legs. All I could feel was the piercing pain. A feeling of helplessness swept over me as I lay there watching the clock counting the seconds before morning.

Early the next day Acie called the doctor's office and told the nurse he was bringing me in. He then helped me get up and dress. We slowly made our way to the car and headed for the doctor's office. The pain never stopped, but it changed in intensity as I moved. The pain was so severe I could think of nothing but what the doctor could do to make it go away.

Acie helped me to the car and doctor's office. After a long wait, I was escorted to an examination room and Acie helped me get on the examination table. After a few moments, the doctor came in. We described the accident to him as he took my blood pressure and examined my back. Without ordering any tests, he said, "It is obvious your wife is having a lot of severe pain. If she isn't better tomorrow, bring her back in." Bring me back in? I knew I could not make another trip back to his office. I wanted to ask, "Can't you do anything, I need to have relief?" I didn't. I was trying to avoid back surgery. The doctor seemed to think the pain would pass with time and suggested over-the-counter medicine to relieve my distress. Acie took me out of the office in a wheelchair.

During the days that followed I was in tremendous pain. The pain became more excruciating each day. I could hardly move. We knew something had to be done. My doctor had gone to a foreign country. A friend of ours, who is a doctor, came to our house to see me and told me time wasn't going to heal this. He called an ambulance and arranged for a doctor to meet Acie and me at the emergency room.

We waited four hours in the examination room. As I lay on that cold steel table it seemed as though my bones were packed in ice. After the third hour, a new sensation replaced my pain. Numbness! It was blessed relief. I wasn't worried about the numbness then, just thankful for the absence of pain. The door swung open and a specialist came in. He moved my legs up and down. A few minutes earlier, I would have screamed, but now I felt nothing, no hurt, no discomfort. The doctor ordered a CT scan to determine whether damage had been done to my back.

The results of the CT scan revealed the need for surgery, so I was given a hospital room. As my body warmed, the numbness was replaced with the excruciating pain once again. The doctor came in and said I had a crushed vertebrate in my lower back. He scheduled surgery for four days later. He had spent about ten minutes with me in the emergency room. He did not know me. After getting settled in my hospital room, I still remember his words as he pulled up a chair to my bedside. He said, "Following the surgery, you will get out of this bed and sit in that chair and you will walk up and down these hallways. There will be no getting out of it. No self-pity party." He was scolding me and pre-judging my behavior. I expressed my dismay to the nurse over his remarks. Why had he spoken to me in that way? I am not one to complain and I have a high tolerance for pain, but I guess the doctor thought I was overreacting. He did not know how badly I was injured. Later we learned the CT scan didn't show all the damage. I was thankful the surgery would repair my back and the pain would diminish over time.

While in my hospital room four days awaiting surgery, I tried to get out of bed to go to the bathroom. Because I could not bend my legs I was having great difficulty. Realizing the need for a bed pan, I called for a nurse. When the nurse arrived I was told the doctor had not ordered a bedpan so she could not give me one. Instead she offered to assist me.

I screamed with each step to the bathroom. I placed a washcloth to my mouth to muffle the sound. I did not want to upset other patients in rooms close to mine. Since I could not bend my legs to sit on the toilet without unbearable pain, I had to stand over it. What once was a basic bodily function had become a humiliating ordeal. It was then that I realized that my colon did not function. The pain was all the way down to my feet. I later learned that great harm was done to the nerve in my foot by walking to the toilet during those four days before surgery. After the surgery I dragged my foot for months before that nerve was restored.

I am learning that while today's medical care is advanced, many times those who administer care are far from knowledgeable and compassionate. One needs to do what is best for one's own body. If you don't, you may be injured for life.

Surgery

It was 11:30 p.m. the night before surgery. A nurse came into the room and asked me to sign some papers for a different doctor to do the surgery. Who is this person? The first doctor came highly recommended. I don't mind saying I was extremely upset by this last minute change. Since back surgery is serious and I didn't want just anyone operating on my back, I was very hesitant to sign the papers. The nurse comforted me by saying this new doctor was more qualified to do the surgery than the first. I felt better by that reassurance and signed the papers. I asked for an opportunity to meet the doctor before the surgery. Also, I asked why the other doctor asked to be removed from my case. The nurse said, "The first doctor felt he got off to a wrong start with you and wanted to back away."

I awoke from the surgery and with each passing minute I was beginning to see more clearly. As the anesthetic began to wear off, I noticed the pain was different. It was not the excruciating, unbearable pain I experienced before surgery. This was different and it felt great! My heart raced as I thought, "Maybe it's gone! Could it be?" Then I realized perhaps it was the anesthetic that was giving relief. Was the surgery successful? Will this incident truly be behind me? I heard Acie ask the nurse, "What was the outcome?" She replied, "The doctor will be here soon to talk to you."

Although the first doctor asked to be removed, he was present during surgery. I thought that was a nice thing for him to do. After the surgery, he came to me and apologized. "The damage on your back was far worse than we could see on the CT scan. You must have taken quite a fall. There were fragments of crushed bone everywhere. The surgeon had to remove the pieces one at a time. Some were difficult to remove, but we feel that all have been removed and you should have complete recovery."

Recognizing my inability to do some things before the surgery, the nurse came in after surgery and asked if she could help me get up to brush my teeth. I was glad to tell her, "Oh no, thank you. I don't need your help now. The pain is so much better."

The doctor later reported that everything seemed to go well in surgery. He instructed me not to lift anything and give my body time to heal itself. I was so thankful to be finished with the ordeal. All I had to do was go home and give my body time to recover from surgery. Thank God! I had many scheduled events on my calendar and I was anxious to get through the weeks of recovery so that I could get back to my life as a public speaker.

Everything is Broken

Shortly after my recovery from back surgery I was asked to speak at a banquet for a rather large group of ladies. The dinner was great and everyone enjoyed the time of fellowship during dinner. After the special music, I began to talk about mother and daughter relationships. About two-thirds of the way through my message, I had an episode of bowel incontinence. I had to excuse myself and make a quick get away. But how? This had never happened to me before. I told the audience I was all right, but I had an emergency and asked to be excused. I requested them to remain seated for announcements and a drawing for door prizes. I asked someone to take over and continue the meeting. As I quickly made my way to the rest room I prayed no one would follow me. By the time I got to the rest room I had soiled myself down to my feet. (sorry to be so graphic). Everything needed to be washed in the sink. As I dried my garments on paper towels, I prayed, "Lord, please don't let anyone come to this rest room until I redress and gain my composure." God heard and answered that prayer. No one came to check on me. I returned to the banquet hall just in time for the dismissal prayer. As guests departed, I autographed books and spoke with people as if nothing had happened. Everyone was having such a good time and they seemed to have forgotten that I had excused myself earlier. God took care of that situation and only He knew my distress.

The next morning I left for home and made an appointment with a doctor friend of the family and later with the physician who performed my back surgery. He suggested I see a gastroenterologist. I asked him if he would refer me to one and he told me, "They're all good, just pick one!" I was disturbed with his reply, but selected one and made an appointment.

When I visited the gastroenterologist he told me he could not help me and passed me off to another doctor. After seeing three gastroenterologists without any results I was frustrated and anxious. Upon visiting the fourth doctor, he said, "Your problem is beyond me. Your condition is serious. You need to see a doctor at UT Medical Research Center at Bowld Hospital who specializes in research work on the Autonomic Nervous System. I will make an appointment for you to see him this afternoon if possible." I visited the doctor at UT Research Center and found he was the first who understood and was willing to talk to me about my condition. He convinced me that I should submit to a number of procedures and tests to shed light on my problem. For two years, 1990-1992, I submitted to every kind of test imaginable.

At the UT Medical Research Center in Memphis I was diagnosed with Autonomic Disorder. The best explanation I can give is that the antibodies which work to keep the body free from germs and diseases are confused. They no longer understand the difference between that which is good and that which is bad. Therefore, they attack the good body parts to get rid of them, thinking they need to knock them out. It has worked its way up through my digestive system. Our bodies need antibodies. How to get antibodies to understand the good from the bad is the big question. Doctors know very little about "Autonomic Disorder." It results in a condition called "Gastro-Paralysis" which is also called "Chronic Intestinal Pseudo-Obstruction (CIP). It is a rare disease that effects my bladder, colon, intestines, stomach and esophagus. I regurgitated everything I tried to eat or drink and could not be connected to a Colostomy, Illeostomy, G-Tube or J-Tube. It was just as God told Acie. My body is broken and he has to take care of me!

Word of my condition spread rapidly. People began praying immediately. Calls came from overseas as well as locally. We were told that in the middle of a conference, the people stopped to intercede on my behalf. Special prayer meetings were held in many places. There was remarkable outpouring of God's love and prayer support from fellow believers.

Temporary Relief

From 1990-1992, I had to use water bag enemas regularly to purge my digestive system. As the elasticity of the colon gave way (like a rubber band loses elasticity), the enemas gradually became ineffective. I had to find another way to gain relief.

In 1992 my doctor prescribed a product called Colyte, an industrial strength laxative doctors use to flush a person's colon, "Drano for humans". This required the patient to mix one and a half cups of Colyte powder with one gallon of water and drink it one glass at a time within a three hour period. It is a powerful laxative that flushes the digestive track purging the system. Doctors prescribe this medication to patients before colon tests or surgery. It had never been prescribed on a weekly basis, but there was no option. I would die if I didn't eliminate my body waste. Colyte was not a treatment, but maybe it would extend my life. Doctors at UT Medical Research Center, as well as those at the Mayo Clinic, had no idea how long it would work for me. I just knew that if this gallon of Colyte medication was the only way I could clean out my body, I had to drink it every third day. Although it was physically draining, I was able to continue my ministry.

When traveling overseas to speaking engagements, I carried half a suitcase of bottles filled with Colyte powder, an empty gallon container, and a 4 cup measuring cup and hoped none of it would break while traveling. I purchased a gallon of water at community grocery stores when needed. At first the medicine worked for me. Then, as the elasticity of my colon weakened, my body began holding the gallon of liquid all day and often into the night before it would begin to expel it from my body. It was torture. I cried and cried. I couldn't stand, walk, sit or lie down. I would hold my tummy with both arms tightly trying to ease the horrible pain. As the sharp pain cut through my stomach, I found the agony too unbearable to express. Besides the horrible pain and loss of dignity, the net effect of this weekly grueling grind was that it was time consuming. The Colyte procedure made it nearly impossible to plan anything, much less a full-time traveling ministry, but I kept going with my weekly engagements. I held every third day open to administer the procedure.

Eventually, the gallon of Colyte lost most of its effectiveness. I asked the doctor for suggestions. His only thought was to take an enema along with the Colyte, which caused excessive vomiting. Acie was so faithful and concerned for me. Even when he was busy at the church during work hours, he would call to check on me. The day of Colyte was always a horrible day of tremendous problems and pure torture! My illness was set in concrete. It overwhelmed me physically, emotionally and spiritually. Acie worried over me with such compassion and deep heart felt tenderness. He literally held me in his arms when the pain was so unbearable I could only gasp for my next breath.

My condition is so debilitating. How does one survive such bleak circumstances? One day the clouds bring a beautiful sense of serenity and reassurance, yet on other days it can bring a bitter resentment as I feel trapped within the walls of my circumstances. When the water overflows, the fire hits and the trials come, sometimes we cannot even see God, but we must know beyond a doubt that God is there all the time. When the pressure comes I must keep my eyes on Jesus. If I don't, I will go down in depression. Depression leads to self-protection. That is when people isolate themselves. Then comes self-pity followed by self-punishment, condemning and blaming self for all that is wrong. Self-destruction is the final step. We need not ever get to that state in life. When depression hits, don't stay in it, go through it, then pull out of it. God will see us through every trial! By the way, it is okay to feel sorry for yourself. To experience fear and depression is natural. Just remember to take it to Jesus. The Psalmist, David said, *"It is good for me that I have been afflicted.*

Why? That I might learn thy statues." God never promised He would protect us "from" trials, but He does promise to protect us "in" trials.

Not For The Faint In Heart

In late 1992, my gastroenterologist arranged for me to see a doctor at the world renowned Mayo Clinic in Rochester, Minnesota. While at the clinic, I was exposed to two and three tests daily. Sometimes a single test would last all day. Every test was stressful.

Our pastor said someone had offered to pay for an airline ticket so that Acie could go with me to the clinic (we don't know who made that offer), but although the flight expense would have been paid, I had to go alone because of the cost of food and motel expenses for two for ten days. It was hard to go alone. I needed Acie there, but there was nothing we could do about that. After all, I had traveled alone for years with my ministry and with all the tests I had endured at the Memphis UT Medical Research Center thus far, how could Mayo be any worse? It could and it was!

I didn't know what to expect. On the eighth day of medical testing, I was told to catch a van the following morning from the Mayo Clinic to the St. Mary's Hospital. I arrived at 5:30 a.m. and was scheduled for an all day test. When my name was called, I was told to undress and place my personal items in a locker. I asked the nurse what kind of test this was and she was very perturbed that my doctor had not prepared me for the ordeal.

I was asked to lay on a cot. There was a monitor placed over my stomach. A nurse walked up with slender tubing draped over her arm. It hung nearly to her knees and resembled layers and layers of garden hose. A second nurse used a can of temporary numbing spray on my throat that only lasts a few seconds. As she applied it, she told me that this was the only time it would be used. It was just to get the procedure started. She then inserted the tubing into my mouth and down my throat. She asked me to swallow over and over as she inched the tubing a little further down my throat with every swallow I took.

The nurses had problems getting the tubing through my body. A trap door in my stomach wouldn't open to allow the tubing to pass downward. The nurses pushed on my stomach to try to force the stomach door to open, but to no avail. They continued to put pressure on my abdomen until finally they could get the tubing through the trap door and through my intestines and colon.

It took more than two hours to push the tubing down my body, but the agony probably masked the true passage of time. When I had swallowed all the tubing, they rolled me to another bed where I was told I must spend the entire day while they ran the tests. The tubing provided the housing for several wires attached to a mechanical recording device beside my hospital bed. The tubing was removed while the wires remained in my body. The machine would react to events in my digestive system, but to what would it react?

The answer came in a short while when a nurse came into my room with a boiled potato, chicken breast and only 1/4 cup of liquid. She told me to consume the food within twenty minutes. "This is very important", she said. "Go slowly with the liquid, that's all you get." I looked at it and thought to myself, "There is no way I can eat with this wire in my throat and only 1/4 cup liquid." But I knew that anything less than total compliance meant doing the test all over again at another time. Pain accompanied every swallow as I slowly ate the food until it was gone. During the process of digestion of this meal, the machine scratched lines on the attached paper. Whatever happened was recorded.

Wait a minute, what if I need to go to the bathroom? Almost as if the nurse read my mind, she said, "You'll need some way to empty your bladder today. I'll get you a bedpan." She had no way of knowing that it had become necessary for me to catheterize my bladder every three hours daily and I was still in the learning process. A bedpan would not work.

My urethra tube is very small, even my doctor has trouble locating it, so how would I insert a catheter with all this contraption in my mouth and throat? (Sorry for graphics here). While I was teaching myself to use the self-catheter, I had to hold a hand mirror between my feet which were propped on the edge of the bathtub, keeping my hands free to insert the catheter while laying on the bathroom floor. I could not talk with the tubing and wires in my throat but I needed to explain to the nurse that the bedpan would not suffice. I motioned for a pad and pencil. I wrote a note explaining my dilemma and asked for someone to catherize me. She said, "There's no one available to do this for you." I was in a hospital. Surely they could call a nurse from another floor to come do it for me, but she said, "That would be against hospital regulations. They couldn't bring in a nurse from another floor." There was no way I could do this for myself in the shape I was in. It was very difficult to catherize myself under normal circumstances. We exchanged a few notes on paper to no avail. I had some self-catheters in my purse in the locker with my clothes. I gave the locker key to the nurse and asked her if she would get one of the self-catheters from my purse and bring it to me. I had to lay on the bed and catherize myself publicly with nurses and three doctors watching me on the machine. I have never been more embarrassed in all my life.

By 9:30 p.m. they had completed the test. They turned off the machine and disconnected it from the wires still inserted in my throat. The wires were finally going to be extracted. A nurse began pulling the wire from my throat hand over hand as fast as she could. I screamed and held my hand up to plead for her to stop. She stopped and said, "Oh, does it hurt? I'm sorry." I wrote on the pad, "Yes, it hurts. Please pull slowly, okay?" She agreed and asked if I was ready to begin again. I really thought had she continued pulling fast on the wires it could have badly damaged my throat. I choked and gagged with every pull on the wires to the point I almost passed out more than once. The nurse would encourage me, "Stay calm, stay calm, take it easy!" Finally, the wire was out! I was told to get dressed hurriedly and get to the front of the hospital to catch a 10:00 p.m. shuttle back to the clinic. This was the last shuttle of the day and I was not to miss it. The stress of the day had taken its toll. I developed a sharp pain in my neck, my left arm and down my side. Sharp pains were piercing my body. I was anxious to see someone back at the clinic about the pain. I feared I was having a heart attack.

The van pulled up at St. Mary's Hospital entrance to take me, along with others, back to Mayo Clinic. From there, everyone went to their different motel rooms. As I got out of the van I found the Mayo Clinic was locked and deserted. The fact that there was no one in the lobby and the lights were dim indicated the building was closed. Only the lobby was open. All patients, doctors and nurses go home each evening. I was alone and there was no one to help me in my distress. I cried as I found a sofa in the lobby to lay on until my pain subsided.

My hotel was only two blocks away. I decided that if I were to collapse and become unconscious, I didn't want to be alone in the lobby where no one would find me until morning. As I stepped outside, there was no one around except busy traffic passing by so I began walking up the street toward my hotel room. When I arrived at the hotel, it was 11:00 p.m. I telephoned another patient whom I had met the day before in the hotel sitting room and asked if she would check on me in the morning.

My pain was so intense I wasn't sure I would make it through the night. We both had more tests scheduled at 8:30 a.m. and knew we wouldn't get much rest that night.

Because the pain was in my neck, left arm and rib area, I was very concerned. I prayed for God to watch over and protect me through the night. I phoned Acie and asked him to pray especially about this. The Holy Spirit comforted me and I dropped right off to sleep, totally exhausted. Morning soon came. I checked with my new friend to let her know I was all right and rushed off to my 8:30 appointment for more tests.   When I saw the doctor, I told him of my chest pain and asked if he would check that out for me. He told me, "That's not why you are here. If you want to get your heart checked, you can schedule some tests with a heart specialist after you are finished with your scheduled tests for this week." The doctor was anything but comforting. I felt a natural impulse to be afraid that I might have developed some heart trouble.

God quieted my spirit as I remembered what Job said in the Bible. He said, "The thing I had greatly feared had come upon me." Fear is not of God. Fear and trust do not go hand in hand. The Christian must decide to have faith and learn to accept God's peace. I did not need to fear. Jesus told us in His Word that He would care for us just as He faithfully watches over the birds of the air, (Matthew 6). Christ died on the cross to save us from our sins. Now He lives in my heart in the person of the Holy Spirit. It is the indwelling Christ who is God's answer to fear and anxiety.

Paul's last letter to Timothy was written under the shadow of a death sentence but he breathed out the spirit of confident victory saying, "For the which cause I also suffer these things, nevertheless, I am not ashamed for I know in whom I have believed and am fully persuaded that He is able to keep that (me) which I have committed unto Him against that day,(the day of His return)". He knew the secret to overcoming fear.

The Mayo Clinic Results

After the two weeks of testing at the Mayo Clinic, the doctor called me into his office to discuss the results of my tests. I can't tell you how desperate my situation was. I was weak and needed encouragement and some good news. The Mayo Clinic doctor compassionately discussed illeostomy, colostomy and the stomach pacemaker and explained why these procedures would not work for me. He confirmed that a surgical bypass would not be effective due to the fact that my pelvic floor does not function. He also told me that a G-tube or J-tube device would only help those whose colon worked, and mine did not. Surgery would not help me. Further test were needed to evaluate the extent of my bladder involvement in the disease. This could be arranged with my doctor in Memphis.

I am grateful that the doctors haven't had to remove any of my non-working organs. The doctor advised me to continue the Colyte as long as possible. "It won't work indefinitely but use it as long as you can", he said. "I am concerned that the colon will lose elasticity with the continued use of the Colyte, and if that happens, I am not sure if the colon would ever regain its elasticity." His comments confirmed the diagnosis of my Memphis doctor, which reinforced my confidence in him. "Can you tell me what started this?" I asked. "Was it the fall or could it have been the results of the surgery?" He responded, "I really don't know. It could have begun by a neurological shortage in your body that may have been there since birth. The fall in the tub may have triggered it.

Was my life ever going to be as it had been before the injury? No, it has not been the same and never will be unless God does another miracle in my body. How did I ever get like this? I will never truly know the answer. I do know that unless God removes it miraculously, I will live the rest of my life with growing complications caused by this disease. God never promised we would be free from sickness and injury. He promises that He will cover me under His wings of protection and lift me up by His strong and mighty healing hands. I need that now more than ever! God is in control of all things, including my body. Every breath I take is a gift from God. He has allowed this to come upon me and He is in control of ALL things. I trust Him to deliver me.

"If God sees best not to deliver me from this chronic incurable illness, acceptance is taking from God's hand absolutely anything He chooses to give us knowing it is good and even perfect, however painful it may be, simply because He Himself has given it. "Acceptance," a little word but what infinite significance it holds for tormented Christian souls! True acceptance can become the wellspring of inner security, serenity and joy. It can ease our pain, our fears, and release our frustration, fill our restless nights with repose, and make even a life of seclusion or helplessness into a life of praise and service."

— Margaret Clarkson

Heaven's Door

There have been times when death seemed near, when the pain was too much to bear. Jesus is there for me and He wants me to talk to Him. I don't fear death because I know I will be with Jesus.

"Fear of the future is part of the burden of those who must suffer prolonged physical illness and weakness, but far into the future shines the glory of the promises of God."

— Margaret Clarkson.

I have family and friends who are in Heaven. They are enjoying eternity with Jesus and have no concern for earthly cares. I know my redeemer liveth, and I know I will see Him on the day He ordains. What glory to spend eternity with my loved ones at the feet of my blessed Jesus!

How can I know I will go there? Jesus said, *"I am the Way, the Truth, and the Life. No man comes to the Father but by me."* John 14:6 (KJV). There is no other way friend, to have the assurance of eternal life in Heaven but by faith in the one who made that possible. John 3:16-18 (KJV) says, *"For God so loved the world, that He gave His only begotten Son that whosoever believeth in Him should not perish, but have everlasting life. For God sent not His Son into the world to condemn the world; but that the world through Him might be saved. He that believeth on Him is not condemned; but he that believeth not is condemned already, because he hath not believed in the name of the only begotten Son of God."* God has promised, "WHOSOEVER WILL MAY COME". That *"whosoever"* is you. He is ready to receive you, if you will come.

Don't trust your situation or your health to last forever. It will not! In fact, it can slip through your fingers in a single heartbeat. Then all you have is your faith. Is your faith based on temporary things that won't last? Or, is it based on the blood of Jesus and His righteousness? *"What can wash away my sin? Nothing but the blood of Jesus. What can make me whole again? Nothing but the blood of Jesus. Oh! Precious is the flow that makes me white as snow. No other fount I know, nothing but the blood of Jesus."* (vs. 1) He shed His blood on Calvary's cross that mankind might find cleansing in the blood. Have you applied the blood of Jesus, praying to receive Him as your Lord and Savior? Ask Him to forgive your sins. Give your life to Him and live your life to His glory doing that which pleases God.

> "Sickness helps remind men of death. Most people live as though they were never going to die. They follow business, pleasure, politics or science as if earth was their eternal home. They plan and scheme for the future like the rich fool in the parable, as if they had a long lease on life, and were not tenants at will. A heavy illness sometimes goes far to dispel these delusions. It awakens men from their day dreams and reminds them that they have to die, as well as live. Now this I say emphatically is mighty good." —John Charles Ryle

"When one has a prolonged progressive illness and they know life will be cut short, sometimes family and friends pretend it is not happening or going to happen. When a bad spell hits, the sick sometimes feel people are hanging around watching and waiting for them to become more ill. The disease filled person doesn't know when they will draw their last breath. It could be they will recover and live another year. They hate not knowing when their life will end, but most of all, they are afraid they will die alone, the nurse will be up the hall and family will have gone home.

They have a real need to talk about death realistically with friends and family. It must not be hushed up or swept under the carpet. The caregiver, loved one or friends must bring it up in conversation when the ill person cannot. To talk about things openly brings relief and support. It makes one feel cared for and loved.

Let me assure those who may be facing death, God will not let you die alone. He will be there for you with the angels of Heaven. Although you will die with the disease unless God brings physical healing, you still have time to live, so live life to the fullest. God wants you to enjoy the time you have been given. Life is worth the living, for as long as God intends us to live upon earth. We are all one breath away from eternity. If we cut our lives short, we will never know what He intended for us. God wants us to choose life. Life must be fought through to the last battle."

— Dorothea S. Kopplin

Life should be precious to everyone. God gave His life that we might live.We are that valuable in God's eyes. Life is God's gift to us. We should value it highly and live every minute as though it were our last. Fill your day with thoughts about others, rather than self. Make every day count for eternity by fulfilling your life's purpose. Go after your dream and fulfill it. Then pick up another dream and work toward its completion. Do everything in the name of Jesus.

Worldwide Speaking Engagements

We made our first trip overseas to Caracus, Venezuela in 1986. We went to do volunteer missions with other Tennesseans for the Southern Baptist Foreign Mission Association. We arrived there on the night of our 25th Wedding Anniversary. The Venezuelan El Presidente was arriving in Caracus at the same time and the people were celebrating his arrival with beautiful fireworks. Just as we were entering our motel for the evening, the fireworks began and we felt like they were celebrating for us too.

My first overseas tour by myself was in British Columbia, Canada in 1993. I began with a TV interview in Toronto and then went to Edmonton for my first of many speaking engagements in Canada. I wasn't prepared for the world being dark in the mornings. When my alarm sounded, I thought it was set at the wrong time of day. I looked out and saw people at the motel restaurant eating breakfast, but it was dark outside. No one had reminded me that it didn't get light until close to 11:00 a.m. I decided next time I'd better do my homework and study the country I was going to visit.

In 1990 I had the privilege of having my twin sister, Carolyn Black as my travel companion to Paris, France. From Paris we traveled to Brussels, Belgium, Amsterdam, Hook Van Holland, Groningen, Vollendam, Liverpool, Exetor, Plymouth, Southampton, London, England.

A pastor in Paris, France invited me to come as the daily speaker for the World Wide Conference and share my miracle. What a wonderful opportunity to share what God had done! The church worship was beautiful and I learned so very much from my host and hostess in France. I spoke at the conference everyday for a week of wonderful meetings. God allowed me to meet so many people and develop many friendships which I have cherished throughout the years.

The conference in France was a fulfillment of God's call. Months before the conference, I began to feel God's call compelling me to take his message by way of my testimony around the world. When I returned home, speaking opportunities began coming from many different countries; first to Paris, France, Switzerland, Wales, Ireland, England, Spain and South Africa. From there, God has opened doors for me to speak in ten countries over the years that followed. I call it "Whirlwind tours" of speaking engagements.

One might conclude that I have been able to "see the world". Although that is partially true, that was not the case. There was little time to do much sight-seeing. My schedule was full, speaking mornings and evenings. It was an exciting time! God has introduced me to the family of God spread around the globe. I have been blessed with friendships that will endure throughout eternity.

The call to travel overseas was not an easy one. I admit my first response to these invitations was, "Who me?" One day I was working in my kitchen when the phone rang. A voice on the telephone asked, "Is this Marolyn Ford?" The lady had a European accent and I could hear it was an overseas call. I hesitated slightly before I responded, "Yes, yes, this is Marolyn speaking." She asked, "Are you the author of the little red book entitled, *These Blind Eyes Now See*?" Yes I am. By now I was really curious. She told me her name and said she was calling from England. She asked if I was scheduled to speak in England at any time? I told her that I had no plans to do so and explained that I didn't have the money to go to London. We talked a while before the conversation took a turn. I said, "The only possible way I can come is if several churches invited me to speak and they would receive love offerings to help cover my expenses. The most important part of the service is the invitation and souls being saved. My message is not just about physical healing, but about spiritual healing. Nothing must interfere with the altar call."

To my surprise she said, "I can get the church pastors to have you in their pulpits." I asked, "How many?" She replied, "You tell me how long you can stay and I will book you in a church every morning and evening for as long as you are here." I responded, "Praise the Lord, I can't believe this conversation is taking place." I had no idea what kind of offerings to expect. Would they cover my expenses? I was willing, but there was no way I had the funds to go. Should I plan for two weeks away from Acie and home? This would truly be a faith venture. In my spirit, I had complete peace that the trip was the right thing to do and, as always, God would show me the way.

Over the years, my overseas ministry flourished. Four couples who ministered greatly to me were Rev. David and Pat Sainsbury, Director, Ministries that Matter, Romsey, Hampshire, England; Rev. Lynn and Bridgett Cowdrey, Director, Associational Missions, Milton S. Sea, England; Rev. Harold and Antionette Peasley, Director of Evangelism Explosion, Florida, South Africa; Rev. Errol and Claudia Wesson, Pastor of the Simontown Baptist Church, Simontown, S. Africa; Rev. Densil and Norma Nenner, Director of Associational Missions, Plymouth, England; and Rev. Cleve and Ann Reed, Director of Associational Missions, Alicante, Spain. These devoted couples, who love God dearly, became my hosts and hostesses, arranged my overseas itinerary and carried me under their arms from one city and country to another year after year on speaking engagements. The Lord truly guides our path when we let Him.

God is truly amazing! I made that trip in faith that God would provide. And He did! His word says, "*Commit thy way unto the Lord, trust also in Him and He will bring it to pass.*" Psalms 37:5 He is faithful to His Word. The meetings were inspiring. The word of the Lord went forth. Hearts were deeply touched by the Spirit of God. People came to find Jesus Christ as Savior.

Pain in Spain

God continued to bless the ministry as I continued traveling year after year all across the USA and to ten foreign countries. Not only did I share my life story of "blind eyes that can now see", I also taught seminars and Bible studies.

A mission trip to Javea, Spain, changed my life yet again. I was there for two weeks and was scheduled to speak every morning in the conference and every evening in churches, except I needed every third day to clean out my digestive system. The Colyte medication (a strong laxative) drained my body of all my strength and left me feeling very limp, but I was there as a speaker and life goes on. Someone said, "Circumstances merely provide you with the opportunity to reveal the extent of your faith in the promises of God."

The conference week had ended and I had been invited to speak one morning at a small church inside a warehouse with barred gates over the doors and windows. It was incredibly difficult getting around in that area of town to park the car. I couldn't imagine what God would do with us here, in a place like this, but He knew! When the invitation was presented, six people accepted Jesus Christ as their Savior. What a joyful exciting meeting it was! Even the angels in Heaven were singing, "Glory to Him who sits on the Throne!"

The following day when I awakened, I began drinking the gallon of Colyte medication to clean out my digestive track. It had not been flowing well through my digestive system. The extreme intense pain brought me to wells of tears all day and into the night hours. I took it for granted that the motel room walls were insulated and would contain the sounds of my crying, but that was not the case. The next morning at breakfast I was informed that everybody in the motel heard my cries, even those going up and down on the elevator. I was so embarrassed. I determined that the next time I had to take the medicine I'd find some way to mask the sound.

Three days went by quickly. Early in the morning I drank the gallon of medication over a three hour period, took a blanket from the bed, wrapped myself up in it and went out on my hotel room balcony. It was a windy day and a bit cold. I sat there in pain and misery with a corner of the blanket over my mouth to muffle the sound of my crying as the wind carried the sound away. I have this zeal for appearing to be healthy and normal. It was important to me that nobody but my host knew I was sick and in pain. I was their guest speaker and didn't want to show myself as weak and feeble, if I could help it. There was nothing anyone could do that would help relieve my agony. I just had to stay with it all day and into the night and work through the hours alone.

> "Grace does not lift a believer above the reach of sickness and disease. Riches will not buy us exempt from it. God allows pain, sickness and disease, not because He loves to vex pain, but He desires to benefit man's heart and mind, conscience and soul, to all eternity." — John Charles Ryle

I had been told that my body would not be able to accept the Colyte procedure forever. In fact, the doctors were amazed by the length of time I had successfully used it. It was quite a paradox. The medicine that gave me back a portion of my life might also be taking it from me. I had no other options. Shortly after the ministry trip to Spain, the Colyte medication became totally useless to me. It would no longer flush out my digestive system. When I swallowed food, I regurgitated and strong acid burned in my esophagus. This caused my throat to swell so badly that my throat would nearly close up.

I have always been a person in control. Even in the loss of my eyesight, I was able to carry myself in such a way many wouldn't know I was blind. One might call that pride. Yes, I am! I am proud of my God and I am proud of what He has shown He can do through me when I let Him. In the lowest valleys of my life, I have known His courage. In my weakness He gives me His strength. In times when I am helpless, He gives me aid. Yes, I've been known as a strong person. I've approached life with vibrant energy, but I'd never felt the loss of control I was feeling now.

My Independence is at Stake

Although I was shy, I had solved my own problems since childhood. I was always confident there would never be a circumstance I would not be able to handle. Growing up in a family of nine on a farm provided a solid foundation of security for us all. We had to look out for ourselves and each other. We were taught to develop strong independent character. I had always been single minded in my pursuit to obtain my goals. I was self-reliant and I knew how to do most anything pertaining to life.

I am a go-getter. I have always had at least ten things planned for each day. My mother always said, "Never put off till tomorrow what you can do today." I have lived by that. For me, anything less is not acceptable. God's Word says, "*Boast not thyself of tomorrow for thou knowest not what a day may bring forth.*" There is never the guarantee for *another day, so whatever there is to do, do it today. "Life is a vapor. It appeareth for a little while and then vanisheth away.*" James 4:14 (KJV). I have approached life with vibrant energy. Even in the loss of my eyesight, I lead a full active life with dignity.

The doctor had previously talked with me regarding the possibility that one day I would have to go on "Total Parenteral

Nutritional Feeding" (TPN) intravenously. I said, "Please don't allow my body to ever get to that point. I enjoy my free flowing independent life and never want to be dependent upon "Nutritional Feeding". I do not want to be connected to tubing, catheters, machines and all that goes with it."

Some people feel that with long-term illness one becomes more well adjusted with time. I find each day, each year, more difficult as the body breaks down and new challenges arise. If you are going through trials it could be because you are bearing fruit for God. If you weren't, Satan wouldn't bother you. John 15:2 (KJV) says, "*Every branch that bears fruit the Father will purge it that it might bring forth more fruit.*" The purging of the tree is difficult.

> "Amy Carmichael has said that the eternal essence of a thing is not in the thing itself, but in one's reaction to it. The distressing situation will pass, but one's reaction toward it will leave a moral and spiritual deposit in his character that is eternal. This being true, then all that God permits to come to one must be working for his good unless he allows it to separate him from God. The only true calamity in life is to lose one's faith in God."
> — Paul E. Billheimer.

1 Peter 5:10 (KJV) says, "*The God of all grace who has called us unto His eternal glory by Christ Jesus, after that ye have suffered awhile, make you perfect, establish, strengthen and settle you.*" Psalm 84:11 says, "*For Jehovah God is our light and our protector. He gives grace and glory. No good thing will He withhold from those who walk along His path.*"

This Can't Be Happening To Me

Time had passed. It was April, 1996. I had made an appointment with my doctor to let him know that I was losing weight and had become dehydrated. He ran a blood test, but it came back with a good report. The following week Acie talked with my doctor in the hospital corridor and told him, "Marolyn is really sick and dehydrated," so he ran a second blood test which also came back okay. I felt so badly. My lips were sticking together; my throat was dry. I told Acie, "I cannot wait until morning for help. Let's go to the emergency room."

When we arrived at the hospital, the emergency nurse said, "Lay down here, you are dehydrated. We'll get the IV going as quickly as possible." When the doctor came in, he immediately admitted me into the hospital. I had become acutely malnutritioned and dehydrated. My body wasn't able to survive any longer without outside help. As much as I despised having to go on nutritional feeding by IV, I had no other choice. This meant much of my independence would be taken from me.

I had suffered through the awful pain associated with taking the Colyte medication from 1992-1996. I thanked God I wouldn't have to go through that pain anymore. Using the Colyte I felt like I had been a prisoner every third day, but now I had to be connected to the TPN bag and computerized pump fourteen hours daily. The doctor was telling me that I had to be put on this awful "Nutritional Feeding Machine." I was rolled into surgery where they inserted a Hickman Catheter into the subclavian vein and began (TPN) Total Parenteral Nutrition. This feeding is administered through IV drips into my blood stream fourteen hours daily. I can take neither health food drinks, supplements, nor additives because they are not predigested. I wasn't familiar with nutritional feeding (Hyperalimentation), but I knew it meant life for me.

At first my positive attitude surfaced as I said to myself, "I'll not be on this long. This will build my body up and I'll no longer be malnutritioned or dehydrated." I thought the machine would only be needed for a few days while I was in the hospital. I wasn't going to be tied to a medical bag, tubes and equipment. I had survived a lot of situations before and this too would only be temporary. How wrong I was.

Laying in the hospital bed the first nights of being attached to the nutritional computer and pump nearly drove me batty. I knew this had become my life support. I found myself listening to this awful sound. The machine sounds like someone gasping for breath. The sound made me nervous. In the middle of the night I found myself wide awake staring at the night shadows on the ceiling and walls, shadows coming in the window from the street lights below. I tried to go to sleep but tormenting thoughts were running through my mind. With it came terrifying feelings of finality, loss, confusion, despair and helplessness. Even the dark clouds moving in the night were spooky. I thought, "This is all a mistake. This isn't happening to me. I am trapped by it all. I'm pathetic." I floated between various moods of fear and self-pity. I thought, "I'll never be able to get off this machine and all the medication and needles. This can't be happening to me!" My heart filled with fear. There were many long anxious nights.

Please don't think I'm ungrateful. Without the TPN I would die. I knew I would have to learn to live with it. This was the beginning of a new era. I wrestled with my inability to cope with all the changes taking place in my body. Never before have I felt the loss of control I was feeling now. My soul and body long to be free, to escape the enclosing walls.

In the months that followed there were horrible adjustments to make. It wasn't only the TPN machine, tubing, medications, needles and bandage changes, but there was also the bladder equipment. Just to roll over in the bed is an ordeal with upper and lower tubing attached. My right leg needs to lay over the top of the urinal bag tubing while the left leg goes under the tubing. I am always having to tuck one leg under and the other one over. Then there is the TPN tubing that I get tangled in. The tubes, bladder and colon pain, hand, leg and feet cramps, all make for restless nights.

My doctors kept checking my blood and adjusting my nutritional feeding intake to get it balanced according to my body requirements. I was in the hospital for twenty-one days while they tried to get everything under control.

Before going home from the hospital, my grandchildren came to see me after I was well enough to enjoy their visit. When they first entered the room and saw me in the hospital bed with the pump machine, tubes and equipment, they seemed a bit withdrawn. They wanted to see me and I wanted to see them. I was still very sick and after they had gone, I didn't remember they had been there.

The second visit was much easier for them because they knew what to expect. Sawyer, the youngest (4 years) remained shy and hesitated to come near. I said, "Come, Sawyer, you can sit on my bed. It's okay." Soon he looked past the IV pump, tubes and bedside urinal bag and saw me. He climbed onto the bed and made himself comfortable. It wasn't easy for Johnny (5 years) and Brittani (7 years) either. Having the children relax with me on the bed was good for them and for me. Had they remained afraid or withdrawn, I would have felt utterly devastated.

Before they would allow me to go home from the hospital, I had to be trained to be my own nurse. A nurse was assigned to teach me how to use the TPN computerized IV equipment, syringes, medications, etc. I was running a body temperature of 103 degrees both days she came to give me instruction. When I expressed my concern that I felt badly and couldn't follow her instruction, she said I would have opportunity to do it myself with her help before going home, and that they would arrange for me to have a Home-care Nurse after my release from the hospital. It was all so very complicated and dangerous. For weeks I felt totally overwhelmed with it all. I didn't think I could be my own nurse.

In John 14:1 (KJV), Jesus said, "*Let not your heart be troubled. Ye believe in God, believe also in me. In my Father's house are many mansions. If it were not so, I would have told you. I go to prepare a place for you. I will come again and receive you unto myself that where I am, there ye may be also.*" When I was acutely malnourished and dehydrated, Acie visualized me in the arms of Jesus. I believe He carries me in His arms through the hard times. Truly "underneath are the everlasting arms".

> For those reading this who may be experiencing difficulties, unending pain, weakness, disappointment, sorrow and varied degrees of imprisonment, "Stay in touch with all the turmoil in your heart, anxiety, fear, anger, sudden shifts between hope and despair. Your true feelings are the closest channels you have for dialoging with God and other loving friends." — Jack Wintz.

I can say without reservation that my God is faithful. He will see us through any problem no matter how extreme the circumstances. His word promises a way to get beyond any situation in 1 Corinthians 10:13. God wants us to stand by His strength, not our own. When my physical ability became diminished, my spiritual abilities were magnified. Life will no longer be the same. I must now see what God has for me moment by moment. And I can say, God has proven to be a faithful friend. Even when everything seems to change, He does not!

Psalms 91:3-5 (KJV) says, "*Surely He will deliver you from the snare of the fowler.*" Every saint will face snares. Who is the fowler? Satan. He is the one setting traps in your way, not God. God is your deliverer. *God says, "You will face perilous pestilence but (vs. 4), "He'll cover you with His feather and under His wings you will take refuge. His truth shall be your shield and buckler. (vs. 5) You shall not be afraid of the terror by night.*" His "truth" is your shield. You defend yourself with God's Word. The "Word" is your sword.

There is a saying, "When life gives you lemons, make lemonade." Lemons are sour, add some sugar and it becomes wonderful lemonade. You can become victorious by taking any illness which comes your way and turn it around for good. Psalm 84:5-6 (LB) says, *"Happy are those who are strong, who want above all else to follow your steps. When they walk through the valley of Baca "Valley of weeping". It will become a place of springs where pools of blessing and refreshment collect after rain."*

"God has given special promises of strength for those who must suffer pain and illness. He has promised to strengthen those who are sick, even to strengthen them on their bed of languishing. He has coveted His own unwearying power to those who are faint and increase strength to those who have no might. He has appointed the measure of their strength and He urges us to take hold of His strength to make up for our lack, that we may be enabled to walk up and down in Jesus Name, spiritually, if not always physically.   He also promises that He will bring glory to Himself out of our afflictions and that we will receive spiritual blessings through Him."

— Margaret Clarkson

Fearful and Intimidating Days

After twenty one days of hospitalization, I was released to go home. As badly as I wanted to be at home, I was almost afraid to leave the hospital. I thought, "What if I measure out and inject too much medication by mistake? What if the unseen bed fuzz contaminates my feeding line? What if I don't see the air in the tubing and it goes to my heart? What if I step on my tubing while getting up or it catches and breaks off at the site? What if the tubing pulls out of my chest at night while turning over in the bed? Blood pours out of my tubing like an open faucet if it is not clamped. If the clamp opens it wouldn't take long for my blood to drain out of my body. The possibility of that happening absolutely terrified me. What if I get infection in the line and I die? The complications with long term (TPN) nutritional feeding are severe blood infections, liver failure and bone disease.

All equipment associated with the TPN and bladder catheriza-
tion had to be delivered to my house that night. The equipment
consists of the following:

Medical Backpack	Surgical lubricant
Weekly supply of nutrition bags	Self Catheter
Small refrigerator to store nutrition	Urinal Catheters
Medical Computer	Leg Bag and Holder
Additives and medications	Urinal Bed side bags
Small and Large syringes	Catheter Holders
TubingIV	Pole
Needles/Syringes	Batteries and Charger
Bandage changes and Tape	Examination Gloves
Alcohol Pads	Under pads

I left the hospital around 9:00 p.m. and the boxes of supplies
were delivered at 11:00 p.m. The home care nurse came to the
house to hook me up to the nutritional feeding bag. The entire
ordeal of coming home from the hospital was overwhelming. I
was very sick and terribly weak. Where would we store all this
stuff? Acie went shopping to find something suitable in which to
store my medical supplies. He came back with three cabinets on
wheels with see through sliding drawers that work like a charm.

I just knew that I was going to be a burden to everybody. Not
only did I feel that my life was ruined, but I had ruined Acie's life
as well. This whole medical disaster is not what I would have
wanted for Acie. Living with the "what-ifs" everyday is a
tremendous load of emotional stress. I have to get my mind off of
self, and think about living rather than this life support system.

Discouragement and doubt walk hand in hand with fear. A
sense of worthlessness and frustration can often become overwhelming. Fear is an evil that undermines our very existence.
For weeks I was a tormented soul facing insurmountable obstacles. Fear grips the soul of man and holds on. It does not lose its

power but we can let go of it. We are only to have one fear. It is an awesome fear of God because of Who He is. All other fears must and can be overcome. We must find God's peace in the midst of our storms. Acceptance of God's will in our circumstances is essential for survival. Life could not be tolerated without it. Acceptance will not be found in the human heart, but you will find it in God's grace. Jesus said, "*Ye believe in God, believe also in me.*" Jesus desires our trust and belief.

Because I was so weak, the home care nurse came to the house daily to hook me up and to disconnect me from the TPN feeding machine. The needles, tubing, medicine bottles and cabinets had to be absolutely sanitary. If my line becomes infected, the infection will go straight to my heart. A little blanket fuzz floating in the air is enough to contaminate a needle. I was lost in the responsibility of it all. During those first months I was emotionally fragile from the stress and the overwhelming fear of it. Many times I cried in Acie arms, "It's too much for me, I can't cope with all the changes in my body and all this medical stuff too." Together we would page through the medical books trying to find answers and understand about the Neurological Shortage, Autonomic Disorder, the colon, bladder, intestine and stomach and how they function. We looked for anything that would help us understand my condition. There wasn't much available. We saw words like "rare" and "chronic". The doctor said they had named "Autonomic Disorder", they had no idea how to treat it.

The first three months were very difficult. Although I was so weak that I could barely lift my head from the pillow, I had to learn to master this equipment. I had much pressure on me to learn quickly how to put the vitamins, medications, lipids and protein in the IV bags of nutritional feeding. I had to know how to dispense the four different types of medications using different size syringes and drawing out the correct amount of cc's into the syringes. I had to remember the importance of using the saline and heparin before and after each injection of medicine. It alarmed me a little when I learned that the medications were incompatible with each other. I thought, "Great, something else to be concerned about."

This mess I was in physically was something I could not repair. The realization of this was horrible. Laying there in the bed listening to my machine pump life and health into my body was serious. I began to realize things would never be normal. I was truly broken and I couldn't fix it. It would have been to my benefit had I used those nightly hours more productively, but I was barely coping.

Knowing God as Savior and Friend helped me deal with the "me-me", "my body", "my condition" syndrome. Too much introspection is not healthy. To comfort me, friends would say things like, "Your ministry as you've known it ends here, but you still have a lot of options open before you. You can work right out of your house." To that I cried, "Help!" There is more for me to do, more challenges ahead. I needed to get my strength back so I could go out. My life needs a lot of activity for me to survive.

Acie has so much love for me. He says that everything he does for me is a joy to him because I make it easy for him. There is so much that he needs to do for me. Many times care-givers get tired and quit, but not Acie. I must be careful that I don't take advantage of his kindness and become a burden. He is so wonderful and has such compassion for me. He also understands the loss I feel at times. I had to give up such a big part of my life. It has been difficult to deal with the losses. Death to a large part of my public speaking and teaching ministry has hit very hard. I had to cancel all of my scheduled speaking engagements overseas and throughout the USA over the next two and a half years. It was hard to cancel the meetings.

What would it take to make my life as meaningful in the future as it had been in the past? How does one survive when all has crumbled? Would it be possible to travel again? How would I manage to do it? Even if I get to where I am physically strong enough to take an air flight, how would I travel with this much medical supplies on board? Supplies can be sent ahead by UPS or Federal Express but I don't always stay in one city for more than one engagement. I move onto another city, another motel. My TPN bag and medicine need to be kept under refrigeration even while traveling. It can never be checked in because there is always the possibility that my luggage may not arrive at my destination. If that happened I would need to enter the hospital for nutritional feeding. Therefore, I must be granted special permission to carry medical necessities on board the plane, thus using more than one suitcase in the overhead rack and also to check an extra piece of luggage underneath. I asked myself, "How in the world would I manage it all? How would I be able to get it all on the air-trans cars, to the motel, and back to the airport?"

I looked longingly at my dismal future then thought of my past years of successful ministry of sharing Jesus in great crusade meetings, conferences radio and TV interviews. I was speaking weekly in the states and overseas. Had I been taking it all for granted, thinking I would have many more engagements? Now I look in the photo and letter albums of memories relating to my ministry. I take them out for a brief look and put them away.

Were the best years of my life behind me? How does one survive when all has crumbled? My ministry is important, but I lost a lot more than my life's work. Where do I go from here? What do I do? How do I cope? How do I go on? Acie and I had to deal with my fearful present situation and find acceptance before we could move on emotionally. Having an illness is intimidating, humiliating and degrading. I have to be careful here. These kind of feelings are not necessarily of God.

The Hunger Goes On

With the passing of time and my inability to digest food, one would think my body would learn no sustenance is coming. That is not the case! After years of this condition, I still remain very hungry and thirsty. It is normal upon awakening each morning to want some breakfast. I dress and make my way to the kitchen. Out of habit I open the refrigerator door to see what is there to eat and then I go to the pantry to see what is there. I stand there a few seconds looking longingly. It brings on such frustration, but I have to look. My hunger at times becomes overwhelming in its intensity.

I asked my doctor if there was anything I could do about this problem. I told him, "It's like being on the first day of a fasting diet that never ends." The doctor told me that as long as I live, the hunger sensation would never stop. He said that the nerves responsible for the hunger sensation are still working sending you alarm signals that you are hungry and thirsty. The fact that you try to ignore these alarms doesn't kill the nerve. Eating is a vital part of normal bodily function. I guess its like the man without legs who still feels his toes! If I go out into the heat of the day and become thirsty and dry, there is no way to get relief, no way to quench the awful thirst. Some days I crave a certain kind of food. Tomorrow I will crave something different. If I am craving fish and Acie eats fish, then I tend to move on to another desired food, maybe it's because I was able to smell the fish dinner. Even though I can't eat, cooking what my body craves seems to give me some type of satisfaction, as well as extreme frustration.

As children, when we were hungry, my sister and I had a saying. "It feels like my belly button is touching my backbone, I'm so hungry!" Not only do I feel continual hunger, but also there is an empty feeling extending from my chest under my rib cage all the way down my body. It feels as if my inner body is a hollow barrel. I miss meal time terribly. I miss the feeling of a full tummy or a cup of hot tea warming my body through and through until it hits the stomach. I don't know how to deal with the pain of not being able to eat or drink. I crave foods. It's the hardest thing in the world not to be able to eat and digest a good solid hot meal. I want to feel the warmth of food in my stomach chasing out the goose bumps. My doctor knows what my bodily functions can and cannot do, and he said, "You must not eat food, it will put you in severe pain," and that it does.

When we were growing up on the farm in Michigan, there were times now and then I'd wake up feeling hungry. I'd make my way down the wooden stair steps and go into the kitchen and get a cookie or a graham cracker. While eating it, I would make my way back upstairs. That little nibble was satisfying and I'd go right off to sleep. I find myself in that same situation, my stomach is always hungry and craving foods. All I have to do is see food and I want it, but at night my hunger pains really gnaw away at me and I can't sleep. I go to the kitchen and bite off a section of a frozen popsicle, chew it and spit it out. I must be very careful not to swallow any or I'll get a terrible stomach pain. After that, I go back to bed. It is probably psychological, but I try anything to relieve the hunger pains. Nothing helps.

Through tears one day, after I had time for recovery and was able to get out of the house, I said to Acie, "Honey, I still want to go out to eat Sunday lunch, Saturday breakfast or go for ice cream with friends like we always have done." I desire the fellowship we have together, but, oh it is hard for me when those meals come out all piping hot and are set on the table. It's all I can do to sit there while they cherish every bite. If they don't, I mentally do it for them. I pray for grace to endure. Everything we do in our society today is centered around food. I love to socialize with friends so I struggle through the meal just to have the fellowship. I don't want to miss another part of life's enjoyment.

I enjoy handling food, smelling and cooking it. At least I can still get some satisfaction from preparing food. I do find it difficult to flavor foods just right when I'm cooking. I can taste it as long as I hold the food to the front of my mouth. There is a taste bud on the tip of the tongue, but it is not nearly as sensitive as those back in the throat area. I can't allow food to go back that far because I would chance swallowing some and end up in severe pain. Acie lets me know if a dish needs more seasoning.

My jaw gets uptight very quickly from not exercising it on food. When it is tight, it hurts to yawn. When I spoke with my physician regarding the tightness, he said I needed to chew on something tough or face the possibility of getting lock-jaw. The jaw muscles need to be exercised just like any other muscle. Since I am not to swallow food, I find that chewing on the outer edge of a pizza crust works best to exercise my jaw. Unlike bread that crumbles, the pizza crust holds together. Then after I've chewed on it with my back jaw, I throw it away. Someone said to me, "Oh well, you can taste and spit out so that's not too bad. Things could be worse." I thought being blind was the worst thing that could happen to me, but not being able to eat and enjoy food is far more devastating. To chew and spit out brings about manifold frustrations. I struggle with this loss every hour of every day. My entire body screams out for the want of food.

This is extremely difficult for me to deal with. God has promised to *"Be my strength, my fortress and my refuge in the day of affliction."* Jeremiah 16:19 (KJV). God's will for me is good, acceptable and perfect. I must accept that this too is God's will for me at the present moment. Otherwise, His healing would manifest itself in my body. Let me add, acceptance of an illness doesn't mean surrender. I may not feel great or understand why God has allowed this awful suffering but in everything, I give

Him thanks. God says, *"Blessed is he whosoever is not offended in me."* I will not ask the Lord why this has come upon me.

A Hunger for God

As our bodies hunger for food and drink, we also have a built-in hunger system to know intimate fellowship with God and to know more about Him through His Word. Spiritual hunger pangs for God are the same as those for physical food.

Our hunger for God is satisfied as we fellowship with Him in prayer and in the study of His Word. Our spirits will be strengthened as we grow to maturity in Christ. Victory over the sins of the flesh will be ours as we confidently put our complete trust in Him.

Remember the charge of David to his son Solomon, *". . . for the Lord searcheth all hearts, and understandeth all the imaginations of the thoughts; if thou seek him, he will be found of thee; but if thou forsake him, he will cast thee off forever."* 1Chronicles 28:9b (KJV).

As we read the Scriptures our spirits are drawn by His Spirit to the awareness of God's love for us. We need to allow Him to move upon our spirits as we feed and meditate on His Word. As we wait upon the Lord and enjoy His presence, He will move in power upon our spirits. As we abandon ourselves to the Lord, He will make us strong.

When we come to the knowledge of how to lay hold of God in prayer, we become so overjoyed with this new enlightenment of the Holy Spirit as He reveals Himself to us that we do not have any more trouble desiring to pray. As with the force of a magnet, the Holy Spirit draws us to Himself. His love is so compelling that we cannot wait to spend precious time alone with God. Our very souls are turned inward toward Him enabling us to enjoy Christ's presence throughout the day. And as we learn more and more to wait before Him, there is nothing like it, for we are drawn deeper and deeper into the love of Jesus. We desire to engage in persevering prayer just to see His power brought down to us. We lay everything else aside to make time to spend with Him.

The secret to spiritual progress is to have a desire to know God's wisdom. The Psalmist wrote, *"As the deer pants for water, so I long for you, O God. Where can I find him to come and stand before him?"* Psalm 42:1-2 (LB). We need to have a strong yearning in our soul that pants after righteousness.

A beautiful hymn written in the 1800's, entitled "Satisfied," expresses the extreme thirst I feel within my soul as I crave and long for something more. It's a song that deeply penetrates my Spirit.

> *All my life-long I had panted*
>   *For a drink from some cool spring*
> *That I hoped would quench the burning*
> *Of the thirst I felt within.*
>   *Feeding on the husks around me*
> *'Til my strength was almost gone,*
>   *Longed my soul for something better,*
> *Only still to hunger on.*
>   *Well of water, ever springing,*
> *Bread of life, so rich and free,*
>   *Untold wealth that never faileth,*
> *My Redeemer is to me.*
> *Chorus —*
> *Hallelujah! I have found Him Whom my soul so long has craved!*
>   *Jesus satisfies my longing;*
> *Through His blood I now am saved.*
>   *- Clara T. Williams*

Those who are seeking God shall find Him real in their lives. Does your soul hunger after the things of God and His righteousness? Are you thirsty for God? Only He can quench that burning desire within you. Seek after God with all your heart, soul and mind.

Take the old hymns of the faith and dwell upon their words. Meditate on them prayerfully and allow them to become the rejoicing of your heart. *"For he satisfieth the longing soul and filleth the hungry soul with goodness."* Psalms 107:9 (KJV).

As we begin to understand the meaning of the fact that Christ is truly our life, we also begin to comprehend the grief He feels when we do not trust Him completely. We are to be so steadfast in His love that nothing can move us. As we say, "I just can't get enough of Jesus."

We need to become as conscious of the reality of God's presence in our lives as is the presence of a friend. We need to sense His presence with us at all times. We can sense when someone enters a room, even though we may not have seen them. So it is with God. We must learn to sense His presence at church, school, work, home, or wherever we may be. As we learn to joy in His fellowship, His presence will strengthen us. Of the many experiences we may have with our Lord, this one is the most important and ought never to cease. As we are in His presence, His love will flow through us to others like rivers of water.

When we abandon everything, our entire existence to God, we recognize that everything that happens in our lives is in His control. His Spirit completely encompasses our souls (mind, will and emotions). We learn that we remain in His presence no matter where we go or what we do. Our sweet fellowship with Him then remains unbroken. We cannot arrive at this through self-effort, but only through total surrender to Him. As we pray for His enlightenment, He will reveal many deep things to us.

Chapter IV

Emptiness

People know I can't eat. Those we socialize with are quite aware of that but when I get around others they often forget and offer me food. We were at a friend's home for dinner. Everyone had served their plate and found a place to sit around the tables. Before me was one last empty plate. I held it up toward our host and said, "Here is your plate, Sue." She responded, "Oh, honey, I put that there for you. Everyone has their food, go get yours." I said, "No, Sue, that's all right." She paused for a minute and then realized what she had done.

Yesterday we visited with other friends whom we don't see often, maybe once or twice a year. Everyone went for cokes at the mall and Jack said, "What kind shall I get for you Marolyn?" Jokingly I said, "Oh just get me a sprite." Then he realized what he had asked me. It embarrasses the ones who forget, but I try to put them at ease.

When our family was living with us, my little four year old grandson, Sawyer, would frequently come to me in the bed and ask, "Mimi, could you eat some food tonight? Just let me bring you some vegetables, they are so-o-o good Mimi. Just try some, please." At other times he would say, "Mimi, is today the day you will be able to eat something?" His little heart of overwhelming compassion brings tears to my eyes. He is so tender and loving toward me. Johnny and Brittani are very loving also, all in their own special ways. We are so proud of our grandchildren - they are all very precious! They are so delightful and a joy to our lives!

While I was blind I often prayed, "Lord, if I have to be blind, let it be for a purpose to further your kingdom work." Now I pray, "If I can't eat or drink, Lord, may it too be for a purpose, then my living will not be in vain."

Our church Minister of Education was telling someone about my situation. He said, "Marolyn has so much to think about just to stay alive. All the needles and varying medications she administers to herself are overwhelming. Some medicine is administered by the IV while others are pulled by a syringe into a needle into her "Hickman" line that goes right into the subclavian going into her heart. She can't eat or take in liquids. Her thirst and hunger pains are inexhaustible. With so many continual aches and pains, I am unable to understand how she deals with them all at the same time. It's like a man in a battle who jumps into a foxhole to avoid the bullets. He keeps waiting for the firing to let up so he can raise his head or run, but it never stops!" I think he gave an excellent overall view.

Were it not for the protection of God, I couldn't do what I do. I often feel the warming of His Spirit and I know He is caring for me. After a conference meeting where I was the guest speaker, a lady said that she saw a radiant glow about me as I was speaking. Thinking the light was coming from a window reflection, she moved several times to reduce the effect on her eyes without success. She then realized the glow was coming from around me. I laughed a little when she told me that after the service. I said, "I don't have a halo, that's for sure." I thought to myself, "But who's to say that God and His angels don't show themselves at times to let others know He is in control? One thing for sure, I am so very thankful for His abiding presence and His ever present Holy Spirit who gives me power to go on.

Exercising Faith

What about faith? Everyone wants to know how to "get faith." Many talk about "getting more faith," or at least sufficient faith to make things happen. Faith is not something we find or muster up. Paul says, *"Yet faith cometh by hearing and hearing by the Word of God*. Romans 10:17 (KJV). Faith is not something we work for, it is a gift of God. This gift is given to every believer at salvation.

However, faith does have to be developed by exercising it. It is like learning to play the accordion. We learn to know where the notes are on the music and where they are on the keyboard. But then we actually begin to play the accordion as we exercise that which we know and put it into practice. So it is with faith. We increase our faith as we exercise it in our walk with God and in our obedience to Him.

We exercise faith every day. I fly to many of my speaking engagements. When I board a plane, I do not question as to whether the mechanics serviced the plane properly or the ability of the pilots to navigate the plane. I just sit down in my seat, fasten my seat belt and wait for takeoff. It is the same with exercising faith. It is already there. I just use it!

Too often we come before the Lord with a spirit of intimidation. We need to ask His forgiveness for our sins and then come before Him as He sees us, forgiven and accepted in the Beloved. When we are forgiven and complete in Him, we are given the right to come boldly before His throne. In Hebrews we are instructed, *"So let us come boldly to the very throne of God and stay there to receive His mercy and to find grace to help us in our times of need."* Hebrews 4:16.

Stop praying for the same thing over and over. Begin to believe God and start praising Him for the answer. It will not be long before answers to your prayers become a reality. The Psalmist says, *"Whoso offereth praise glorifieth me. To him that ordereth his conversation aright will I show the salvation of God."* Psalm 50:23.

God wants us to take Him at His Word. Sometimes we think our problems are either too big or too small for God and that we shouldn't bother Him with them. When finances aren't available and nothing is going our way, we neglect to turn these needs over to the Lord and trust Him to supply the need. The Apostle Paul says, *"I pray that you will begin to understand how incredibly great His power is to help those who believe Him. It is that same mighty power that raised Christ from the dead and seated Him in the place of honor at God's right hand in Heaven."* Ephesians 1:19-20.

There is nothing God cannot do for us. He has promised to supply all our needs according to His will. Charles Allen wrote, "God is our source of supply and His blessings are not limited by the human resources that are available." We must never forget that He will give us everything we need to carry out His plan for our lives upon this earth.

We need to develop a faith that's unmovable, steadfast and secure; a faith that will stand the test when mountains come into our lives. If we look to our own unworthiness and weakness, then we will be defeated and go down in despair. 'Believing' is useless without doing what God wants you to. *"Faith that does not result in good deeds is not real faith."* James 2:17-20.

We must act upon our faith or our faith is dead. We are admonished in Hebrews, *"Looking unto Jesus, the author and finisher of our faith..."*

Hebrews 12:2a (KJV). Applied to prayer, "author and finisher of our faith" simply means God put the desire or need before us. He planted it in our spirit to begin working toward or praying for that desire or need. In that sense He is the "author" of it. He makes His desire, our desire, in order that we will pray and work toward the fulfillment of it. Then He also is the "finisher." He began the work in us. He put the desire there before us. Now, by faith, we are praying it through and working it out. He becomes the "finisher of our faith" as He makes that thing come to full reality.

We can be assured that God hears our prayers as we kneel before His throne. From that moment on, we must believe that we have already received that which we and God have agreed upon in prayer. Our actions then must move toward the success of that for which we have prayed. The answer has already come, so we must move in that direction. We must lay the foundation, make preparation and do whatever is necessary to bring about the desired end.

It is an incredible thing to learn that God stands behind His promises. His promises are exactly like the laws of nature. When you throw a ball up, gravity pulls it down. It must happen and it always will. God's promises are equally as certain. When He makes a promise and we meet the conditions of that promise, we can bank on the fact that He will fulfill it. He has to. His Word cannot fail to produce.

We must not allow fear and doubt to keep us from receiving all that is our inheritance in Christ - the eternal riches of His glory and the abundance of things hoped for. Paul wrote, *"Don't worry about anything; instead, pray about everything; tell God your needs and don't forget to thank Him for His answers. If you do this you will experience God's peace, which is far more wonderful than the human mind can understand. His peace will keep your thoughts and hearts quiet and at rest as you trust in Christ Jesus."* Philippians 4:6-7(LB). When we are at peace that God has answered our prayers, we need to stay with it. Our confidence must be in Him.

The Bible says that the entrance of the Word gives light (Psalm 119:130). The devil will cause us to be blind to what God really says in order that he can keep us from walking in that light. Hosea wrote, "My people perish for lack of knowledge" (Hosea 4:6/KJ). We have not studied to fully understand and know what God has promised to us as believers and, therefore, we fail to receive the blessings God has for us. We must learn to grab hold by faith and to receive the benefits of God's Word. Abraham *"staggered not at the promise of God's word through unbe-*

lief; but was strong in faith. . ." Romans 4:20 (KJV). We, too, must have that kind of faith in God.

R. A. Torrey said, "*Prayer is the key that unlocks all of the storehouses of God's infinite grace and glory. All that God is and all that God has is at our disposal in prayer.*" What an incredible, powerful statement!

Power of Prayer

Great power was released when Jesus came to His Father in prayer. When Jesus prayed, things happened. His disciples noticed this, and it changed their lives. When we go before God in prayer, we must believe Him for what He can do, and great things will happen in our lives too! God delights in answering the prayers of His children.

Andrew Murray states it like this, "Live in the Word, in the love and infinite faithfulness of our Lord Jesus. Even though it is slow and though we may stumble, the kind of faith that always thanks God, not for the experience, but for the promises on which it can rely. That kind of faith goes on from strength to strength, still increasing in the blessed assurance that God Himself will perfect His work in us."

Our first work ought to be to come into God's presence, not with ignorant prayers, not with many words and thoughts, but in the confidence that the divine work of the Holy Spirit is being carried out within us. This confidence will encourage reverence and quietness. It will also enable us, in dependence on the help the Spirit gives, to lay our desires and heart needs before God. The lesson for every prayer is, see to it first of all, that you commit yourself to the Holy Spirit. And in entire dependence upon Him, give Him first place in your life.

Let the Holy Spirit motivate you, your feelings, your desires. Let joyful eagerness surface. Never wait for feelings before you begin to do what you know God wants you to do. The Scriptural order is that God blesses you first, then blesses others through you. God's people see God's joy, love and peace in you, then they want to get that joy and peace also.

I have prayed so earnestly that the Lord would enlighten my understanding into the deep things He has for His children. I have asked God, "What is the power of the resurrection that Paul wrote about? What are the things God desires to do for and through His children that are greater than we could ever ask or think? Where is this mighty working power that is to flow from the child of God?" I asked God, "Show me what this 'fullness of God' is that I am to be filled with." It was on my knees in prayer that God began to show me some of the eternal riches of our inheritance in Christ.

God has sent His Spirit to tell us, and His Spirit searches out and shows us all of God's deepest secrets." 1 Corinthians 2:10b. And so I prayed, "Lord, by your Spirit, show me what all this means." This gained insight into God's Word has helped me tremendously in dealing with my illness and the shutdown of my digestive system and bladder.

Could I Physically Handle This?

When my blood levels are low, I need more blood. After receiving blood, my levels are more normal, but as each month goes by, the levels constantly drop. That has happened three years straight. I had just been given blood three months prior so it was at a time when my blood levels were leaning more toward normal than any other time of the year. An invitation had come for me to speak at a very special church. I had prayed that this pastor would invite me to come share my testimony with his people. He had invited me years before but at that time I was unable to go. This was an invitation I had longed for and I could catch a direct flight between Memphis and my destination.

Traveling with Parenteral Nutritional Feeding requires me to take quite a lot of medical supplies wherever I go. If the travel involves air flight, I need to gain special permission to exceed the FAA maximum limit for carry-on baggage. My makeup and medical supplies fill two overhead suitcases and cannot be checked as luggage below because it might not reach my destination on time. It has to be carried on board the plane. My purse is a large one with room for five or six 8 x 10 spiral notebooks containing my lecture notes which I study while traveling. My garment bag and larger suitcase can be checked and stored in the compartment below. Northwest Airlines graciously permit me to bypass their carry-on luggage regulations.

After an intense hospital stay and months in the bed, I had been laying down and sitting up around the house. Although I was still weak and my recovery was a slow process, I had been able to go out sightseeing in the car a few times. My thinking was if I can go sightseeing, I could handle the ride from my house to the Memphis Airport. And if I could get that far, then the rest of the way would be sitting in my wheelchair with someone pushing me to the gate and I would sit the rest of the way on the plane. After all, I had progressed out of the bed and I had been sitting around the house about a week or two. When I arrived at my destination I could go directly to my motel and rest all Saturday afternoon, evening and Sunday morning.

Not really knowing whether or not I could physically handle this, I accepted the invitation as guest speaker. Feeling a peace that God wanted me to speak at this meeting, I decided I would put myself to the test and see what my limitations would be. God always empowers me with strength beyond myself, and supernaturally equips me for the ministry He calls me to do. When I didn't have the human strength to minister on the whirlwind tours to Spain, South Africa, Switzerland, Europe, Belgium, and France, God empowered me. It was then that I was having to drink the gallon of Colyte every third day. Anyone who has the Colyte procedure knows how it drains your strength. The fact that I had to administer the Colyte every three days, and that my body couldn't relieve itself of the Colyte for many hours, made it difficult and painful. God administered His strength to my weakened body and empowered me for that task.

Now here I was, trying to go again to minister in the name of Jesus. I did not realize how challenging this trip would be for me physically. This would be the first time I would be seen or heard publicly after canceling my meetings over the past two and one-half years. I did not know if I could handle the airport, traveling, motel, packing, unpacking and tending to my needs with all the medical supplies. I did not know if I could handle the audience and the delivery of God's miracles. I knew I was shaky and wondered if it would make me nervous to stand before a crowd in my weakness. I had prayed much about this trip and the meeting. Several times while waiting for the date of my departure I considered not going through with it. The responsibility of a meeting is awesome, but the part of my personality that likes challenges and the Lord my God won the debate. I knew it would be extremely difficult, but the success of the meeting would not be in doubt.

As I stepped out into the unknown, my commitment and God's hand guiding me outweighed the risk of fulfilling my obligation. The ride to the airport and the flight were more intense than I had anticipated. Upon my arrival, my transportation hosts were wonderful in caring for my needs. She too had been in a wheelchair after recovering from back surgery a few years prior. They understood wheelchair problems and made every accommodation to meet my needs. In case of an emergency, I had my doctor's telephone number, as well as the numbers for my home nursing care company and the company that delivers my medical supplies.

Knowing I would not have strength to travel and speak on the same day, I arrived at my destination a day early. The ladies of the church had a nice gift basket placed on the dresser of my motel room. Rather than fruit, which will spoil and is most difficult to travel with, they had all kinds of things in my basket; mints, crackers, candy bars, a can of nuts, note pad, post-it note pads, lotions, creams and several tapes and books the pastor had written. I was thrilled. Acie would love the nuts, candy and crackers and I could use the other items. They were so very thoughtful and kind to me during my stay.

Since I was scheduled to speak Sunday evening, once I arrived at the motel on Saturday, I stayed in bed until late Sunday morning. Around 10:30 a.m. I got up and showered, put on my make-up, slip, hosiery, and robe and fixed my hair for the evening meeting. I propped the bed pillows up and got back into bed under the covers to keep warm. I had not met the pastor and was thrilled to have the books he had written. This would give me a way to get to know him. Therefore, I spent the day reading, praying, resting and recuperating from the trip. Also, reading and spending time in prayer edified my spirit in preparation for the meeting.

My host, a lovely couple, came by my motel room and we did just a little bit of sightseeing on our way to the church. Upon arrival, I stopped by the powder room to make my final adjustments before joining the pastors, their wives and some board members in the church. We had a powerfully anointed circle of prayer. Anyone could go out with confidence and high expectations from God after that kind of prayer before God's throne.

God had led in all things and I was so thrilled to be there. The service began with singing and worship. It was time to enter the sanctuary. The pastors lined up and seated in my wheelchair, I was ushered in by the pastor's right hand man. A sea of friendly faces focused on me. It seemed they were greeting me and assuring me of their prayer support. The singing continued. I could not believe the excitement of the audience. Deep within I wondered, "Would I give out physically or faint before them? Would my saliva glands produce the moisture my mouth and throat needed for me to completely share my life story? Would my voice tremble terribly thus showing my extreme weakness? Would the audience be turned off by that tone of voice? Could I hold my audience in the palm of my hand as I always have done before I became engulfed in this illness? Laying aside my anxieties, I knew I could trust God with all of it. Everything had been bathed in prayer and I knew that my being there as a guest speaker that night was God's plan for me and the church.

It was time for me to speak. The pastor introduced me to the audience and announced my name as the speaker for the evening. About two thousand people rose to their feet giving praise to God, clapping, cheering, welcoming me there. It was a lengthy hand clapping and I was glad because I had to be pushed to the platform. Once there, I sat on a stool and was given a hand microphone to make my presentation. The ovation continued for what seemed to be five more minutes. I had such mixed feelings of gratitude, excitement, and joy. As the applause died down, the audience became intensely silent. It was as though they were holding their breath waiting for my first words to be uttered. I had been so engrossed in the worship and singing that I failed to prepare ahead for my introductory words. I thanked the audience for their great applause and loving prayerful support. After that, things went well because God was with me. His strength was my strength while I delivered His message of faith and hope. The response during the time of invitation was the working of God. It was a fruitful service. "To God Be The Glory for all the Great Things He does!"

After the invitation had been opened for people to come forward for salvation, prayer and rededication, my host asked if he could usher me out to rest, but I wanted to remain in the sanctuary for most of the invitation. I wanted to let the Spirit of God rest upon me and see the many who were coming to Jesus, trusting Him to meet their need that night. However, I did make my escape before the crowd was dismissed.

Once I returned home, it took a week to regain the strength I had lost making the trip. That is the only flight I have tried to make for a speaking engagement since I was put on nutritional feeding in 1996. The trips I had taken before becoming ill were strenuous. The trips I have taken during my illness are nearly impossible and hard to endure, but I love every minute of my ministry and speaking engagements. I know the work I have done for God will endure throughout eternity. There is no greater joy than to be busy about the Master's service. *"Come near to God and He will come near to you."* James 4:8a (NIV)

I have taken other engagements but have traveled to those meetings in our van which is equipped with a wheelchair lift. That first time out publicly was difficult physically, mentally and emotionally, but challenging as well. I am not eager to be seen publicly in a wheelchair and/or hooked up to my nutritional feeding. (I have a portable backpack to house my TPN bag when I go out for an evening.) If I need to catch an evening flight home after a morning meeting then I need to connect to my TPN feeding before going to the airport. Due to my bladder problems, I need to connect the urinal leg bag and strap it on as well. I am tired of being sick and weary. In spite of all the embarrassment, hardship and difficulty, I feel better if I stay involved. I'd like to keep so busy in ministry and serving God that I wouldn't have time to spend on thoughts of my illness. God does expect us to take care of ourselves, but I can do that wherever He leads me.

Those who invite me as their speaker are so kind and thoughtful. Sometimes they leave a "basket of goodies" in my motel room to welcome me. That little extra touch brings warmth and love upon arrival. If you plan to do this for a guest speaker, give items that are resealable, items they can use later and that travel well in a suitcase. Your guests will appreciate anything you do for them. When the conference is lengthy and requires meals and lodging for several days, I am assigned a host and/or hostess to care for my needs. A host sees that the speaker is placed at the front of the lunch and dinner line or is served early to allow time for a few minutes of rest before the next session begins. If the host is well informed, this will relieve the speaker of many pressures like pushing through a crowd of people to get to the next meeting area, or workshop room, or getting items from one area to another, etc. I always thank God when I am introduced to someone who will be my host during the conference.

"Do not pray for easy lives. Pray to be strong men. Do not pray for tasks equal to your powers. Pray for powers equal to your task! Then the doing of your work shall be no miracle, but you shall be a miracle. Everyday you will wonder at yourself, at the richness of life that has come to you by the grace of God."
—Dorothea S. Kopplin

John assures us, *"For whatsoever is born of God overcometh the world, and this is the victory that overcometh the world, even our faith."* 1 John 5:4(KJV).

Prayer is powerful. It is through prayer that His power is made available to us. Prayer unleashes the power of the Holy Spirit through us to our world. Reach out and touch God in prayer until He pours out His Holy Spirit upon you. When your life is clean, you can come before His throne of grace with holy boldness.

The desire to have "power with God" needs to be the number one priority of our Christian lives. If you desire to have God's power, seek it and pray for it continuously. Let that one desire absorb your every thought and prayer more than anything else. The Psalmist David wrote, *"Be delighted with the Lord. Then He will give you all your heart's desires."* Psalm 37:4.

In an earlier Psalm David said, *"The one thing I want from God, the thing I seek most of all, is the privilege of meditating in His Temple, living in His presence everyday of my life, delighting in His incomparable perfections and glory."* Psalm 27:4. Do not allow other desires to crowd out your main objective. The quality of time you spend in prayer will determine the power of God that you will have in your life, work and ministry.

The Apostles prayed, *"And now, O Lord, hear their threats, and grant to Your servants great boldness in their preaching. After this prayer, the building where they were meeting shook and they were all filled with the Holy Spirit and boldly preached God's message."* Acts 4:29, 31. The anointed Word of God is powerful. It breaks every yoke of bondage. It is God's will that all Christians be filled with His power. Jesus said, *"For the Scriptures declare that rivers of living water shall flow from the inmost being of anyone who believes in Me."* John 7:38.

In The King's Service

Some people ask me, "What keeps you going? How do you find the strength to resist your infirmities and tell people about Jesus?" God is my strength. *"I can do all things through Christ who strengthens me."* Philippians 4:13 (KJV). How could I be happy if I stop telling people about Jesus and what He has done for me? Other people ask me, "Don't you ever feel like curling up into a little ball and laying there till you die? You have so much wrong with your body." They say that out of love and understanding kindness. Sure, I have discouragement and I could think that way if I wanted to, but I don't want to quit living life to its fullest until my work on earth is done and He has finished preparing that heavenly place for me. When that time comes, what Christian would want to stay? Somewhere hanging on the wall, I saw a framed picture that read something like this: "The Lord put each of us here for special assignments and achievements. At the rate I'm going, I'll live forever."

When you are free in your spirit, you will find that there is joy in sharing Jesus wherever we go in Jesus' name. People want to know God. They want to really find Him. There is a vacuum inside the soul of mankind that will never be satisfied or filled until you come to know Jesus and invite Him into your heart and life. Only then will you find completeness. God will give life to your spirit and that vacuum will be filled.

Testimonies like that of Roy Brunson keep me working. Listen as he tells his story: "In 1988, I was on a plane trip from Dallas to Memphis contemplating suicide because I had been fired from my job as an executive with the nation's largest direct marketing company. An attractive and neatly dressed woman sat next to me. Her face seemed to glow as she identified herself as a speaker and author. She was nice enough, but there was something different about her that was hard to describe. Then, out of the blue she started asking me personal questions; 'Did I go to church? Was I a born-again Christian?' I was very rude to her, as she had interrupted my suicide planning. Then I made the mistake of asking her what God had done for her anyway? She proceeded to tell me. She shared the story of the wonderful miracle God had done for her and how He restored her sight after being blind for thirteen years. She then told me that Jesus loved me and what He had done for me. I became frightened and wondered if God was real. A week later I gave my life to Christ and I thank God almost every day for placing the "blind lady that can see" on that plane to witness to me. That lady was Marolyn Ford, a messenger surely sent from God!"

You never know who will benefit from your testimony, and there is no way you can know the results until the Holy Spirit multiplies it and you meet Jesus. The treasure laid up in Heaven is not gold; rather, it is the lives that you touched for Jesus. Roy has told "our" story to thousands from the state of Tennessee to Ukraine. He tells me that over 1000 souls have given their lives to Jesus as a result. Those 1000 souls belong to God now because I told my story to the passenger in the seat next to me on the airplane. How can I stop or even slow down? The fields are white unto harvest. If we don't tell people Jesus saves, who will? We can rest when we get home!

The Stress Of My Illness

The stress of my illness is so great that the tears flow frequently; however, I have a very healthy outlook on life. If and when I fall into a depressed mood and descend to the pit of gloom, it doesn't take long for me to jump out of it. Generally all it takes to cheer me up is a visitor, Acie coming home, a day of bright sunshine, or just a telephone call. I cannot stay in the dumps. There's too much to be joyful about when you know Jesus truly does care for you. Jesus is the same yesterday, today and forever. Meditate on His unchangeable love, power and wisdom. Let the joy of the Lord flood your soul. I have to let the joy of the Lord fill my soul. That's not always easy to do, especially when weighed down with the mental stress of an illness.

Emotional distress induced by illness plays a very vital role in coping with disability and disease. The state of my mind can make the situation critical if I remain depressed for too long. However, fear and depression are not bad feelings, it is normal to have some fear over the disease, over what is going on within my body, and it is normal to go through periods of depression over it. Denying I have an illness will not help to lift my spirit and it will not make it go away. I try to be honest with myself about my illness. It's hard to cope with, tiresome, painful, debilitating, embarrassing and I have to talk about it openly. It doesn't mean my faith is weak or that I am not accepting God's strength or peace. It's not something I can push under the carpet. It's not going away - so I face it. I'm going through it and sometimes I am angry, but I tell God all about it. My illness is not a punishment and neither is yours. God loves me - God loves you!

John Charles Ryle, D.D. lived from 1816 to 1900. He wrote, *"Sickness is often one of the most humbling and distressing trials that can come upon man. It can turn the strongest into a little child, and make him feel 'the grasshopper a burden' (Ecclesiastes 12:5). It can unnerve the boldest, and make him tremble at the fall of a pin."*

Pressure affects people of all ages and in many different ways. Husband and wives want to be better partners. A child makes "A's" and "B's" and parents overlook it. He comes home with a "C" on his report card and parents react, pressuring the child. What is this "C" on your report card? You should do better. Teenagers feel peer pressure. They want to live right and show respect for their parents and honor their moral codes, but if they do, their friends call them "square, old-fashioned or, out of it." Friends pressure them to do drugs and drink. On the job, adults are pressured by their co-workers to produce more, work a little harder and keep up. Pressure comes from business losses and financial difficulties and illness.

People want to throw up their hands and run. They run to alcohol, partying, sex or sit for hours before the television hoping the pressure will vanish. When they stop running, they find the pressure still there because problems and pressure don't just go away, they have to be dealt with."

- Author Unknown.

When our Christian lives take on pressures like those described by Paul, we have the opportunity to experience the power of prayer. Because of the pressures, we can come boldly and expectantly into God's presence in prayer, knowing that He will answer. He will deliver us from every trial.

Whatever God speaks to your heart when you are reading His Word, learn to rest upon that Word, for it is the sure foundation for your faith. Don't be discouraged because you don't feel His power. Don't let how you feel hinder your faith. Accept God's Word by faith apart from your feelings.

It takes all the strength and effort I have to keep going. One day I was feeling really torn up about life as it is for me today. Crying, I told Acie, "I can't remember which day of the week today is nor which week of the month this is." Sometimes I pause and hesitate in conversation trying to pull up certain lost words in the middle of a sentence. My mind doesn't click fast enough. It is difficult for me to concentrate. It takes such mental effort. I have to keep up with ordering all my nutritional and urinal supplies. When supplies don't come in, I sometimes forget about it or can't remember to reorder or remember what the order was. I get so confused with everything and sometimes can't remember what I need to do. My doctor appointments and physical therapy take up all my time. People and medical staff think that because I am ill, my time is not valuable. The doctors somehow feel I should think it's a "good outing" to see the doctor and enjoy being at his office two or three hours; like I don't have anything else calling for my time, no deadlines, no real activity, duties or schedule. It seems that they think only their time is important and they over schedule appointments, thereby mistreating their patients. There is no time to do what I need to do. I was trying to cope. Seeing no end to it at all, I gave way to tears as I shared with Acie my frustration. I have to let the tears flow to relieve my soul of the inner agony brought on by the stress of my illness, or I could not go on another day. The door to my soul must open to relieve the pressure that wells up inside. My illness overwhelms me physically, emotionally, spiritually and socially.

We need to be strong willed when Satan attacks. We do that by keeping our mind stayed on the Word God has given us. *"Thou wilt keep him in perfect peace whose mind is stayed on thee."* Isaiah 26:3. To have perfect peace in the midst of our storms, we rest our faith on God's promise to us.

Faith that Prevails

John 15:7 says, *"If ye abide in me and my words abide in you, ye shall ask what ye will and it shall be done unto you."*

The reason God can say, "you can have whatever you desire," is because if you are abiding in God's word and His Word is truly abiding in your spirit, you're not going to ask for something that the Bible doesn't say you can have. So, therefore, because you are abiding, you will ask according to His word and God says you will have it. The only way we can have that kind of faith is to base our prayer on things given us in the Word.

Whatsoever Ye Desire - Desire is the substance. Desire is the secret power. The Bible says *"Seek ye first the kingdom of God and His righteousness and all these things shall be added unto you."* "Seeking God" will link us with our desire. Then we can depend upon His promise where He says, *"He will fulfill the desire of them who fear God and keep His commands.* Psalm 145:19 (KJV).

If God tells us to do something, we should just do it. Godliness is within our reach because we possess the life of Christ. If we are always wrapped up in thinking about our old nature and paying attention to it, it becomes more and more active. Self-discipline and self-denial are necessary to decrease our desires for sin and wrong. We must take our minds off our sins and turn them inward to focus on God's deliverance. As we turn our thoughts to the new man within in Christ, then the old man will become weaker and weaker. Fires which are not kindled will die. Abandon ourselves to the Lord and He will make us strong.

Begin each new day by saying, "Oh Jesus, I love you, I love you, I love you." Rejoice in the God of your salvation. Allow His warm, tender presence to flood your soul. Pray with the Psalmist, *"How I love your laws! How I enjoy your commands! 'Come, come to me.' I call to them, for I love them and will let them fill my life. Never forget your promises to me your servant, for they are my only hope. They give me strength in all my troubles; how they refresh and revive me."* Psalm 119:47-50. *"Stand ready to help me because I have chosen to follow your will."* Psalm 119:173. Quote Scripture to God and He will honor HisWord. Many Christians cover their sins by saying, "I have no convictions against this. Just because you think it is sin doesn't make it sin for me." The Holy Spirit does not have two sets of standards. He will not tell one Christian that what he is doing is right and tell another the same practice is wrong. Sin is sin, right is right, wrong is wrong for every believer. There is no double standard with God. However, we believers are not to judge one another regarding these matters, because each of us knows what we regard to be sin in our individual lives will vary according to our knowledge of God's Word. We are only accountable to God for that which we know and understand to be good or evil.

Realize that God never takes away our free will. We have many choices to make and He will not make us do anything against our will. When our spirit loses contact with God, we are as dead. It is up to us to pursue God personally and individually.

We must ask the question, "Do I desire to know the Lord and to have a deep, close fellowship with Him?" This is possible for us as we are sensitive to the presence of the Holy Spirit within us. We must be cautious not to grieve Him. We can do this by failing to be sensitive to the prompting of His voice to our spirit. We need to recognize His prompting and conviction as the very power of God working within us. The Holy Spirit will reveal Himself to us daily in many ways. We must accept Him and His presence as He communicates within us. We must accept His leading and wooing, respond to Him in love and unquenchable faith, and trust Him to do all that He says He will do, for He cannot lie. Talk to the Holy Spirit when you are alone. Don't just ignore Him. Learn to know what grieves Him, what makes Him angry. He is a person who hurts, responds, perceives, speaks, comforts, and loves. He wants to be loved. He desires our fellowship, but He will not force Himself upon us unless we invite Him to do so. He desires to do so much for us. He is the power of the Godhead.

"Call to me and I will answer you and I will tell you great and mighty things, which you do not know." Jeremiah 33:3 (NAS). *"Now glory be to God who by His mighty power at work within us is able to do far more than we would ever dare to ask or even dream of - infinitely beyond our highest prayers, desires, thoughts, or hopes."* Ephesians 3:20.

Get your prayer promise firmly planted in your spirit. That is the foundation for your faith. Use that verse against the attacks of Satan, against doubt and unbelief which will rob you from receiving the blessings of God. Commit your need to God's faithfulness. The desire of your heart needs to become the expression of your lips. You are making your request based on the already revealed will of God. Accept it by faith. Receive it into your spirit and thank God for it because He is the author and finisher of your faith. He authorized it when He placed the desire within you. He compelled you to pray and work toward it. He's the finisher of your faith. No one needs to struggle with a lack of faith.

Your "desire" is the underlying force around which all your actions revolve until that desire becomes reality. Not to believe you have it until you have it is not faith at all. "Desire" and "belief" are the power behind our prayers. Faith is a choice. Faith is trust, substance, evidence of things not seen.

Doubt may come, but use your weapon. God's Word is your sword. Constantly affirm in your spirit that God's promises are true. Isaiah 55:11 (KJV) says God's Word will not return void. *"We are to cast down imaginations (that's human reasoning) and every high thing that exalteth itself against the 'knowledge of God,' and bring into captivity every thought* (doubt and fear) *to the 'obedience' of Christ."* 2 Corinthians. 10:5 (KJV).

Faith depends upon the believer living by faith in the invisible realm. All of our difficulties that are connected with prayer can be swallowed up in the adorning assurance, "This is my God, He will bless me." If you seek God, you will receive the power to know you have received that which you are asking Him for before it is received. "Blessed" is that one who has his eyes and heart fixed upon God alone, who refuses to rest or give up until he has "believing acceptance" that he has received. Heavenly blessing and answers to prayers must be spiritually recognized and accepted before you feel or see it, even in the midst of contrary circumstances. This is where persevering, prevailing fervent prayer comes into existence.

This reminds me of a time when I had tucked away $200 so well I couldn't find it. Days passed and I had looked everywhere. At that time, $200 was like $2,000 to us, and therefore, I was very anxious to find it. I prayed, "Lord, please help me to find it." One day, God gave me a particular scripture verse, *"Keep on looking and you will keep on finding...."* Luke 11:9b. I based my faith on that verse. With my heart lifted in praise and thanksgiving to God, I began looking again, and found it that very day. To be sure, God hears, He answers and He guides. He is faithful to His Word!

Joyful Encouragement

In March, 1997, Religion Writer, David Waters of The Commercial Appeal Newspaper had written a lengthy article about my story. Following one of my very stressful days in 1998, Mr. Waters telephoned and asked if he could write another article about me for Thanksgiving that year. I was thrilled to have him do another article, but so much had happened I knew it would be difficult for me to give him my story verbally. I mentioned to him that I had been working on a manuscript based on my story from 1990, the year I fell in the Jacuzzi, through the present time. Although it was in rustic form, he could get the story from my manuscript if he wanted to read it. He was pleased with that suggestion and asked if he could arrange a time to interview me after he read the manuscript. He also asked if he could watch me hook up to my nutritional feeding to get a greater understanding of how that is done. That was fine with me.

Arrangements were made for the interview. Photographer Robert Cohen came and followed Acie and I around in order to snap some photos for the paper. That was awkward, sometimes uncomfortable, but fun. David Waters wrote a series of articles about me for the week following Thanksgiving, November 23-29, 1998. He did wonderful work on each day's article, keeping his readers in suspense all week as to whether I lived or died. The title was "Faith To Endure." The Commercial Appeal is far reaching and the articles were posted on the Web. Praise the Lord for using my story for His Glory.

An hour after talking with David, a publisher telephoned me regarding the publication of my manuscript. I was praising the Lord as I shared with Acie the exciting day I had. I was rejoicing because God is doing this and my suffering will not be in vain.

Medical Information

I have "Autonomic Disorder", a disease which causes the body to work against itself. The antibodies, which kick out all the trash keeping the body free of germs and diseases, are confused and are destroying the good parts of the body. In 1990, the disease first started in my colon and bladder; therefore, my doctor referred to it as "Gastro-Paresis" or what is otherwise called, "Chronic Intestinal Pseudo Obstruction" (CIP), the most severe form of abnormal Gastro-intestinal motility. It causes disfunction of the involuntary nerves and muscles of the GI tract. My doctor said it is the wrong name for what I have, but until they come up with another name for it, he used "Gastro-Paresis" (CIP) because it is a disease wherein the digestive contractures become slow and inefficient and/or stop. It can occur in any part of the digestive tract, and in some cases, like mine, it involves the bladder and stomach. Pains become severe and debilitating as the disease progresses. Because of my bladder disfunction, I need to self-catherize daily and use the bedside urinal bag while on the nutritional feeding. Nausea sets in frequently throughout the day which causes me to regurgitate bile. The Mayo Clinic doctor said that it is probably a Neurological shortage I may have had since birth, and that the fall in the Jacuzzi triggered the Autonomic Disorder which is causing more and more of my body to disfunction.

My blood doesn't show that I have Sjogren Syndrome Disease, but I have all the symptoms of the disease. It is a neurological disorder that causes the body's immune system to work against itself. Because my body's defense system is upset with the autonomic disorder it has begun to destroy the secretion glands that produce lubrication. White blood cells infiltrate the glands that secrete fluids. Autoimmune Disorder causes elevation in the liver and low blood levels. The salivary glands and inside of my mouth are affected. This creates a problem with smell, taste, tooth decay and mouth sores. It dries the mucous membrane lining in the gastrointestinal tract, windpipe and trachea. I am very susceptible to infections and pneumonia. It affects the esophagus all the way down with burning dryness of the throat, difficult, painful swallowing, acid reflux, a burning in the stomach and nausea.

I was told that the vomiting of bile can be very damaging to the teeth, especially to the roots under capped teeth. The Autonomic Disorder causes lack of saliva. My mouth is dry which is very bad for my gums and mouth tissue. To keep gums and mouth tissue healthy, they must stay wet. At night, I awake with my mouth and throat so dry my lips stick to my teeth and my tongue to my mouth like Velcro. At night, it becomes so dry that my mouth feels like an open shell of crust. I awake choking and quickly reach for my spray of lemon water to wet it down. The water soaks in and is absorbed by the crusty film, then I have a thick paste which I need to deal with before going back to sleep. The struggle goes on until morning. Once I am up and my tongue is moving, it is easier to maintain saliva in my mouth. However, it frequently goes dry on me in the middle of conversation. When that happens, I begin choking and coughing. I move my tongue way down in my throat area and usually that helps to regenerate the glands to produce the moisture I need.

Acie says that when I am asleep sometimes I struggle in great distress with an abnormal shortness of breath. He gets really concerned about it. I am in enough distress that it awakens him.

My tear glands are not producing enough moisture for my eyes causing them to become dry and to itch. Severe burning and a sensation of gravel under my eyelids form frequently during the day. This can cause severe damage to the cornea. Upon awakening each morning I cannot open my eyes for pain from the dryness. I squint to peek between the lids for a few hours waiting for the moisture to resurface. If I come in contact with a breeze from fans, air conditioners, air ducts, passing automobiles or sometimes the airflow from someone's fast bodily movement, my eyes will become excessively full of a sensation of gravel. When my eyes become overly dry, the pupils dilate and light becomes so bright I have to squint or close my eyes completely. I never know when this dryness of the eyes will come upon me throughout the day. It is happening more and more frequently and lasting longer as the disease progresses. My skin, voice, ears and nose are greatly affected by this lack of moisture.

I thought when I lost the function of my colon, bladder and digestive ability, I wouldn't survive the grief I felt over the loss and the pain I had to endure. Now the "Autonomic Disorder" has progressed further with an entirely new set of pain and illness. I wouldn't be here today if it weren't for my Lord who gives me "Grace To Endure."

My body is cold. I wear a half slip, two pair of heavy underwear, two sweaters and still get goose bumps at 74 degrees temperature. In winter, I wear three pairs of underwear and two sweaters indoors. At night, I use several hot water bottles and microwavable heating pads to warm my sheets and keep myself warm. I prefer water bottles over electric blankets or pads because there are times when I find myself lying in a pool of water because my catheter has come loose. An electric blanket may not be too safe when that happens.

We like the house cool, so during the winter months I use an electric heater in the bedroom. It takes nearly an hour to hook up to the bed-side bag and catheter, to connect the tubing and prepare the feeding bag and syringes with the correct dosages. It really gets tedious night after night without a break. When I am ready for bed, I unplug my heater and warm up under the blankets with my hot water bottles.

Everything I do becomes a real chore and creates enormous stress. I get weary quickly. Many times I feel I can't handle it and sometimes panic in despair. My emotions are intensified by the helplessness I feel at times. Acie is so compassionate. He is long-suffering and has a lot of fortitude. He hangs in there for me. He seems to be able to look into my soul with understanding and holds me while I cry. Tears are important because tears cleanse the soul, one's mind and emotions. I am very much aware of the toll a sick person in the home takes on everyone in the family. Therefore, I refuse to have a public pity-party and I do not talk about my weakness and pain continually, but neither do I withhold my feelings from my family. A day never goes by that Acie doesn't ask me about it. We talk quite openly about how I feel. Acie always asks directive questions regarding how I am, but I will not be a burden beyond what is necessary. I try to think good virtuous thoughts and keep busy. In Philippians 4:8 (KJV) we are told, "*Whatever things are true, whatever things are honest, whatever things are just, whatever things are pure, whatever things are lovely, whatever things are of good report; if there be any virtue, and if there be any praise, think on these things,*" and also Proverbs 23:7 (KJV) says, "*As a man thinketh in his heart, so is he.*" "In the midst of suffering, trust that either your burden will lighten or you will receive the strength to endure."

—Jack Wintz

Who Am I?

With age comes the weakness of body, aging of the skin, bones, joints, hair and the realization that I'm not as young as I use to be. Life has changed gradually as the years have passed. Wrinkles and pains have increased and with that comes adjustments and acceptance.

When an illness snatches good health from one so quickly, it is devastating. One day you are vibrant, healthy, energetic and suddenly it's gone. Having to give up cherished activities over night is a difficult adjustment to make. The medical complications are bad in themselves, but suddenly you find you have become an observer in the world around you and you can no longer be an active participant. When people ask how you feel and you say, "weak", they often respond and say, "We all know how that feels." However, unless they have been struck down with an ongoing severe illness, they can't comprehend what weakness of that kind is. I am referring to the kind of weakness one feels when the body is struggling just to survive. It feels as though life has been sucked right out of you.

It's devastating when your body suddenly ages. It's so sudden there is no time for psychological adjustment. It's a mental and emotional shock to look in the mirror one day after having been bed ridden a few months and see how your body has deteriorated. You don't like what you see anymore. You think back over the years of how well you took care of your body, never allowing yourself to become over weight in adulthood. You stayed out of the sun and used plenty of skin creams. Your skin was thick, muscles firm. Now, suddenly, as you look in the mirror you notice all that loose thin skin. It is no longer firm and tight and you know there is not much one can do to restore that which has been lost. You can exercise and try to rebuild the body, but the strength is gone. You are still the same on the inside, but even your personality has had to make changes for survival. If anything good has come from my medical troubles, it is my hair. It had started to turn gray, but has gradually turned back to the blonde color I had when I was young. Every gray hair is gone and I am again a natural blonde. Even my hair dresser is surprised!

There comes a time when you accept the fact that you can only be the best that you can be on the outside, and what really matters is the person on the inside. That person is still there. You have to accept what is left of you or you will be one miserable unhappy person. Those who love you, love you for who you are on the inside and not just the outer layer. You are still a worthwhile person. God's Word says, *"Beauty is vain, but the woman who feareth the Lord, she shall be praised," "Her price is far above rubies."* Proverbs 31(KJV)

Chapter V
From Tragedy To Triumph

Our daughter, Sharon, has a beautiful gift of music. She sings like a bird and plays the piano. While her life has certainly had its trials, her response to the emotional valleys of life demonstrates her overcoming spirit and deep faith in God. There was a time when we didn't think she would pull out of the valley, but God was faithful and she accepted His grace to go on after her first husband, John Roberts, was killed in an automobile accident at 26 years of age on September 11, 1993. John was serving in the military and was stationed at Ft. Campbell in Kentucky.

John had been in Germany for more than a year. Because of her pregnancy, it was best for Sharon to stay here in the states. Therefore, they had been apart until just before Sawyer was born. John came home for the baby's birth and then had to go back to Germany to finish his military time there. He had only recently returned home to set up housekeeping with Sharon and baby Sawyer. They were so in love and just beginning life together in their home.

Sharon and John lived in Dover, Tennessee not far from base. Their son, Sawyer was one year old at the time of his father's death. I was in Louisiana for the weekend. I had taught an all-day ladies conference at one of the churches. It was late in the evening when Sharon telephoned and said, "Momma, I can't find John. He's not home yet and I know he left the base over an hour ago. I don't have a car so I can't go looking for him but I am afraid something has happened. What should I do?" I said, "If he had a flat tire on his way home, it would take him an hour to walk back to the base if he needed help. Give him another half hour then call me back if you haven't heard from him. Two hours passed. Still there was no word. "Sharon," I said, "I telephoned Dad and told him what's happening. He is coming to you. It will be 3:00 a.m. before he will arrive. Just know he's on the way. Have him call me when he arrives." Things didn't sound good.

When Acie arrived at Sharon and John's house, he immediately knew what had happened. Several ladies from around the neighborhood had gathered. Sharon was weeping as she told her Daddy that two soldiers had arrived at her door around 1:00 a.m. telling her that John had been killed in an awful car accident. Acie immediately telephoned me in Louisiana. At dawn on Sunday I canceled both meetings where I was scheduled as the guest speaker for the day and flew back to Memphis. Our hearts were so crushed. We couldn't believe this awful thing had happened. We loved John and our hearts were in pain as we grieved for John, his family, Sharon and Sawyer. We hurt so for them. We had such deep, deep sorrow, disappointment and despair.

Grief is painful, but to grieve is healthy. Grief becomes less intense as time goes by, and the grief periods should come in intervals further and further apart as time passes. It is difficult to work through grief because sometimes you feel that if you give up the pain, you've given up on the person you lost, and that's not true. Grief is a natural process. God enables us to work through our grief period and He enables us to go on with life.

Closing a Door on Life

Just as soon as I returned home from Louisiana on Sunday morning, we drove to Dover to get the food out of the refrigerator and turned the unit off. We gathered up necessities; disposable diapers, other baby needs, and temporarily closed the house to return to Memphis with Sharon and Sawyer. The closing of the house was so final, and leaving Dover was difficult. It was like we were leaving John there. They were a family and that was their home. Sharon's life would never be the same again. It tore us up to have to lock up the house and leave it. That was John, Sharon and Sawyer's life, which was now a closed door. Sharon wanted to return to the place of the accident, so she and her Daddy drove over there. We felt so sorry for Sharon and the emptiness she felt. She was young, a new mother, and had a husband who loved her and now he was gone. It was a nightmare. The sadness was more than we could bear.

The funeral was held at the Broadmoor Baptist Church in Memphis. Before the day of the funeral Sharon told us that she was pregnant and that she had intended to tell John about it on the evening that he was killed. The news of the pregnancy was a mixed blessing. Sharon was so deep into her grief she couldn't pull out. As time passed we hoped that maybe the baby girl growing in Sharon's womb would restore her joy and help her through the grief process. She was so happy to be pregnant with another of John's babies and it was a part of John that would linger, Sawyer would have a sister.

Sharon came to live with us in Memphis. It was not the circumstances any of us wanted. It would be hard for Sharon but with God's help maybe we could make her recovery a little easier. However, Sharon sunk into a deeper depression. She lost her will to live and spent most of her days in bed. She had become immobilized with grief.

Another Great Loss

It was at that same time I was coping with the emotional adjustment to the loss of my colon and bladder function. I was grieving over my own loss and under great stress. This was a very difficult time for me. I felt I had more than I could bear. I was barely making it through my own hardships day by day. That was where I was emotionally when our much loved son-in-law, John died and Sharon was threatening suicide. We hoped the coming of the baby growing inside of her would give her greater purpose for living. The spark in her personality was surfacing and we began feeling better about her progress.

The baby's due date was upon us and the doctor was checking Sharon weekly on the baby's progress. Suddenly, there was no heartbeat! Baby Amanda Ruth had died in the womb April 23, 1994 at the time delivery should have occurred. Sharon had to wait over the weekend to enter the hospital four days later to deliver her baby. The naval cord had twisted tight at the tummy cutting off the baby's life-line. Sharon buried Amanda with her Daddy feeling that John had Amanda and she had Sawyer. That thought seemed to bring her comfort and helped her through it for the time being.

Life, A Precious Gift From God

Sharon needed to press on with life. Thinking maybe it would help, she decided to return to her home in Dover. After living there a few weeks, one day while I was talking with her on the telephone, she spoke freely about a plan for taking her own life. The losses in Sharon's life had grown too large to be covered by any desire for living. As the weeks went by, she couldn't get a grip on life and went further into despair. She was overcome with depression. Although going through such a low time in her life, Sharon was still very wise and knew she needed help with her grief. She went to the hospital emergency room in Springfield hoping to check in as a patient on the Psychiatric Ward of the hospital, but the doctor said she didn't need to be hospitalized. He told her that what she was feeling was normal grief and it would pass and lift with time. Sharon said, "But I can't handle the loss." The doctor then arranged an appointment for her with the psychologist in the building across from the hospital. She tried to get help from that doctor, but neither of them took her seriously when she told them she couldn't handle the grief. She told them she would take her life.

Discouraged, she telephoned me from near the doctor's office. She was crying in despair. I asked her to carefully drive back home to Dover and wait for me to get there. It would be 5:00 p.m. before I could arrive from Memphis. I knew I had to get to her and do it quickly! Sharon promised to wait for me to get there.

When I arrived at her home, she was sitting in the car with a gun ready to do what she said she would do. Sawyer was strapped in his car seat behind her. I knew beyond a doubt she was serious. I said, "Sharon, we love you. Sawyer loves you. He needs you. To waste your life is a shame. God gave you life. Do you want to be remembered as Acie and Marolyn's daughter who committed suicide?" I begged her to think of our love for her and little Sawyer's needs. "Who would rear Sawyer and care for him? How would he be able to handle not only the loss of his daddy, but his mother too? Think of all the emotional problems he would have growing up. Think about how much he needs and loves you." I hoped her love for him would change her decision. In tears we embraced and cried for what seemed an eternity. She and her Daddy made the necessary arrangements in Memphis to get the help she needed. Sawyer lived with us during this time. We praise God for giving Sharon new hope and strength to go on. A hope to build upon one day at a time. "When you trustingly bear deep sorrow, your heart grows in wisdom and grace."
— Jack Wintz

Our church family ministered to us so faithfully during those months while Acie and I were helping Sharon and Sawyer to adjust and caring for their needs. Friends sent cards and helped us through the time of struggle. God will bless them for helping us. He says, *"Give and it shall be given unto you, good measure, pressed down, shaken together and running over, shall men give into your bosom. For with the same measure that ye meet withal, it shall be measured to you again."* Luke 6:38 (KJV)

One year after John died on September 11, 1993, and five months after baby Amanda's death on April 29, 1994, Acie's father died in Louisiana on August 19, 1994. Sharon had a profound love for her Grandfather and his loss only compounded her growing dismay. At her Grandfather Ford's funeral, however, Sharon spent a lot of time with her cousins in Louisiana and that helped draw Sharon out. Her sparky spirit was coming back once again and we were encouraged seeing this change in her.

A Gift From Above

One year later we went to Michigan where Sharon's cousins on my side of the family live. While there, Sharon's cousin Eddie spoke to her about a really nice guy with whom he had worked a couple of years prior, named John Bouman. John was a single parent living in Texas. Eddie felt that if he could get them to talk on the telephone together they might encourage each other. Eddie asked Sharon if she would mind if this fellow John telephoned her. She agreed that it would be all right, but she wanted him to know she didn't want a boyfriend or to remarry. Eddie telephoned John in Texas and told him about Sharon's sorrow. John telephoned Sharon in Michigan the following day. Many telephone calls followed as we returned to Memphis. John Bouman and Sharon fell in love with each other's spirit. They spent hours courting each other over the telephone in the months that followed. By September they were engaged, and they married January 1, 1995.

John has two lovely children, Brittani and Johnny. They had been asking, "Daddy, when will you get us a new Momma?" They were ready to receive Sharon as their Mom. Sharon fell in love with them and cares for them as though she had given birth to them. They are really great kids. Sawyer enjoyed having a brother and sister. I believe the merging of the two families was hard on the boys. Johnny was 4 years old and Sawyer was 2 years old. Johnny had to share his room and toys with Sawyer. He had to share what was his, and no longer was the baby in the family. Sawyer missed having his Momma's attention all to himself. They were too young to express how they felt. It had to be a major adjustment for them both.

At the time of this writing, Sawyer is six years old and loves to sing as he plays. He is very happy and full of fun. He talks a lot and is quick to show affection. He can entertain himself for hours with Legos, puzzles and books. He goes to bed at night with a book in his hand. He will push to the limit to see how far he can go before he gets into trouble. Johnny is eight years old and enjoys history, which comes easy to him. He loves to work more than play. One day when he was 7 years old, he came to his mother and asked, "Mom, what can I do?" Mom replied, "Just give me a few minutes to finish what I'm doing, Johnny and I will be right there." Later when she entered the kitchen, she found that he had washed the dirty dishes, dried them off and put them away. She found him finishing the job by wiping the counter top. He sees what has to be done and does it without being told. He sings, "God Is So Good" as he works. Brittani is ten years old, loving and affectionate. She will share what she has with everyone even though she may end up with only one piece for herself. She is a giver and a good little mommy. She knows how to feed, diaper and take care of her two little sisters. She loves make-up and pretty nails, as all little girls do. She is quite a beautiful young lady even at ten years of age.

John is a skilled carpenter who does beautiful work building and remodeling houses. He has the ability to build an entire house, plumbing, electrical, the works - from ground up. Most of all, John loves the Lord and moves on faith knowing God will provide that which is necessary. He is a faithful steady worker and cares for his family lovingly. I compare his love for Sharon and the children to the craftsmanship he displays in building homes where quality comes first by a large investment of thoughtful labor.

John is such a blessing to our family. He has such a loving spirit about him. Both he and Sharon are mature beyond their years due to what they have experienced in life while so young. But, the two of them are very playful together. They both love adventure, camping, hunting, fishing and water sports. They make a fantastic couple. John works long hard hours on the job, but then he takes a day off and says, "Kids, let's go to the park", and away they go to picnic or fly a kite. John reads the Bible to his family nightly. The children have memorized scriptures that will stick with them through life.

Our family is so blessed because we see God's directive hand leading in the circumstances of our lives and the lives of our children. Our daughter Sharon demonstrates a deep strong love and a lot of wisdom in rearing her children. She uses every opportunity as a means of helping them to learn how to handle life. When she has to scold or discipline her children, she explains to them why what they did was not best and then shows them how to handle it the next time. She uses it as a teaching experience and explains to them what happened and why they reaped the results.

Family Love

Sharon, John and the three children moved from Texas to Memphis and moved into a house that he purchased to remodel. As the remodeling of the house progressed they eventually had to move out and begin work on the kitchen and bathrooms. We suggested they save their rent money and move in with us temporarily while they finished the work on the house. In October,

1997 they moved in with us. I was so happy they had chosen to move in with us. I felt Acie needed activity in the household, and having the children here with us was good therapy.

I hook up to my nutritional feeding around 6:00 p.m. and get in bed to rest. That's as far as I can go for the day. People commented about how lonely Acie seemed to be since I had become ill and how worried he was over my failing health. He truly felt I was going to die. It was a very difficult time for him and he needed the children so desperately. He worked puzzles, played games and read books to them. On his day off, he would take them to get an egg biscuit and give them time to play in the tunnel at the indoor playground. Then he would drive to the dollar store and allow them to choose a toy. He lived for the children and loves them dearly. They truly filled a need in his life. The children call us "Mimi" and "Poppie."

John and Sharon are both very good cooks so Acie said, "You can come live with us; you buy the groceries and do the cooking. I'll eat what you cook. That will be your rent." They agreed. They bought the groceries and Acie ate their food. With my Dutch background, where cleanliness is next to godliness, I wanted to make sure the house would be kept tidy and clean. It went very well for all of us. John was very sensitive to Acie's feelings about things. Something could be weighing heavily upon Acie regarding the church work and John would pick up on it. He'd say to me, "Mimi, have we offended Poppie?" I'd say, "No, John, it's nothing you've done. It's just something going on at work." It was nice that he and Sharon were both sensitive to our moods. We had seven people in our house. You talk about keeping up with the cleaning, laundry and cooking. It was upon us!

I love to cook for my family now and then. I can't do it often, but when I am going to prepare a meal, I start three days in advance. The first day I shop for the groceries. The second day, I chop vegetables and make pie crust. The third day all I need to do is throw it all together and put it in the oven. By the time I get the table set, it is mid-afternoon and generally that's as far as I can go with it, so the family takes over from there.

Sometimes I would sit with the family for a short time while they ate their meal. Usually, I was too tired so I would go to my bedroom, hook up my nutritional feeding and get in bed. From my bedroom, I enjoyed listening to them talking, laughing and enjoying their meal together in my kitchen. They were sensitive to my need for rest and were happy to have a meal prepared for them once in a while when they came in from the days work of hard manual labor. The kids worked hard helping Daddy clear off the land and building the houses. Little Johnny was learning how to pound those nails into the boards just like Daddy. I have a loving family who encourage me and care for my needs. I try to avoid talking too much about my illness but often my friends and family do talk about it. I am so glad they do because it makes me feel wrapped up in their love.

Caring

It brings much comfort to me when others talk with me about my hardships and troubles. I have many friends who care about me and really want to know details surrounding my day by day difficulties. They notice when my eyes look weaker or my legs feeble. That's getting down to the nitty-gritty and expressing understanding. I thank God for them.

I have noticed that I need to be careful when somebody asks me, "How do you feel today?" Although the person asks, they sometimes are not in a caring, compassionate mood, nor do they feel like listening to my troubles. At other times, I sense they are in the mood and I can respond quite honestly. If you are ill and feel the need to talk to someone, it's a matter of sharing yourself with the right person at the right time. Good friends are honestly concerned and give great support one day, but may not the next. That's all right, sometimes people are preoccupied with their own difficulties. They can't always be there for you. Telephone another friend. There is someone else who is in the mood to listen and help you bear your burden. "Let your suffering open you to a deeper capacity for loving, to cherishing the person who enriches your life."

—Jack Wintz

As a family, we often sit and talk about things. I am so thankful for my husband, family, brothers, sisters and friends who do not create a vacuum around me. Silence is devastating. My family and friends care and I know that. They are a part of my circumstances. My illness affects everyone. I feel sorry for those who are ill whose families and friends may not show love, compassion and support. I couldn't survive without that. I am so blessed. People who are too busy in their own world to give attention to those who are ill are most pitiful indeed. It's human nature to show compassion when confronted with another's misery. Only the most calloused individual ignores sick folks and walks away selfishly and untouched. The love of God speaks of service with compassion that is purposeful and involves personal service.

Standing by those who are ill, bed-ridden or isolated is a great ministry. In Matthew 25:36 (KJV) Jesus says, "*I was sick and ye visited me...*" Those who visit the sick are kind, tender and willing to obey the Father when He calls. It takes time and devotion. God works through people to do His work. If we are not willing to give of our time, how can God show His love and compassion to the sick? You will have no greater joy than to do that which God prompts you to do. Do it today! You'll be glad you did.

King David wanted to buy some land. The owner of the land wanted to give it to the King, but King David wanted to give it to the Lord and he didn't want to give God something that didn't cost him. He said to the land owner, *"Neither will I offer burnt offerings to the Lord my God of that which doth cost me nothing."* I Chronicles 21:24 (NIV) Those who want to do something for God and help others and are not afraid to encounter expenses and difficulties are truly servants of God.

Steven Grellet was a French born Quaker who died in New Jersey in 1955. Grellet would be unknown today except for a few lines which serve as an inspiration to many: *"I shall pass through this world but once. Any good that I can do, or any kindness that I can show to any human being, let me do it now and not defer it. For I shall not pass this way again."*

Marriage Is Giving

Acie's care demonstrates his love for me. A day seldom passes that he doesn't express his love to me, and no matter what I ask him to do, he does it cheerfully. In fact, I don't think I've ever heard my husband complain about anything (other than to trim the lawn close around my flowers and blueberry bushes.) He shows the love of Christ in the way he loves me. Jesus told husbands to *"Love your wives as Christ loved the church."* Ephesians 5:25 (KJV). He sets a good example for any man to follow.

Where does the deep love between us come from? The Bible doesn't say to marry the one you love but it does say to love the one you marry. Marriage is not based on sex or good looks, it is based on marriage vows and commitment. When a person accepts these vows and makes this commitment to each other, they agree and "choose to love" the other person. You can choose not to love someone, but you don't just fall in and out of love. Love is a choice, an unconditional choice. We have chosen to love each other in sickness and in health, for richer, for poorer, till death do us part. We are committed to that with a strong cord of love and respect. Everyone has good and bad characteristics. Acie and I dwell on the good things. We love, respect and appreciate each other. We treat one another as we want to be treated, loving each other through thick and thin. We don't blame one another when things get bad because "bad" is a part of life. We learn to trust God with the things we do not understand and don't try to *"lean on our own understanding"*. We rather, *"acknowledge God and He directs our path."* Proverbs 3:5-6 (KJV).

How does my condition affect our relationship as husband and wife? Acie is the best medicine I could have. He comforts and encourages me. He tells me he couldn't make it through life without me. Oh, how he makes me feel great! He is my "caregiver" and my "lover." He says, "You're easy to take care of. It's a joy for me to have the responsibility. Anything I can do for you, I want to do it." He spends time on the computer looking up information about my condition. He tries to anticipate what the right response might be under every circumstance. He has read books on caring for the sick in the home. We often talk about what he has read. This brings closeness, comfort and understanding. If either of us has to go through a trial, we go through it together. If you don't, it will tear you apart. Together we take one day at a time. We look at the big picture and strive to make our home life happy and as normal as possible.

I was sitting on the sofa one day, feeling really down. I was depressed about my losses, my disability and life in general. It has been a hard toll and is difficult to bear. I felt like my body had aged beyond my years. Acie came over and sat beside me. He put his arm around me and drew me close to his side as I continued to express my dismay. Acie then reached over and lifted me onto his lap. He wrapped his arms around me as if I were a baby. Placing his head against mine he held me close until I stopped crying. He told me, "Marolyn, I love you just the way you are. I am so sorry you have to go through so much pain and suffering all the time. I love you and I am here for you. Whatever

I can do to help, I will do for you." He is so wonderful about my need for his touch and reassuring words.

Touching is the key to communicate warmth and personal acceptance. It lets you know you are cared for and loved. Touching brings emotional security. Words of acceptance need to be verbalized on a regular basis or one will be left in confusion, unsure of personal acceptance.

Emotional Security

I do not know how much my individual physicians know and understand about my overall well-being. One doctor treats me for this, another for that. Sometimes I get the feeling that no one knows half the problems I have to deal with, but they try and they are doing the best they can. I have good doctors who are compassionate, but it seems at times they think the only stress I live under is that which pertains to their specialized field of medicine. It would be great if they would look at the whole picture and work with me from that viewpoint with some degree of understanding. But I know they cannot do that. The medical profession is so specialized. It's just that there are times one needs to feel like your doctors also see and understand the total picture. Being assured of this brings emotional security. Sometimes it seems that there is no one but my sweet Acie who seems to see or even begin to understand the tremendous load of stress that comes weighing heavily upon me from all sides.

I get the feeling that those who work in the medical profession think that if you are on nutritional feeding then you should feel good, energetic and healthy because somehow that provides all that the body needs. There is no way it can. That is not the way it is. Scientist cannot produce everything the body produces from the foods we eat. There are nutrients my body needs for survival that cannot be put into my TPN feeding. Doctors cannot do much about my physical weakness or my blood levels running below normal. There are many problems associated with my disorder. My Doctors are doing the best they can for me and I am thankful for them.

I'll never adjust to having to be dependent on high-tech nutrition and being on a machine with tubing entering my chest. I feel like I am a full time nurse and never get relief. I am faced with insurmountable obstacles dealing with life day by day. I pray for strength to persevere in spite of overwhelming circumstances. In order to take a medication, I must first draw some saline into a syringe, clean off my tubing cap with an alcohol swab and inject the saline. Then I draw a medication into a syringe, add saline to dilute it, clean the tubing cap again with the alcohol swab and inject the medication. Then I again take a syringe, draw up more saline, clean the cap with alcohol and inject more saline into the tubing. Then I do the same with a syringe of Heparin which needs to be injected into my Hickman tubing after each dose of medication. Heparin is used to keep the line from clotting and blocking off. Finally, I clean the cap with alcohol again. All of that for just one dose of medication, whether it is day or night. When I leave the house I must ask myself, "Do I have my surgilube, indwelling catheters, self-catheters and bedside bags, leg bags and straps and tubing, as well as nutritional tubing, syringes, medication, alcohol pads, needles, caps, etc." - everything I need while away. I can't forget my medical supplies, not even one item.

I am so thankful God chose to restore my eyesight before this illness came upon me. As always, God knew what He was doing. He knew I could not be my own nurse without good eyesight. The extra physical attention takes time and makes me feel like I can't get anything else done because it's constantly calling for my attention. This is a great stress factor for a personality like mine. It drives me and I resent that. The pressure upon me is ceaseless. The emotional stress of my illness affects me greatly. I feel hemmed in by my circumstances, imprisoned by it all. I suffer endless agonies. Pain's companion is loneliness, a penetrating loneliness. It is always present. No one can feel the pain that racks my body and mind or the thick sadness that lingers deep inside my soul. I tried to deal with the physical limitations, but I don't know how to deal with this overwhelming sadness caused by the illness that has overtaken my body.

"Even though my suffering seems endless, it has taught me to look to Jesus until I climb over the mountain that obstructs my pathway. I need to lift my faith yet higher and higher to be able to live above despair and continue on with my work until healing comes. No matter what kind of suffering and torment we experience, we need a faith that is greater than our suffering in order that the suffering loses its power to discourage us. We are not to look to our suffering, its violence or strength of its attack, but look to God who promises us the victory."
— Dorothea Kopplin

Once when we were laying in bed with our arms around each other I asked Acie, "Honey, are you okay?" At that moment Acie says he realized he was all right, but although we are husband and wife, and he is so very compassionate with me, I am still alone in my pain. Even Acie is alone in his pain over my loss of health. Although we talk about it frequently, he too is alone and suffering in his grief. Our lives will never again be the same. We suffer a great agony of loss. Friends sympathize but suffering is essentially within one's self. I cannot find words to communicate it. To suffer is to be alone. There are times when I get weary and tired of fighting the battle.

Acie tries so hard to delve deep into my soul to gain understanding of my inner-most feelings. The sealed places of the human spirit cannot be opened. These feelings cannot be pulled up to the surface and verbalized. They go too deep and are so painful. Acie tries so hard to be there with me. Not very many husbands stand by their wives like Acie stands by me, loving

me, supporting me, encouraging me. I thank God for giving
me Acie.

*Because the physical distress consumes all my energy, there are times
I cannot pray. I lose concentration and I can't follow through to pray
coherently. I find a sustained mental attempt to reach out is impossible. In my weakness I cannot even put two words together and voice
them to God. The desire is there, but I cannot focus my mind. For
months I could only say, "Oh God", or "Lord, help me." I couldn't get
beyond that in my prayer life. Jack Wintz spoke to this when he said,
"Stay in touch with all your turmoil, fear, anxiety, anger, the sudden
shifts between hope and despair. Your true feelings are the clearest
channels you have for dialoging with God and loving friends."*

*"It's only by faith that we are enabled to look beyond the confines of
our hedge (illness) and see God as a God of love at work in us. We need
a faith great enough to transcend the suffering to which we have been
committed. Faith strong enough to help us bear our crushing burden of
frustration and sorrow. Faith deep enough to crush our fears - where do
we find that kind of faith? "Faith cometh by hearing, hearing by the
Word of God", but here the sufferer is faced with an insurmountable
problem. Most sufferers find that any degree of intense concentration
and sustained mental effort is literally quite impossible, and the problem of how to maintain any sort of workable relationship with God in
the face of such difficulty is the single greatest problem in the lives of
suffering Christians. The very energies that make it so imperative that
we live deep in the Word of God also makes it nearly impossible for us
to study it intently, even to read it meaningfully at all. It takes real
physical and mental energy to approach scriptures in such a way that
they may be transmitted into spiritual power and this strength we do
not possess.*

*How does the needy soul, beset by difficulties like these, absorb enough
of the Word to produce the faith he so sorely requires? Just to express
and to do daily data, with this devitalizing and demoralizing situation*

is in itself a task calling for almost heroic effort. Only those who live in this way know it takes all the strength we have just to endure.

When one is unable to read or concentrate upon that which he has read, then memory must serve. Happy indeed is he who has furnished his memory storehouse with the plentiful harvest. Pain and weakness rob the sufferer of sustained passages of scripture so that only fragments remain to surface the mind. God uses the fragments that remain in our consciousness to nourish our longing soul. Fragments of scripture can minister to our spirits and sustain us through many trials.

There is an inability to concentrate for even a few minutes, wandering thoughts make it impossible to repeat a single scripture in its entirety, and it is equally impossible to pray in a sustained way. When you feel you cannot formulate a prayer there are ways in which we may reach out to God even in our weakness. We must cultivate these."

— *Margaret Clarkson*

When I feel stronger physically I find myself saying, "I'm sorry Lord, I didn't mean to leave you behind." I find I am asking forgiveness for neglecting my Lord. I believe it is a trick of the devil. Many lives are ruined by the spirit of guilt rather than strengthened by the spirit of faith. When we neglect to pray, it is sin. If due to your suffering you are unable to pray, that is not sin. God reaches out to us when we can't reach out to Him. When we can't pray we need a faith strong enough to endure the loneliness it brings and a faith strong enough to know God understands and will carry us through. When choice scripture verses cannot be brought to the surface of one's mind, the bits and pieces will sustain one in weakness. Romans 8:26-27(KJV) says, *"Likewise, the Spirit also helpeth our infirmity; for we know not what we should pray for as we ought; but the Spirit himself maketh intercession for us with groanings which cannot be uttered. And he that searcheth the hearts knoweth what is the mind of the Spirit because he maketh intercession for the saints according to the will of God."*

Has God moved away from me? No, but if you think that then perhaps you need to rethink your own relationship with God and determine who holds whom in whose hand. I don't have the strength to hold onto God. I don't need to hold on because He holds me and I am safe in His arms. My faith in God endures because God's love endures. Thank God! "When you find it hard to pray, surrender to the emptiness, or rather to God just beyond it. God is close to the brokenhearted."

— Jack Wintz

Frequently I find myself crying on Acie's shoulder in exhaustion and despair. I am emotional but not depressed, not mentally weak. Generally I have a healthy outlook on life, but there are times I cry until there are no more tears. It seems that the tears somehow wash away the emotional stress restoring a peace in the midst of the storm and a calm dependent spirit like a lamb picked up in the arms of the Good Shepherd. God hears us when we cry out to Him. When we cry, God cries with us. He is merciful and compassionate, loving us more than any person can comprehend. *"The righteous cry and the Lord hears them and delivers them from all their trouble."* Psalms 34:17 (KJV) I am learning to receive the resurrection power of Jesus Christ into my life by faith all the time.

"Be linked in spirit with suffering people of every place and age. United with them, let your compassion come to life - in prayer, words, and actions that help those who suffer. When deep suffering or loss befalls you it will take time to be set free of the trauma of your broken heart. Remember that through it all, God's healing love is at work. Releasing the tears opens the window of healing. Let the tears flow forth honestly within your soul and with treasured friends."

— *Jack Wintz*

Despair and depression are tools of the enemy. If Satan knows anything, it is how to use these destructive weapons against us. We need to resist the attacks and fiery darts of the wicked by using the "Name of Jesus" and by standing upon God's Word. I am covered by the blood of Jesus. Satan can't keep me down. He has no power beyond that which I allow him to have in my life. I have God's awesome power within me and I appropriate that power to be an overcomer.

Sometimes people need psychological counseling to know how to stand against their emotions. Make sure you go to God first. Confess your sins, clean your conscience and reconcile your feelings of guilt. No doctor in the world can free you from the distress caused by guilt. That is a spiritual matter and only the great physician can expose and heal in that area.

Christians should be careful not to allow themselves too little sleep. Few of us can do with less than six hours sleep and still be well in body and mind. Go to bed early. You get your best sleep before midnight. Get up early because to remain too long in bed is a waste of time. That is unbecoming for a saint who is bought by the precious blood of Jesus. The time you have should be used for the Lord. If we sleep more than is necessary for the refreshment of the body, it is wasting the time the Lord has entrusted to be used for His glory, for our own benefit and for the benefit of other believers around us.

Advance Preparation

A lady from our medical insurance company telephoned me around the middle of the year, 1996. She asked what doctors I had appointments with during the past three months and what tests they had run. Then she asked what doctors I had scheduled appointments with during the next three months and what tests they may want to run. Three months later I received another call and she asked the same questions. This time it made me nervous. Her questions made me uncomfortable and I wondered if they were going to make trouble for us because my medical bills were so costly for the company. In mid-October they telephoned again and this time I realized they were trying to protect us from financial disaster. My medical care is extremely costly and she wanted to let us know that we were soon reaching the $1 million cap on our insurance policy. She said that if I had to enter the hospital one time in 1997 we would cap out. In order to have financial protection we could make a switch to a policy coverage that did not have a cap. We could only switch in October and the time to switch was upon us. We were grateful to the company for bringing this matter to our attention and guiding us to the right choice. We switched to an HMO.

The change meant I would no longer be under the care of the UT Medical Research Physician who knew and understood all the medical problems connected with my illness. I had been with UT Medical from the beginning and they were most knowledgeable about my case studies. The thought of changing doctors was frightening, but I knew and understood that we didn't have a choice. We had to maintain insurance coverage. They were very thoughtful to help us with the change. We were blessed to find someone who helped us through the difficult interviews. We selected a primary physician who was compassionate and somewhat knowledgeable about my illness. Then we selected what we felt to be the best gastroenterologist, urologist, neurologist and blood specialist from the HMO listing.

Acie and I decided it would be wise to meet all the new doctors before January 1, 1997. I needed to know that my new doctors had my medical records and knowledge of how to treat my condition. In case of an emergency in January, I needed to be acquainted with them.

It was a blessing that we were able to meet those new physicians Christmas week. I became very ill January 3, 1997, and had to enter the hospital through emergency care. I had contracted pneumonia, a urinary tract infection and also a possible infection in my Hickman line. Hickman line infections are hard to diagnose when fever is coming from other areas. I was far too sick to talk with the physicians. We were so thankful I had given all of the new doctors copies of my medical records and had talked with them just two weeks prior. They knew me and I knew them.

Out of the Hospital and Back In Again

When I arrived at the hospital, the emergency room took me in, but could not admit me to a room. All beds were filled. There was no vacancy in either of the two Baptist Hospitals in Memphis. They tried to get a room for me in the Baptist Hospital in Mississippi, but they were filled also. The Baptist Hospital called the Methodist North Hospital and they said, "Yes, I could come there. By this time, it was almost midnight. I waited in the Methodist Hospital Emergency room for a couple of hours only to hear a doctor say, "I'm sorry, you have a nutritional feeding bag and we are not equipped to help you here." We were sent home to wait until morning.

The following morning my doctor was able to get me admitted into the Baptist East Hospital. I was one sick girl. The nurse knew I needed immediate treatment. For eleven days I dropped in and out of consciousness. I was in bad shape. Acie phoned my twin sister, Carolyn and she flew in from Michigan because things were not looking good. Carolyn arrived in Memphis and had just walked into my hospital room on Sunday when the doctor came in behind her and said, "You need two pints of blood immediately. Do you know anyone compatible?" I said, "This is my twin sister, Carolyn, will she do?" I do not remember him being there or saying that to him, but they said I did. However, I do recall having several hallucinations.

They told me later that I hallucinated because my electrolytes were extremely low. I thought I had bugs trapped in my bed sheet. I thought that the sheet had rolls of little pockets on it with bugs in them. I was told that I picked the bugs out of the pockets one by one. When I caught one between my fingers, I would set it free by releasing it while saying, "Pin...g". Then I'd catch another bug and say, "Ping" and each time I would set one free.

For days I thought that the Broadmoor Baptist Church, where my husband is on staff, had been robbed and we were at the police station taking care of the paperwork. I said to my sister Carolyn, who was with me at the hospital, "I need a bed, I can't stand here while they do all this paper work. Look, there's a bed over there in the prison cells. I'm going to bed." Carolyn said the nurse came in at different times asking, "Marolyn, Marolyn, do you know where you are?" I replied, "Yes, we are at the police station. We are trying to get everything worked out here.

Many friends were there to help. So many people stayed with me at the hospital during the long days and nights. I had no knowledge of their stay with me, and didn't even know who washed my dry mouth out with flavored swabs (little pieces of cherry, orange and lime flavored sponge on a stick) and cleaned up my messes.

As soon as my body temperature dropped close to normal, the doctors released me from the hospital so I could recuperate at home where I wouldn't be subject to so many germs. I was released with a ten day supply of antibiotics by IV drip, but I continued to get sicker. My home nurse who tracked my progress was convinced that something was definitely wrong. He immediately got in touch with my primary care physician. She called for an ambulance to pick me up at home, take me to her office for some tests and take me back home to wait for tests results.

Around 10:00 a.m. the following day, I received a telephone call from my primary care doctor. She feared I had a blood infection. She said, "I have an ambulance on it's way to pick you up. It will be there in 10 minutes. Pack your bags and be ready to go to the hospital. I have arranged for you to have a heart test before you check into a room. We need to know whether or not the infection has reached your heart and there is no time to waste here. When you get to the hospital, go immediately to such and such room for the tests. The hospital technician is expecting you. The test was run. It is a matter of life and death if that infection reaches the heart. I was scheduled for surgery to remove the Hickman Catheter and insert a new one. This experience took place the first of the year. (Remember, I had just selected my new physicians and talked with them during Christmas week concerning my medical condition in case of an emergency.) I was really glad God had directed me to plan for the "what ifs".

Special Connection

Acie met Steve Elliston who married a sweet lady in our church named Linda. Linda told Steve about my medical condition and Steve then wanted to get to know Acie. It seemed they had a special connection yet unknown to Acie.

Steve's first wife, Carolyn, whom he loved dearly, suffered from Gastro-paresis and Sugar Diabetes. She had to deal with some of the same type of medical conditions I deal with. Carolyn regurgitated her foods and was put on a stomach tube and IV feeding as her body grew weak and helpless. Steve was beside her throughout the long illness and ministered to her every need. After many years of illness, Carolyn had a stroke and God took her home.

From Steve's point of view and first hand experience, he is able to talk with Acie about his fear and difficulty in handling my illness. He knows the anxiety Acie is going through not knowing whether or not today may be another day of rushing to the hospital with me lingering between life and death. Steve went through that many times with his wife, Carolyn.

One day before I was put on TPN, Acie and I went to dinner with Steve and Linda. After eating, I asked if I could be excused from the dinner table. (I was having trouble regurgitating my food intake). That day Steve realized I was having difficulty holding my food down. He had seen the symptoms before and understood what was happening.

He and Linda know and understand the problems I have with the doctors and referrals to specialists; the delays in being able to get the help I need and the frustration of being told, "This too is related to your nutrition and autonomic disorder." It seems to me if everything is related to the autonomic disorder or the TPN, then there is no reason to try and correct any new problems.

Steve is retired and therefore, when Acie needs him, he is able to help the ladies of the church when I am hospitalized so Acie can go about his church work. (He is employed and needs to put in hours like anyone else, but the church is so good to allow Acie time to be with me.) Both Steve and Linda have been pillars of strength to us.

Linda would usually come to the hospital when she got off work. More than once, she carried my hospital clothing home and returned them clean and pressed. They take good care of me and continually volunteer their assistance.

I thank God for such wonderful friends who care!

Lord, Please Ease The Pain

I have terrible muscle cramps in my hands, feet and legs. My colon and bladder go into spasms producing unbearable pain day and night. Some pain comes early in the evening when I first try to relax and usually remains until morning. My fingers freeze up while reading, typing or peeling potatoes and carrots. With these cramps comes intense pain. It is not uncommon for me to have muscle cramps in my hands at the same time my legs and feet are cramping. This goes on sometimes all night. The pain is so great, I must move quickly to stand up and apply pressure on the cramp for relief. I get tangled in my urinal and TPN tubing and can't get out of bed fast enough. The pain is so great and nothing seems to help. I can't get the rest my body needs to cope with my weakness. The doctor increases my protein, calcium magnesium, liquids in my nutritional feeding bag, but that doesn't help either.

My bladder problems are a continued source of stress. The bladder spasms are hard to endure. During these times every nerve in my body feels like a dentist has hit a nerve in my tooth with his drill. It causes saliva to come down and cover my teeth. When my bladder has a spasm, saliva covers my teeth as every nerve in my body is set on edge. I stay perfectly still and catch my breath after each piercing streak of pain. Because I can't take anything by mouth, the only medication I can try to fight pain with is a Tylenol suppository.

Sometimes in the middle of the night, the TPN tubing disconnects from my Hickman tubing (which comes out at my chest), and the TPN computer beeps to alarm me that the catheter has come loose. Other times, the tubing to my urinal bed-side bag comes loose, causing the bed to become so wet it is necessary to change the bedding. If these situations are not enough to keep us up all night, the steady noise of the TPN machine will.

When I first became ill, I made crocheting my hobby. I made several afghans but I have had to lay it aside because my hands cramp so badly. I have difficulty pulling out the plunger on the syringes that I use daily for my medications and urinal catheter balloons. It is difficult to do much of anything with my hands.

My neurologist prescribed an electric scooter for me. Staying off my feet is medically necessary and greatly reduces the amount of muscle cramping. I am weak and cannot push my body weight in an independent wheelchair. The electric scooter is a blessing. With it, I am mobile. However, being confined to a scooter or wheelchair takes away my ability to enjoy the world around me. I can look on but I can't get involved because the steps are too many, the beach is too sandy, the hall is too narrow, the aisle is too crowded. The scooter/wheelchair gives me freedom and also hampers my freedom. I can't just go when or where I want and do what my heart desires. Sometimes I feel I am in bondage to the scooter. It is something I have to learn to endure.

I have always been free in spirit to hug friends and family. I reach out to them and they reach back to me, but the wheelchair presents a gulf between us. Sometimes God lays the desire upon me to hug someone who would least expect it and when I do they beam all over. People need hugs. God says, "*Be ye kindly affectionate one to another.*" Ephesians 4:32 (KJV). Being led of the spirit in that spontaneous action of love is beautiful but difficult when hampered by a wheelchair. I miss the simplicity of being able to hug those I love without the scooter between us. It seems when I feel the need to reach over and give someone a hug (example, when we enter the home of a friend), they are standing too far away from me. I can't step closer and conveniently pass on that hug. Now, more often (when at church) the hugs become an affectionate love pat on the hand. Either way it has to be, I thank God for all the love we encounter.

Some people behave awkwardly and walk behind a person in a wheelchair, but my friends are very thoughtful to walk beside me and allow me the privilege of joining in conversation with them. Acie likes to walk beside my scooter while putting his hand on the back of my scooter seat or my shoulder. That way we both move at the same rate of speed and communication is enhanced. Acie is a very good communicator. He wouldn't push me through the mall or walk beside my scooter and not talk with me as we go from store to store. Not that we have to be in conversation all the time, but communication between marriage partners is good.

Yes, people are so good to me and I am so richly blessed. But, I still fall into the self-pity syndrome. We all compare ourselves with others. I see someone who is bound to a wheelchair and usually I identify with them, but then I see this person pull himself up into a van and drive off. He can go anywhere he desires. We go into a fancy restaurant or mall food area and those who can't walk still are able to eat. I am not allowed to drive and I cannot eat. What could be worse? What could be worse? Not knowing God. I could not handle it if I did not know God has a purpose in this.

From February through July, 1997, I had regained some strength and seemed to be holding my own. As the year passed, my strength was fast leaving my body. I talked with my doctor about my weakness during my August and September visits. In October, I had Acie go with me to the doctor. He is good with my doctors and they listen when he tells them my strength is failing. When he describes my condition they seem to understand it well. If I forget to ask the doctor something, Acie may remember to bring it up. It is good for him to hear what the doctors say because he is concerned about the different issues and questions being addressed. When we both hear what the doctor says, we can discuss it together in the days that follow, and develop greater understanding, especially about troublesome matters.

The doctor had been telling me that my weekly blood reports were just fine. During this October visit, I asked the doctor if there was a different blood test they could run because I was getting very weak. In November I had Acie go with me again to see my doctor. I said, "If my blood tests are fine, then why am I so weak? I can't even open doors - something is wrong!"

A few days before, I had to go to Fred's Dollar Store to make a purchase but found I could not open the door. I tried to open it just enough to stick my toe in the door, but my strength was totally gone. I could not get in. Embarrassed with myself I quickly rushed back to my car and waited for someone to drive up, park and go in, so that I could enter the store with them. After making my purchase, I waited for someone going out to open the door so I could get out of the store and back to the car. Not long after that incident, I could no longer open car doors or turn the knob on the house door. I felt my strength had gone as low as it could possibly go. I couldn't get help from my doctors. I felt so badly.

By the end of November I had developed intractable mouth ulcers. Since my doctor was not in at the time, I had to see a substitute doctor for medication. The doctor asked the nurse to touch each ulcer with a silver nitrate stick. The following day I developed twice as many ulcers, so I returned to the doctor's office and they touched the additional ulcers with the silver nitrate treatment. Sixty or more ulcers covered my mouth, tongue, soft palate and throat. I was in misery! This doctor did not know that the silver nitrate would cause the ulcers to multiply.

Time Out, the Baby is Due

The following day, December 3, 1997, our daughter Sharon gave birth to our fourth grandchild, Jessica Lane. Since it was a scheduled birth by induced labor, we all planned to be present at the hospital for the big occasion. Yes, me too. Nothing would keep me from being there!

Acie pushed me in a wheelchair to Sharon's hospital room. Something was wrong with me. I do not remember going to the hospital and being pushed to Sharon's room. Nor do I remember the birth of baby Jessica Lane. Later when I asked Sharon about what had happened on the day of Jessica's birth, where was I and why did I not remember her birth, she told me that I had fallen asleep in the wheelchair. Her husband, John, picked me up and laid me on the sofa in her room and I slept through the entire event.

We learned later that I wasn't asleep. It was as though I was comatose. I wasn't aware of anything around me. We drove home that evening and went to bed for the night. After a night of rest, I woke up and dressed for the day. I cannot recall any of these events to this day. As a matter of fact, as I am writing my story, I had to ask Acie how I could have been present when Sharon gave birth to Jessica and not remembered it. Since Sharon's last pregnancy resulted in the death of her baby, Amanda Ruth, I was determined to be there for her at the birth of this baby. I wanted to be there to reassure her that all was going well and to comfort her through the birth of Jessica Lane.

Acie tried all week to convince me to be admitted to the hospital. I have a hard time admitting that I am sick enough to go to the emergency room. I grew up feeling that you should be half dead to go to the emergency room. Acie explained to me that I was terribly sick and needed to be hospitalized, but I refused to let him admit me. After all, I had been to the doctor twice in the past two days. I guess I am hardheaded and a bit stubborn. Seeking help, Acie told his friend, Steve that I needed to be hospitalized, but I was against going into the hospital and he could not talk me into it.

I Really Did Pull Through

On December 5, my mouth was so terribly swollen and painful with ulcers I could not bear it. My tongue was so enlarged that I held it between my open teeth so it would not touch anything. I had visited the doctor about my ulcers two days straight. He was not my regular attending physician, but I suppose he should have admitted me to the hospital then, he did not. I felt that it wouldn't do any good to go to the emergency room because the doctor had already done all he could for me, or so I thought.

Poor Acie did not know what else to do, so he actually tricked me into going to the hospital. He called our "Home Care Nursing Institution" and requested they send a nurse to evaluate the situation. When the nurse came to see me, she called my primary care doctor and had me admitted. I was semi-comatose at that time. I did not know I was in the world during the eight days that followed.

From August to December, I had been telling my doctor I was getting weaker and weaker. They kept telling me that my weekly blood tests results were fine. I felt that either the blood reports were not showing them what was wrong, or the doctors were signing and filing the blood reports weekly without reading them. There was nothing we could do.

While in the hospital, we learned that doctors have learned not to touch mouth ulcers with silver nitrate because it causes them to multiply. We learned from the hospital blood tests that my blood hermatocrits were "17" and 37.4 is normal. That explains why I was so weak. My spleen was at upper limits of normal and my liver was enlarged.

Again, I had hallucinations all week. I remember thinking Acie and I were living back in the "horse and buggy days" and we had been kidnapped. I thought the dark wall at the head of my bed was the side of an old barn with worn out boards. I thought I was in the barn laying on an old mattress, which was stretched over an old wooden table and chair top. I kept saying to Acie, "We need to get out of here. They're going to kill us. I could see three men through the cracks in the barn board where we were being held prisoners. They were playing with their guns, shooting wildly at nothing. I recall begging Acie, "Come, let's run for our lives. We've got to get out of here. They are drunk. Maybe we can escape."

Hallucinations went on day after day. Friends came to visit me. Acie said I would talk to them but I had no memory of their visit just minutes after they walked out of the room. I was told that I said funny things. For example, to one man I said, "Would you like some pie to go with your coffee?" as though he was a guest in my home. He didn't even have a cup of coffee with him.

To relieve the unbearable pain I was suffering due to the ulcers, I was given a medication called, Delaudid. I would become semi-conscious for a short time but still was not aware of anything much around me. I had no idea of the seriousness of my situation. I cried and pleaded for something to relieve the pain.

I do remember the night nurse coming in and finding me rolling in excruciating pain night after night. The pain medication had worn off and I had to wait two hours for more medication. I was in torture and could not wait for relief. I trembled in pain. He felt such compassion and tried to comfort me by rubbing my forehead and sitting by my bedside to help me through the long hours. I recalled holding onto him and cried, "Please don't delay in getting the pain medicine to me. I don't think I can make it." Acie was also there with me. He wouldn't leave me at night while I was so sick, in and out of consciousness. The doctor spoke with Acie after I had been there a week and she said, "I don't see any way your wife will pull through this. You need to prepare for her death and if by chance she does pull through, she will be in a nursing home for the rest of her life." I didn't know anything about this until a month later after I came home from the hospital. Acie told me that he had purchased burial plots for which we were making payments. I can't imagine the burden Acie was carrying upon his heart. He loves me so much and the thought of losing a partner and seeing me that sick had to be so painful for him.

Thirteen days of torture and pain had passed when I finally regained consciousness. Acie gathered me up in his arms and in spite of my terrible condition I could feel his deep sincere love for me and I knew he was glad to have me back. There was no way I could have survived the hospital stay without Acie. He gave me such emotional support. When I was afraid and in severe pain, he was there comforting, hugging and loving me through it.

Again, the ladies of the church stayed with me throughout the days I was hospitalized. Oh, they were so good to do that! This was my third hospital stay and they were always there to help. Some ladies stayed with me during the day and others stayed at night until after I came through the crisis. I had suffered with such a dry, sore throat from medication and lack of saliva they moistened and medicated my mouth regularly. I choked on the dryness frequently and then I would dry heave with nausea. It was a constant battle and these gals were so good to me. They really cared for me and made me comfortable with them as they were nursing me. They were wonderful!

After I began to respond to treatment and realize where I was, a doctor who was not one of mine came into my room on Sunday evening and said, "Do you know that you are the talk of the hospital staff? All these doctors are talking about your case." He said, "The digestive system just doesn't shut down like yours has done. We have never seen anything like it before." They obviously had studied my medical test results from U.T. Medical Research Center and Mayo Clinic. A couple of days later I was dismissed from the hospital to recuperate at home with home nursing care and Nutritional Feeding by IV.

I cried as David cried unto the Lord out of anguish and hurt, "Oh, God, I am desolate and afflicted. The troubles of my heart are enlarged. O bring me out of my distress." Psalms 25:16 (KJV) "My God, My God, why has thou forsaken me?" Why art thou so far from helping me?" Psalms 23:1 (RSV) *"I am weary with my groanings. Every night I flood my bed with tears."* Psalms 6:6 (RSV). God didn't receive David's anger. Instead David became aware of God's loving arms offering him comfort and understanding. Then David said, *"I truly came through the shadow of death."* He said, *"O Lord my God, I cried unto thee and thou hast healed me. O Lord, thou hast brought my soul from the grave. Thou hast kept me alive, that I should not go down to the pit. Sing unto the Lord O ye saints of His and give thanks at the remembrance of His holiness"*, Psalms 30:2-4 (KJV). God has kept me alive also. We give Him glory and praise with a thankful heart.

Faith is Built Through Adversity

God does not promise us a life of ease. He tells us that suffering and trials will come. Our attitude in handling them will determine the development and growth of our faith. Jesus prayed three times in the Garden of Gethsemane that if there were any other way to bring salvation to mankind other than the cross that the Father would release Him from His suffering. He prayed, "My soul is overwhelmed with sorrow to the point of death. Stay here and watch with me." Going a little farther, he fell with His face to the ground and prayed, *"My Father, if it be possible, let this cup be taken away from Me. But I want Your will, not Mine."* (Matthew 26:39b NIV).

Jesus suffered and was tempted as we are, but He overcame temptations by the Word. Therefore, we are to speak the Word when we go through suffering and temptation. We claim the victory through the use of God's Word. There's power in the Word. Learn to use it boldly.

Someone has said, "There's nothing God and I can't handle together." Paul assures us, *"No temptation has seized you except what is common to man. And God is faithful; he will not let you be tempted beyond what you can bear. But when you are tempted, he will also pro-*

vide a way out so that you can stand up under it" I Corinthians 10:13 (NIV). *"A righteous man may have many troubles, but the Lord delivers him from them all;"* Psalm 34:19 (NIV). It is not that we will never be sick or have difficulties, but when we do, God is there to deliver us.

We are often tested and tried in order that we might learn to pray and seek after God. Why do we stumble around in unbelief? We often cannot see any possible way for our needs to be met, yet God said He would provide. He has the answer to every problem we face already available for our taking. Micah the prophet said, *"As for me, I look to the Lord for His help; I wait for God to save me; He will hear me."* Micah 7:7

Home Again

I returned home from the hospital in December, 1997, with a home care nurse. I was too weak and sick to help myself. When I arrived home, Acie pushed me in the wheelchair through the door and there stood Sharon, John and our grandchildren; Brittani, Johnny, Sawyer and in Sharon's arms was our new baby Jessica Lane. Sharon cried, "Momma, we didn't think you'd come home from the hospital." We all cried and rejoiced. The Lord had spared my life once again.

Oh the joy of seeing my family as they waited to receive me back home from the hospital. Sharon placed the baby in my lap just briefly so I could say hello, give her a kiss and hug. Then I gave each of the other grandchildren a big hug and told them how much I loved them. They are precious children; all very well behaved and well disciplined. Each one has his or her own unique and special way and we are very proud of them.

That night, Acie dreamed we were in heaven. I was in a different part of Heaven than he was. I had been completely healed. There were no feeding tubes, alcohol pads or medications. My personality was very outgoing, cheerful and entertaining. I was telling everyone what great things God had done for me.

I recall the sinking feeling when, nearly a month after I was dismissed from the hospital, I realized I had no memory of the days before I entered the hospital. I had missed my daughter giving birth to her baby. I was there in body, but not in mind. I have no memory of being at the hospital or that the baby was delivered right there in the room where I was. I don't remember going home that evening, undressing, going to bed, redressing the next morning, or anything about that day. Evidently, I was active, but my mind wasn't involved. I was so looking forward to being there for Sharon, to hold her hand and bring comfort. That is if I could get past her loving husband, John. I wanted to rejoice with them following the birth, especially since she had lost her last baby, Amanda. I don't understand how I could have been there that day and have no memory of it.

The home care nurse was with me until January 1, 1998, but I remained bedfast through March, 1998. It wasn't until April, 1998 that I gained enough strength to sit up in the living room for short periods and go for an occasional ride in the car.

Acie, You Are My Sunshine

My husband, Acie, is the associate pastor of Broadmoor Baptist Church, Memphis, Tennessee. It is a large church which keeps him extremely busy. He puts in long hard hours beyond the call of duty. He is a good pastor and tremendously loved by the people. He is also my encourager, my love and support. He carries a beeper so I can reach him any time of the day and he telephones me frequently throughout the day to make sure I am all right.

In January, after the home care nurse no longer came, Acie, once again took over as my nurse. We worked my needs around his work schedule. Therefore, our mornings began earlier than usual so Acie would have time to help me before going to work. First, he would bring in a thick towel to place beside me on the bed. Then he would get my tray, a glass of water and prepare my tooth brush with tooth paste so I could brush my teeth. Meanwhile, he warmed a washcloth so I could freshen up. When I finished, he put away my towel, tray, toothbrush, etc. and helped me change into fresh clothes for the day. After I was dressed, he brought my makeup and mirror to me and would comb and style my hair as best he could. He would help me disconnect from the nutritional feeding and get me all the necessary syringes and medications to insert into the tubing of my Hickman line. Then there was the matter of the urinal bedside bag which had to be taken care of. Acie is so good and more gentle than the doctor when it comes to inserting the urinal catheter. He would put the water in the balloon with a syringe and remove it each morning.

After the morning routine at home, Acie would leave for the church office. Each evening when he came home from work, he bathed me and washed my hair in the bed because I was too weak to get in the tub. After several months, I was stronger and he helped me get into the bathtub. Acie soaped me down and bathed me and then had to literally lift me out of the tub. As the weeks passed, I could get on my knees in the tub after a lot of hard work, but I couldn't get to my feet to stand without Acie's help. The doctor said it would take six months for my blood to build up.   Acie was so tender, kind and gentle. He did so much for me day in and day out for four months. He washed my hair, dried it and really seemed to enjoy styling it. He tried to make me pretty. I knew I looked bad due to my illness, but Acie always told me I was beautiful to him. I will be eternally grateful for Acie's unconditional love and support.

I feel like a vegetable wasting away while others wait on me. Laying in the bed is difficult for me. When I am feeling really bad I like to get around friends. It energizes me. When my arms and legs feel so bad they drag and there is hardly strength to move, I get in the kitchen and begin chopping vegetables to make chicken soup. Involving myself in activity is my salvation. No, I am not a hyper person. I just like to be active. When I am down in the bed I am totally miserable. I was born with this inner drive. The worse I feel, the harder I work. My mind is way up front and my body just better stay with me. I feel the need to go to bed, but I can't. I just keep pushing forward and will not give in to, nor acknowledge, the reality of weakness until it literally knocks me over. I push way beyond what is healthy. It is a sin to mistreat (our body) God's holy temple. It is something I must conquer.

Angels of Mercy

Upon my arrival home from the hospital, I was greatly surprised and extremely moved when again, the ladies of the church took care of me daily for sixteen weeks while Acie was at work. There was always someone dropping in to see me. One of the ladies, Martha Jane Edwards, had taken the responsibility for coordinating daily sitters for me for as long as I was bedfast and needed care. So many people were calling to ask if there was anything they could do for us and since most people in the church knew Martha, we directed their calls to her. There were so many who offered to help us. Each one was asked to bring their own lunch to relieve Acie from the concern of their lunch needs. She recognized that Acie didn't need any more responsibility or concerns placed upon him. He was going through a very difficult time caring for me before and after work. He was under great stress. The ladies stayed with me until Acie came home from work each day. Martha was our "life saver." She even organized food being brought in for Acie's evening meals. She saw to it that there was only enough for one person so he wouldn't need to worry with leftovers. They were to deliver food in throw away containers so Acie didn't have dishes to return every week. I was so grateful and Acie appreciated the hot meals he received each night.

The girls who cared for me were informed of what they needed to do for me. Little things like changing my sheets, heating water for my hot water-bottle at regular intervals; bringing my medication to me when necessary; draining the urinal bag and other such needs. The girls were wonderful and I didn't feel intimidated by their daily care. They made me feel at ease and comfortable. Sometimes one would wash a load of clothes while staying with me and then the lady who came the next day would ask whether or not I needed some ironing done. They all seemed to have their special something they wanted to do for me. A gift of three shelves for knickknacks had been given to me. One of the ladies saw the gift and asked where I planned to hang it. When I told her, she said, "Can I do that for you - would you trust me to hammer nails in your wall?" I said, "Yes, I'd love for you to hang that for me." She hung the shelf and placed the knickknacks that had been given to me on the shelves. Everyone was so helpful!

People care for me in different ways. They give constant attention, frequently calling me to see how I am feeling. Others come to visit for brief periods of fellowship while others drop off bouquets of fresh flowers weekly at the door. God has also given me a lady who sews and adjusts my clothes. My pants size went from size 8 down to a junior size 3 slim. That requires quite a lot of sewing. One sweet wonderful lady has telephoned me morning and evening since 1990 when my physical shutdown first began after the fall in the Jacuzzi. She has never failed to check on me daily. She is a real encourager.

Another came to me while I was still in the hospital and asked if it would offend me if she volunteered to clean my house for me. Mind! I thought that was a wonderful offer! I told her, "Yes,

I'd be grateful to have you clean my house." She said that she had prayed asking God to give her something she could do for someone as a service to God, that wouldn't take away from her business she had at home. God laid it upon her heart to clean my house so she took on two helpers. This is such a great blessing from God.

After I had been home recuperating for some time, another friend called to ask if she could take me out for a drive when I felt up to it. She kept reminding me that she wanted to be my driver. After my strength started improving, we did just that. She then explained that she felt God telling her to take care of me, and help me get to doctor's appointments, the grocery store, drug store, bank, etc. I do not go in at the bank, post office or drug store. She goes in for me and takes care of my business while I wait in the car. She takes me to physical therapy aerobics three time weekly. I call her my "Professional Chauffeur" and "Wheelchair Pusher." She has gotten it down pat! No one can do it as well as she does. She has an incredible sense of humor and keeps everybody around her entertained. As we were leaving physical therapy one day she said to one of our friends, "See ya day after tomorrow. That will give you something to look forward to."

I have an electric scooter with a lift in our van, but Acie takes that to work everyday so my chauffeur and I go everywhere in her car. The trunk will not hold my folding wheelchair. No matter where we go she has to go into the building (sometimes taking the elevator up to the doctor's office) to locate a wheelchair for me. She pushes it out to the car (sometimes in the rain) and helps me into the chair. Then she pushes me into the building to take care of business or to my appointment. She pushes me back to the car, returns the wheelchair to its proper place, and comes back to the car where I am waiting. We may make three or four stops while we are out. It is unending and a lot of work for her. When we go to the grocery store, she not only goes through the routine with getting me an electric scooter from the store, but when we return home, she unloads the groceries and helps put them away.

She keeps a jacket or afghan in her car for me if I get chilled. She is very considerate of my cold body temperature (hypothermia) although she is a warm natured person. She is tender and compassionate with me. She says she is my angel sent by God to take care of me. Every hour she is caring for me she feels she is serving the Lord. She doesn't mind if it takes us all day to do what I need to do. How very blessed I am to have such friends. It is God's provision. God said, *"Casting all your care upon Him, for He careth for you!"* I Peter 5:7(KJV) *"The Lord is my shepherd, I shall not want."* Psalms 23:1(KJV)

I am embarrassed with the way my body has fallen apart and deteriorated. My strength has dwindled. My neurologist prescribed water aerobic therapy three times weekly. I wear floaters around my rib cage when I am in the pool and float in the deep water so that I do not put my weight on my legs while exercising. If I am on my feet I get severe cramps. Exercise is very difficult for me because I am terribly weak. My chauffeur has to help me get out of the pool and into the wheelchair. She then pushes me into the dressing room and starts the shower for me. While I rinse off, she rinses out my swimsuit and gets my clothing out of the locker. By the time I have showered and dried off, I get a shortness of breath which causes heavy breathing. My saliva glands do not produce proper amounts of fluid for my throat so I begin choking from the dryness in my chest. If I exert myself too much, I take on shortness of breath, and become dizzy headed and nauseated with a tingling numbness in my hands and feet. I was told this is caused from having low hematocrits in my blood levels. My chauffeur has her hands full helping me. Because I'm exhausted and sick after working out and taking a shower, she helps me get dressed and changes my medical bandage on my chest. It is hard for me to deal with the need to have other people do basic things for me such as dressing and undressing me when I am too worn out to do for myself. Survival is what it's all about, and acceptance.

The Lord has blessed me with many angels and two are my chauffeurs. One who drives me where I need to go in Memphis, from the doctor visits to the grocery store and everywhere in between. Then there is another who is my out-of-town chauffeur. She drives me to speaking engagements. When we arrive at the motel, she unpacks my suitcase, presses and hangs the outfits I will be wearing to the meetings, and remakes the bed just the way I prefer to have it done. She does everything for me and more; just like my other helpers. When we arrive at the meeting place, she opens the back door of the van and unloads my electric scooter and brings it to me as I wait in the car. She helps me into the scooter, then gets the suitcase of books out of the van, and we enter the building to find the person in charge. It may be the church pastor, the women's meeting director, or the President of the Organization. While I am being briefed on details regarding the meeting or meetings, my chauffeur is attractively setting up the book table. After the meeting, she works the table and then packs remaining books in the suitcase and waits for me to finish talking with people. She is much loved and usually talking herself. She is a very delightful European girl. I thank God for her willingness and availability to travel with me.

We return to the motel and she can't do enough for me. Knowing how totally exhausted I am following a speaking engagement, she helps me by getting everything hooked up for my nutritional feeding and bed-side urinal needs. She sets the hot water kettle and when it is ready, fills my water bottles and tucks them in the bed. (I don't have enough body heat to warm my sheets.) She opens the bed for me to get in. This girl is something else! When morning comes, everything goes back into the suitcase. After the long drive home she comes in and unpacks all my clothing and medical supplies. She puts everything away, including placing my empty luggage in the attic storage. She will not leave until she has me all tucked in bed once again. She has a real gift of serving. Both of my chauffeurs have the "Gift of Service." God has called them into this ministry of helping me. Both my chauffeurs treat me like royalty. You would think I was the Queen of England. They love the Lord and support me with their prayers. They both love to talk. People like that and I do too.

I feel very insecure knowing just how to relate my needs to my angels. They are sent from God to help me and I am so very grateful for them, but I have a hard time asking them if they will do this or that. If I don't ask, they will not know how they can best meet my needs. I don't want to take them for granted or "use them". I certainly don't expect them to jump to respond immediately to my every need. They have their own luggage to unpack and groceries to put up and floors to sweep. I want to be considerate of those whom God has sent to help me. I am not comfortable having to receive this kind of help from others. It makes me feel the pain of my loss and my inability to care for myself. Although this is so difficult for me, I am so grateful for those who help me and I thank God for each and everyone.

The Lord has given us another dear friend, a business manager, who handles all my medical insurance papers and invoices. There are bills for the urinal needs, nutritional needs, pathology lab, ambulance services, doctors and hospitals which are difficult to interpret. Our medical bills are approximately $300,000 a year. It overwhelms us. We were lost in it all when our friend asked if we would trust her enough to handle this for us. Since she works in the medical field she understands billings and insurance. She said she wanted to relieve us of this stress. We could never keep up with all the claims and medical statements. She asked if she could do it as unto the Lord. She is truly a gift from God and we are so grateful for all she does.

My friends know what is going on in my life and what could happen should my condition deteriorate. God knows how much we need and depend on our dear understanding friends who stand by us. There are so many who do. I thank God for all those who have done so much to help us. I wish I could name them one by one. "Get well" cards have come from Switzerland, Africa, Spain, Belfast, Scotland, France and England. We have received hundreds of cards and letters. People are so thoughtful. There is a genuine outpouring of concern and affection coming our way. It is so encouraging to have everyone's love and prayer support. God has sent so many to meet my needs. They keep up with my weekly difficulties with a generous spirit of love and understanding.

Life in the Wheelchair

At my physical therapy sessions, I enjoy getting to know others in the pool who are suffering from loss of body function due to a stroke or a disease. I find myself connecting with these people in ways I never felt possible.

Those who are afflicted and in wheelchairs respond to me when they see me in my electric scooter or wheelchair. It is a contact made by the look in the eye from somebody I've never met. It is an unnoticed emotional contact. Sick people, young and old, relate to each other and are linked in spirit in a silent way. Their eyes seem to say, "I understand", or "I am sorry you are afflicted", or "I'm here if you would like to talk." It really helps me to have that contact with others who are hurting. They may not have the same debilitating physical weakness I have, but we relate and gain strength from one another. It is really neat.

The adjustment to the wheelchair/electric scooter was difficult. It's a little like when I was blind and had to adjust to walking with the assistance of a white cane. I felt so embarrassed when I had to use it in public. It told everyone I was blind and I didn't like that. My eyes did not show blindness and I wanted to appear normal around those who didn't know I was blind. To look at me, one would not know I am sick, but the wheelchair stands out like a sore thumb. I am thankful for the chair because without it I could not get through the house, go grocery shopping, rolling through the mall or enjoy the freedom it gives me. I need it to get around, but there are great difficulties when one is dependent on a wheelchair. To carry a pan of water from the sink to the electric range, or dishes from the refrigerator to the table with one hand when your body is too weak to carry it with two hands is a real problem. I need one hand to operate the scooter. Have you ever tried to sweep a floor while in a sitting position? It's impossible! Be considerate of the extra time it takes a handicapped person to complete a task. I am blessed. The doctor said I am not to walk from room to room, but I can walk some within a room so I don't have to do everything with one hand all the time. However, I cannot be on my feet very much or I will be up all night in pain.

When I have laundry to wash, I divide my clothing into piles according to color then fill the laundry basket with a load. I pull the basket with the wash load from the bedroom to the laundry room behind my scooter. I do the same thing when I have the wash load dried and folded. I pull the load behind the scooter to the bedroom. I water my flowers and blueberry bushes the same way, pulling the garden hose with my scooter across the lawn. When at the mall, I must be very alert to people around me and careful not to run over children and the feet of adults. I am especially cautious when passing a baby stroller. So often they come out from between the clothing racks unexpectedly, it scares me. Next is the problem of tablecloths draped over tables in the middle of the store aisles. My wheels could run over the cloth hanging to the floor and pull everything off. I am really shy of the china and crystal department.

I have a bell on my scooter like a bicycle bell, only this one is a yellow rubber duck head. The children, as well as the adults, can't resist the temptation to squeeze my yellow duck and make him talk. The younger children point and say, "Momma, Momma, see Big Bird!"

My yellow duck (it's showy, but I love it) really comes in handy when we are shopping for groceries. When someone is standing in the aisle, I can't pass their grocery cart with my wide scooter. It is difficult to get their attention from a distance so if a child is sitting in the grocery basket, I pull my scooter within reach of the child. They love to play with the yellow duck and soon they have their mother's attention, and so do I. They move and I can get through.

Often, when I'm not feeling well and am too weak to operate my scooter, Acie will push me in a wheelchair through the mall. He likes the exercise and it gives me a chance to get out of the house. But, if I need to do some shopping, the wheelchair isn't best. I cannot roll it by hand, so if we are looking at clothing on racks, I can't circle to see what is on display on the other side. Acie begins doing the shopping. He holds up this and that to see what I think about it. That is sweet of him, but like all women, I want to see everything on the rack, so I need to be pushed around to the other side. It takes some of the enjoyment out of shopping when I have to depend on someone to push me rather than having the convenience of my electric scooter, but I am so thankful Acie wants to push me. I love to be out with Acie and meet friends, or go out to lunch with them.

Saying Good-bye

July, 1998, John, Sharon and the kids made a family decision to move to Alaska. John's boyhood dream was to live in Alaska. He envisioned himself fishing out of the holes in the ice and shooting game for food. Sharon has always said she was born 50 years too late. She had dreamed of living in deep snow country where life was adventurous. Before they married, John asked her whether or not she, as his wife, would be willing to move to Alaska if he chose to do that one day. She was all for that. Together they decided they would move to their dream country and raise their family.

John was nearly finished remodeling their house in Memphis and they had been thinking for some time of their desire to live in Alaska. The house could be sold, and they would be free to make the move. They decided if they were going to make this move, it would be best that they go now. The children would be in high school and college later, and they would not be able to go. After that, they would be too old to tackle the long hard winters. They put the house on the market and asked God to sell it that weekend. It sold the first day they made it available. They were fully persuaded that this was God leading them in that direction.

There were people who were critical of their decision to go to Alaska and live. Some couldn't believe our only daughter would move so far away and take our only grandchildren from us, especially during a time when I was so ill. Others reacted in a positive way. They envied their spirit of adventure and wished they were also going.

We gave them our blessing. I admire someone who has a dream and fulfills that dream. John and Sharon are full of adventure. I told Sharon I would not expect her to give up their lifetime dream based on my health. So I said, "You go with our blessing.

I do not want to hold you back or dampen your spirits." We do miss them terribly.

After the children moved to Alaska, our cooks were gone. Both John and Sharon did the cooking while they lived with us and they are great cooks! Acie loved all the good food. We sure do miss our children! Now it is just Acie and me. I can't cook every day, but when I do, he is so appreciative. He tells people, "It is a sacrifice of love for someone who can't eat, to go to the store, buy groceries, come home and prepare gourmet meals for me."

Sharon is good about calling us weekly and sometimes more often. She shares all their joys and excitement with us, the beauty of the area in which they live, and the fun they are experiencing. They live in a house at the end of the world. The vast ocean below is a stones throw out their front door, and a snow-capped mountain is not far away from their back door. Soon the winter snows will be at their front door. Even the kids love it there. Sharon says, "It's like they are at a resort all the time."

The children enjoy walking up the mountains and having a picnic. They couldn't wait for the first snowfall. One day Sharon called and said, "Momma, it looks like there is a white cloud hanging over the mountain. It's the strangest thing I've ever seen." She called me later and said, "Momma, the cloud has lifted, but there's four feet of snow on the mountain. I didn't know that cloud was snow! The next day the snow fell another eight feet as the cloud covered the top of the mountain again. Suddenly, it reached ground level and the children went tobogganing, sledding and started taking ice-skating lessons. They all went out and tried fishing from a hole in the ice. They were overjoyed with the winter activities, fun and excitement while awaiting the birth of another sibling.

Hannah Grace was born April 6, 1999, blessing their family with another bundle of joy. They now have 3 girls and 2 boys, each with their own special personalities. Jessica has Sharon's outgoing laughter and fun personality. At fifteen months, she entertains the family and the family entertains and spoils her. She loves all the attention she gets and now will need to share that with Hannah.

The snow has melted; mud season has passed. The bears have awakened from winter naps, and come into town occasionally. Therefore, they must keep an eye out for bears. Little Johnny went camping in the woods and is now talking about fishing for salmon and hang gliding off the bluff. They will also be hunting for meat supply for next winter. They must be careful riding their bikes because if it's too steep, they may lose control coming down the mountain.

Filling The Gap

After our children moved, to fill the gap of loneliness we adopted several young couples from our church whose parents live in other states. One couple has a baby, Ashlyn. Acie loves to play on the floor with Ashlyn like he always did with our own grandchildren. These couples have accepted us as their "parents away from home" and they drop in every couple of days. They come and go like they belong here. They cook for us and we cook for them. We go on family picnics together, shop and buy groceries together. Baby Ashlyn really accepts "Poppie" as her granddaddy and playmate. We really enjoy each other's company. Even though I can be mobile with my nutritional IV, I need the bed rest so they spend the evenings with Acie and then later they visit with us in our bedroom, as do the rest of our friends.

The really neat thing was that when we shared with Sharon and John that we had adopted these young couples who are about their age, they told us they had made friends with a couple about our age who have become like Mom and Dad to them. I say, "Isn't that wonderful! God always provides!"

Strength Made Perfect through Weakness

In my weakness I have difficulty remembering holidays and special events. Even though I participate in the holiday's activities, I can't remember it afterwards. I have been so sick that I failed to recognize when it was my birthday, Acie's birthday, or our anniversary. I get mixed up with which week we are in or the day of the week. Even now I go through the motions but I don't know whether it's Monday or Friday, whether this is the week we are leaving on vacation or maybe having house guests. I ask myself, did I do this or that? I start a task only to come upon it later and see I didn't finish what I started. Some days I tell Acie I want to telephone our daughter, Sharon, because I have not talked with her in days, when in reality I just talked with her the day before. Suddenly I am dealing with problems I thought would come later in life. I should not be facing them now.

August is a special month because we were married on the 14th and Acie's birthday is on the 26th, which is also the day God gave Acie the best birthday present anyone could ever have received. On that day in 1972, He gave sight to my blind eyes. Our lives have never been the same since. In early August, 1998, I was sad when Acie came in from work. It had been one of those days where I held back the tears all day. One thing we have always enjoyed was going out to dinner on Mother's Day, Father's Day, birthdays and anniversaries. Celebrations are always with food. Now that I can't eat, how do we celebrate?

We were married August 14, 1962, and while driving from Michigan to Canada on our honeymoon, Acie sang to me several times daily, "Beautiful, beautiful blue eyes, I'll never love brown eyes again," and the song, "You are my sunshine, my only sunshine. You make me happy when skies are gray. You'll never know dear how much I love you. Please don't take my sunshine away." Because I had trouble remembering dates, birthdays and anniversaries, Acie made sure I'd have a constant reminder of our honeymoon.   On August 14, 1998, the day of our 36th wedding anniversary, Acie found this "sunflower plant" that's movement activated and sings our song, "You are my sunshine, my only sunshine. You make me happy when skies are gray. You'll never know dear how much I love you. Please don't take my sunshine away." He had it gift- wrapped and gave it to me as my anniversary gift. We've had a good time laughing with it. It's a conversation piece. It brought back so many good memories of our honeymoon, and even though we couldn't go out and eat a special anniversary dinner at a fancy restaurant, Acie brought joy to my heart with the singing sunflower plant.

Just before Acie's birthday in 1998, I said, "Let's go somewhere really special for dinner and celebrate your birthday. I'll just sit and watch you eat, but at least I will be with you." That went over like a lead balloon. My heart longs to do that, but knowing that neither of us would be comfortable, I began to cry. I go with Acie when he eats at most restaurants, but we have not gone to a special anniversary-type restaurant together since I started on nutritional feeding in April 1996. I didn't believe I could handle that, but I thought maybe I could try. I felt if we could do that maybe somehow I could put life back to normal somewhat. I miss special dinners on special occasions more than words can tell. Acie was right, he always knows best. It would have been more than I could have dealt with.

It was soon August 26th, Acie's birthday. We didn't go out to a special restaurant to eat because Acie wouldn't have enjoyed going to a fancy restaurant knowing I couldn't enjoy the food also. He didn't want me to bake him a birthday cake because he is not eating sweets. Even though I had given him a birthday gift, it seemed that his birthday just came and quietly passed by. I just couldn't get anything together to make the day special for him. We've always had special meals with cake and ice cream for birthday celebrations. (Actually, his birthday cakes turned out to be pies. He likes pie better than cake.) When I realized I had not done anything more to celebrate Acie's birthday other than to buy him a gift, I felt terrible. I couldn't seem to zero in on it. I can't seem to realize special days are here until they've passed me by. I had purchased the gift quite far in advance, so I would have that on hand and available when the day came. I felt badly. I said, "I am so sorry Acie that I didn't do something more to make your birthday special. " Acie is so kind. He said, "I know you have trouble concentrating on those things. Don't you give it another thought because I understand your limitations. I know you cannot remember last Christmas when we were all together. We had a special Christmas dinner and the tree with all the gifts, but you were there in body only. You were too weak to get much involved. I understand that you can't zero in on these things, it's okay." Jack Wintz wrote, "When deep suffering (or loss) befalls you, it will take time to be set free of your trauma or broken heart. Remember, that through it all, God's healing love is at work."

November came and it was time for Thanksgiving week. Everyone is going to enjoy "Thanksgiving Day dinner" with their families. I haven't been able to eat a Thanksgiving Day dinner in three years. We had gone to Michigan to visit my family in the spring, so we would not be having dinner with my family this Thanksgiving. Acie's mother will be with his brother, Hersholt and their children and grandchildren so she'll not be alone. Acie wanted to make the day easier for me. He surprised me and said, "I have a motel room reserved for us in Nashville. We'll go on Thanksgiving Day and make it a special day." I am so blessed to have a husband like Acie. His love is patient, kind, protective, and unfailing.

Home with my Parents and Family

It's always exciting to go to Michigan and visit with my family. I come from a very large family, and we have gone to see them every year of our thirty-six years of our married life. We feel family relationships are important and need to be cultivated. It's easy to become busy with life and neglect those we love most.

July, 1998, we arrived in Michigan and had a nice evening planned with my twin sister, Carolyn, and her husband, Bill; my oldest brother, Don, and his wife, Karen, and two friends who had lost their husbands in death recently. We felt they would enjoy the evening.

Upon arrival at the restaurant, one of the girls said, "Lets go to the little girls room before they seat us." So we followed her. Before we left the rest room, Carolyn, being quite protective of me, especially when I am connected to my nutritional feeding, said, "Is your tubing all securely tucked in so it will not catch on something or get under the wheel of your scooter?" I said, "Yes, I am holding it tight in my hand." She opened the bathroom door for me to exit, and we went about 8-10 feet around the host counter to be seated. Somehow, within that short distance, my TPN tubing caught on something. I didn't see anything it could have caught on, but I felt a jerk on my tubing at my chest. I looked down and I was shocked to see my tubing lying there on the floor. I then looked at my Hickman line and blood was pouring out like a fountain. I immediately said, "Somebody call 911, I need to go into surgery." My lap and hands were full of blood. The cap, as well as the clamp, had pulled off the line, and there was no way to repair it other than to have it replaced. The ambulance arrived in about five minutes, and we were on our way to the Holland Hospital. Acie was thinking, "Oh no, we've come to Michigan for Marolyn's funeral." He didn't know what to think. He just thought the worst. (So much for the great dinner evening with friends.) I knew I would be all right because the paramedics were able to clamp the tubing and stop the blood flow, but Acie didn't know that. He was in the van following the ambulance to the hospital.

Everyone was at the hospital by the time the doctor arrived. He was a doctor who specialized in "Hickman lines" and "Portocath" surgery, and was a friend of the family. When my sister-in-law, Karen, saw him come in, she spoke to him and asked, "Have you been called in to take care of Marolyn Ford? She is Don's sister from Memphis." His reply was, "I knew God had something special for me here tonight."

God was watching over me. I have two ports on my Hickman line. For several weeks prior to our trip to Michigan one port was blocked either with a blood-clot or crystallized medication. Whatever it was, it could have broken loose at any time, and the blockage could have gone right into my heart. That made me uncomfortable. My doctors had tried three times to clean out that port with medication, but were unsuccessful. I really felt the Hickman line should be replaced so I wouldn't have to live under that threat. When this strange accident happened, I felt it was God's protection over me. The Hickman line had to be replaced, and I was freed of that constant concern.

Troubled Waters

My sister, Carolyn, and her husband, Bill, had transferred their condo week from Orlando, Florida, to Myrtle Beach, South Carolina, and had invited us to join them in June of 1998. Ever since I became ill in 1990, I had this great desire to vacation on the ocean shore and experience the fun of ducking under the high waves on a windy day. I really didn't think I'd ever get to do that again because of the weakness of my body. Well, we did it! I can't run my electric scooter on sand, so I asked Acie and Bill if they could carry me out far enough into the water so I could duck under the waves (it's a good thing I only weigh 94 lbs.).

Oh, it was such fun! Bill held onto me and Acie went back to the beach shore to get the camera. He wanted a snapshot of me in the ocean waves. We had ducked under three or four waves. It was just as exciting as I envisioned it would be, but I was worn out. I said, "Bill I'm too exhausted. I need to go in." We had only been out a few minutes, but I was really huffing and puffing, so Bill helped me to the shore. I savored every moment of my experience in the ocean waves.

Meanwhile Acie was on shore. As we were coming toward him, we noticed he was waving for us to come to shore. We really didn't think anything about it because we were coming out. It wasn't until we came to shore that we realized all the people were looking to their left down the beach. We could not hear Acie calling to us, neither could we hear the life-guard blowing his whistle. Acie said, "There was a shark, a six foot sand shark in the water." He was between us and the beach, but he was moving on down the beach in shallow water. It wasn't the kind of shark that attacks people, but, if aggravated, they have been known to hurt people. Acie was quite frightened for our safety. It added a lot of excitement to our venture in the water.

Day by Day

The years 1996-1998 were difficult. My goal was just to try to keep going. I had accepted one speaking invitation out of town and a couple of meetings in town. It's exhausting for me to speak at a meeting. Over the years, I have been encouraged by so many people who come up to me following my meetings and say, "What a blessing to hear you speak. Never stop telling that wonderful testimony and teaching seminars and conferences."

I know that Satan doesn't like it when I speak at meetings. Could it be that my physical illness of today is a direct result of Satan's attack upon my ministry and life? He is the one who *"comes to kill, steal and destroy." "God comes to bring us the abundant life."* (John 10:10).

When I see spiritual transformation in the lives of people, I must continue to go, telling of God's great love and inviting those to Christ who do not know Him. Some who invite me to speak at their meetings don't know about my current condition, but they have heard of my miracle of restored eyesight. I will continue to give my testimony of *These Blind Eyes Now See*, but I will not stop there. How can I say what God has done for me and fail to mention the miracles he is still performing in my life today. It's a miracle I am alive. It's a miracle I am up and semi-active. I want people to know how God is our "Provider" as well as our "Savior", not just our "eternal salvation" but our "daily salvation."

God gives me the strength to get through each day. I really have to be ready to give, when sometimes I want to take affection, love, and encouragement. When I think I can't physically go on, God lifts me up by His power and helps me through the difficult days. Yes, my life testimony does go far beyond that of my life as a blind wife of a minister. A woman who sees today because the Lord Jesus brought sight to my blind eyes after thirteen years of walking with a white cane and reading Braille. God has given me other miracles. God has spared my life four times in the last two years. People want to know about it, and they need to see how God works today in helping those who are His children.

When I am out on a speaking engagement, I need the loving prayerful support of people who lift me up before the throne. Then God sustains me with his super empowering strength and anointing. I never minimize the power of intercessory prayer that covers me and my ministry. I ask men and women everywhere to pray not only for me, but also for the Holy Spirit's anointing, salvation of lost souls, conviction resulting in changed lives, healing for individuals and families, and for

God's spirit to reach down and touch people's lives in a real way. My life and ministry is that of edification and building faith in God's people.

People say, "I don't know how you are doing all that you undertake." Dorothea S. Kopplin said, "It is the greatest of all mistakes to do nothing because you can only do little. Do what you can." In the Bible Paul said, "*When I am weak, then I am strong.*" 2 Corinthians 12:10 (KJV). The more things get out of control, the more I need to cling to God. My role as a public speaker has won a great deal of affection for me. My illness has created a new level of public support. I am left on this earth for a purpose, and that is to fulfill God's plan. Every breath I take is from God. I am surviving on God's strength. My digestive system is not functioning. My blood remains below low-normal, but my ministry continues to flourish.

Everyone has a purpose on this earth. Since illness has taken my ability to travel far and wide, I have to find God's purpose for my life for this period of time. I expect one day I'll be able to take on full time ministry again, perhaps even overseas. I may be able to speak in a European country by the time you are reading this book. God can restore my health in full today. Amen? God can give me strength for each task or perform another healing miracle before you finish reading these pages.

I try to be optimistic about my future. I am thankful that I am able to take a few engagements once again. A change in my environment is rejuvenating. I am trying to feel my way back into the ministry and praying that God will continue allowing me to serve Him through my speaking and teaching ministry. I love sharing in meetings. It is a real challenge to me. I am overjoyed with anticipation of that. I have accepted a couple of meetings recently to "test the waters" and am learning my limitations in regard to the ministry. I have to limit my speaking engagements and travels, as I start back very slowly. My wheelchair or electric scooter, medical equipment, and supplies go where I go. God says we are to endure hardness as a good soldier.

God will let me know what I can and cannot do as I step out and try. God doesn't allow us to look ahead into our future, but it's healthier for me to look ahead, schedule some meetings and try, than to sit and grieve over my losses. God is empowering me to rise above my circumstances. The Lord will let me know when I am strong enough to tackle the work. Until then, correspondence keeps my "four walls" transparent so that I can see beyond the boundary of my confinement. Let me hear from you. God might allow me to share my story at your meeting. Accepting invitations to minister gives me hope. It's inspiring and uplifting. I can be a giver rather than a receiver. When I am standing before an audience, I am my strongest. The Holy Spirit invigorates me for the task and delivery of His message. Yes, there will be difficulties ahead, but what I do with life now can give meaning to the illness. Being able to impact the lives of others makes blindness and the wheelchair worth it all.

It is very difficult for me to come before a congregation of people and share my story. Talking a lot causes a trembling weakness in my voice and heaviness in my chest. While speaking, I sit on a four-legged stool for physical support. I become totally exhausted and need two or three days to recover my strength, but that's okay. Just let me tell people of Jesus and His love for mankind. Dorothea S. Kopplin said, "Do not criticize your part in the play of life; but study it, understand it, and then play it, sick or well, rich or poor, with courage and with proper grace."

Chapter VI
Insurance Troubles

It was November, 1998 when we received a letter that our medical insurance coverage would be switching to another insurance company. There were two policies to choose from; one was HMO and the other had a "cap" on it. Due to the expenses of my Parenteral Nutritional Feeding, we would cap out very soon and have no coverage, so we had to choose the HMO.

We read the HMO policy they were offering and realized there would be trouble ahead. The policy reads they would cover Nutritional Feeding disposables, Diabetes disposables, but not bladder disposables. Immediately I telephoned some medical supply companies from whom I had received my bladder disposable products and asked them how much they had billed the insurance company for their supplies during the year 1998. Roughly speaking the cost was between $8,000 - $10,000 that year. These are medical necessities and the cost is beyond that of a monthly house note. We were in trouble. This is enough to ruin anyone financially.

We started doing our homework on this and began calling the insurance company explaining our need. We had full coverage with our company prior to this switch. To receive less coverage than what we previously had wasn't right. The switch had been made and we had no vote in the matter. We would not receive medical coverage for the bladder disposables under the new company. After weeks of dealing with many different people involved in this insurance process, we finally were able to get to the "top brass." We felt surely they would see the seriousness of our situation; they would understand my medical need and make an exception in this case. We made appeal after appeal to no avail in the months that followed.

Discouragement was weighing heavily upon us. The stress of this was too much for the both of us along with the stress of my illness. Our hearts were heavy ladened. As Acie walked nightly around the park, his soul cried out to God in prayer. God had given him scripture verses that he planted his faith on. The very week he would feel hopeful and encouraged about it, would be the week I would be defeated over it all. Then when I arose to faith in hope, his spirit would take a nose dive. When his spirit was up, he would make the telephone calls and plead our case in search for answers. Then when he became too burdened to handle it, I would be up in spirit and able to make the contact seeking help. The verses God had given us were:"*And all things whatsoever you ask in prayer, believing, you shall receive.*" Matthew 21:22 (KJV). "*He that spared not his own son, but delivered him up for us all, how shall he not with him also freely give us "all things*.*"* Romans 8:32 (KJV). "*According to His divine power hath given unto us "all things" that pertain unto life and godliness.*" 2 Peter 1:3 (KJV).

I said, "Lord, I am placing a period after "life" in this verse. You are telling me you have given unto us "*all things that pertain to life.*" That's my insurance, Lord, that's coverage for my bladder supplies. That's what is pertaining to my life right now. You said you had given us everything pertaining to life. All things, whatsoever, are freely given to us, thank you Father for your provision."

The Word became our sword and we used it daily casting down doubt and defeat. Our confidence is God and His Word held us strong. Another appeal had been made to the insurance company. About ten days later we received word that the insurance company had turned that down also. It was more than either of us could handle. We were overcome once again with anxiety and despair. Acie had thought he had found a glimmer of hope, a light at the end of the search. He had contacted anyone who might be able to help us. He worked through the primary care doctor's office. My doctor tried to get coverage for the bladder supplies through the Home Health Care, Disability and Medicare. Medicare said I do not qualify for Home Health Care because I can get out of the house. We cannot get the coverage we need through Disability, Medicare, or the state TennCare program because they do not cover much on the Parenteral Nutritional Feeding, which costs far more than the bladder supplies. We would be in bigger trouble taking either of these options. The stress of seeking week after week, month after month, had taken its toll on both of us. Usually we were able to encourage each other, but all hope seemed to be gone.

When it seemed all had failed, Acie began contacting the hospitals, medical supply warehouses and distributors to ask if there would be any way we could purchase the needed supplies at a discount price. There was no where else to turn. We truly had come to our wit's end and didn't know what else to do. Our minds and emotions were so stressed we couldn't bear it any longer. It's bad when husband and wife get discouraged together. This time we had both hit despair in the same weeks.

God says, *"Ask, and it shall be given you; seek, and ye shall find; knock, and it shall be opened unto you. For every one that asketh receiveth; and he that seeketh findeth; and to him that knocketh it shall be opened."* Matthew 7:7-8 (KJV). Prayer is more than just asking. We went seeking and knocked on every door possible. Prayer is asking, seeking and knocking. *"Faith without works is dead."* James 2:26 (KJV). We were both standing in faith on God's Word once again.

We had both been under heavy stress regarding my medical coverage for four months when God gave us another verse in March, 1999. *"Cast not away your confidence which has great recompense of reward. For ye have need of patience that after ye have done the will of God ye might receive the promise."* Hebrews 10:35-36 (KJV). In our hearts we said a mighty, "Praise the Lord!"

Two days later, Acie was able to locate someone who could get the supplies at a lower cost. Although we received word again the first of April that the insurance company would not cover the medical necessities, we are praising the Lord that He has made a way possible for us to get the supplies at a discount price. That was our answer to prayer. God did not give us insurance coverage, but He is our supplier and meets our needs day by day.

We have fought this battle standing on the Word as God has spoken it to us. "Endurance" is the key to answered prayer. God says we are to have patience and not grow weary in our asking. But why does He ask us to persist? Our endurance does more than promote God to act. Prayer releases power - Holy Spirit Power. The Holy Spirit lives in the believer. We are the vessels, the temple of God, His dwelling place on earth. Therefore, as referenced in John 7:38 (KJV), His power comes from within and flows outward touching others. Just as the rivers of the waters of life come from the throne of God (Rev. 22:1-2 (KJV)), we are to release the river to flow from us and touch others. Church friends and family have been so wonderful to assist us financially through the tough times.

God talks about the businessman whose occupation is on the storm tossed sea in Psalms 107: 23-28 (RSV), *"They that go down to the sea in ships, that do business in great waters; they see the work of the Lord, and His wonders in the deep. For He commandeth and raiseth the stormy wind which lifts up the waters thereof. They mount up to the Heaven, they go down again to the depth, their soul is melted because of trouble. They reel to and fro and stagger like a drunken man and are at their wits end. They cry unto the Lord in their trouble and He brings them out of their distresses. He maketh the storm calm so that the waves thereof are still. Then they are glad because they are quiet; so He bringeth them unto their desired haven."* God raises the stormy winds of life; we go down to the depths, our soul melts with trouble. Like these men on the troubled sea, we come to our "wits end". If we look up the meaning of "wits end", we find it means, "we just don't know what else to do." There are times we come to our "wits end" and we just don't know what else to do.

One Day at a Time

God is so good. I praise Him for His unending grace. I live daily supported by His mercy and grace. My red blood cells do not mature after entering my body. Much of my blood chemistry runs low and doesn't come up to normal. I received blood in January, 1997, but by December it was dangerously low and they had to give me blood again. My blood levels were greatly improved in January, 1998, but as the year progressed, my blood chemistry dropped monthly. In October, my iron supply dropped to 16 (normal is 45-150). My doctor decided to give me iron two hours daily for six days by IV drip. My platelets, hematocrit, hemoglobin and my white count are always low. My GGT and Alkaline Phosphatase SGOT (ast), SGPT(alt) counts are always high. People on nutritional feeding (TPN) stay "anemic" because the intestines do not absorb nutrients.

Paul E. Billheimer wrote, "Yielding to self-pity, depression and rebellion is a waste of sorrow. Those who have unsuccessfully sought healing, and who submit to resentment, discontentment, impatience and bitterness against God are wasting what God intended for growth in love and thus, for enhanced rank in the eternal Kingdom."

Several months ago, Acie was anxious and concerned. I, too, had been anxious and frustrated about my declining health. I was totally unprepared for the reflection that met my eyes the day I took a long look in a mirror and saw my frail skeleton. It was far worse than I had realized. I felt my life slipping away, helpless, and empty. We both were frightened over possibilities ahead. We had to make a decision to be in control of our emotions. We would take control of our negative feelings and start exuding joy, confidence, and purpose. This is difficult to do when one is so weak and ill. It is only through our inner spirit (God in us) that we can be strong. One can feel horrible, but determine with God's help to be happy.

When a person maintains a strong healthy attitude, he or she can send out mixed signals. The strong attitude of not giving-in is an excellent coping tool and self-protective strategy, but also becomes an invitation for misunderstanding about the intensity of your situation.

"Misunderstanding meets the sufferer on every side. The effects of the ceaseless pressure of pain on the human spirit cannot be understood by another. More painful to bear than the illness itself are the misunderstandings, the criticism, the well-intended, but totally wrong judgments passed upon the sufferer by those healthy. The heartbreak of this constant ebbing of the tides of human hope within us keeps these evils ever near. Those misunderstandings come because others have not walked in the sufferer's moccasins and cannot fully comprehend the need. Most do not even try to understand because it is too deep and complicated."

—— Margaret Clarkson

In spite of that, God says, *"Let the 'joy' of the Lord be your strength."* So I try to be cheerful and controlled by God's power and might. A person seeing me might say, "But, you look so good," or "You don't look ill at all," or "How can you be so ill when you look so well?" (Even when I was healthy, my face held my weight. That's my blessing now. My body is nothing but bones and skin, but my face is not bony.) These remarks might be a compliment, or become hurdles in your attempt to cope with the illness. It would be easy to sit and wallow in self-pity, but life is too short to be living miserably. People reach out with compassion and understanding in the best way they know how. People who are sick need to receive compassion wholeheartedly and receive strength and encouragement from it. I am coming to terms with my illness, and I am always glad to be alive. I know first hand of God's power to heal. Now I must learn about God's grace to help me endure illness until God, through His marvelous power, manifests another miracle in my life.

Margaret Clarkson wrote, "Breathe before God the Holy name of Jesus, knowing that nothing is more precious to Him and nothing is more feared by the powers of evil than this strong word - JESUS! By the strength of that name, we can live through the hours, days, weeks and even a life-time of sorrow whether we can pray normally or not."

So often we can only cry with the ancient prophet, "Oh, my God, I am ashamed and blush to lift my face to thee." For God in His mercy will hear. Our prayer life may be, and probably will be, a fluctuating thing. We may be tempted to give up, feeling that the Lord is God of the hills, not of the valleys, but God promised that every valley shall be exalted and the glory of the Lord shall be revealed, and so we persevere. I Kings 20:28, Isaiah 40:4-5. But we must be patient. Such victories are not won in a day. It was only after Abraham had patiently endured that he obtained the promise, and so it is with us." "*We must run with patience the race set before us, looking unto Jesus, the author and finisher of our faith.*" Hebrews 6:15; 12:1-2
— Margaret Clarkson

Many people take their health for granted, especially when they are busy enjoying life to the fullest. No one ever pictures himself or herself battling a chronic, debilitating, progressive disease. One should not be governed by what used to be or live life with "if-only." If you allow your disease to permeate your every thought and deed, it certainly will. "If only" thoughts will take you prisoner if you dwell on them. Life with a disease is just that, life! To accept it is to move on, to integrate the disease into your life, but to deny it from taking over your every thought.

"Accepting" a situation is reaching a plateau of balance and purpose in life.

Saved by the Blood

God in human form entered the world as a baby, named Jesus, to live according to the Father's will. While He walked on earth, He healed the blind, lame, and sick. If that was God's will then, it is still his will today. My belief is based on the fact that God never changes. Jesus not only came to earth to heal and teach his disciples, His ultimate purpose was to come and die on Calvary's cross for us. God and Jesus are one. John 1:1(KJV) says, *"In the beginning was the Word, and the Word was with God, and the Word was God."* The Word refers to Jesus. He came and dwelt among men. He came to earth to give his life to shed his blood for our sin. Only His blood can cover our sin.*"And almost all things are by the law purged by blood; and without the shedding of blood there is no remission of sin."* Hebrews 9:22 (KJV). We would have to pay the price for our sins if Jesus had not paid the price for us.

Jesus came to earth to give His life so you would not have to spend your life here on earth, as well as in eternity, without Him. Do you believe in Him and the things He says? Can you believe, by faith, that Jesus is the Lamb slain for your sin? Would you ask Him to forgive you for your sins? Would you believe that His death on Calvary's Hill was so that you might be covered by His blood and find God's redemption for your soul? Will you ask Him to save you from your sins to make you a part of the family of God?

God has provided a complete salvation which is to be enjoyed in complete triumph. It is our responsibility to die to self and live unto God according to the finished work of Jesus Christ on the cross.

Andrew Murray wrote, "We are to lay hold on the blood and make its power active in our soul. Where the blood is honored, believed in and appropriated as the power of our full redemption, therein is the way opened for the fullness of the Spirit's blessings on our individual lives.

We think of the blood as an event that happened 2000 years ago. Do you see the blood as present and real today? Do you know what the blood can do? Honor the blood and its power to overcome every hindrance. When Jesus died, His blood had power to conquer sin and death. So that Jesus was brought again from the dead by the blood of the everlasting covenant. When I rely on the blood, Jesus makes its power glorious in me. The blood is all-powerful in its effects. We often limit the continuance of its activity to a period of our own active cooperation with it. As long as your faith is actively engaged with it, the blood will manifest its power to you. Commit yourself to the sanctifying power of the blood."

God says, "*Whatsoever touches the altar shall be holy.*" Exodus 29:37. In the Old Testament we learn that the blood had the power to cleanse and sanctify anything that the people laid upon the altar. This remains true for us today. What I lay on the altar is sanctified and made holy. I must believe that what I have given is accepted by God. Only then can the blood exercise its power.

The only sin God will not forgive is the sin of disbelief. His blood covers every other sin. If you want your heart to be clean, Jesus stands with arms outstretched saying, "*Come to me, all you who are weary and burdened, and I will give you rest.*" Matthew 11:28 (NIV). If you don't know Him, today can be the start of the "new" you. He's waiting now. He is knocking at your heart's door. Will you let Him come into your heart? If you want to invite Him into your heart, here are the four simple steps:

Admit that you are a lost sinner. *"For all have sinned and come short of the glory of God."* Romans 3:23 (KJV).

Believe that Jesus can save you. *"That if thou shalt confess with thy mouth the Lord Jesus, and shalt believe in thine heart that God hath raised him from the dead, thou shalt be saved. For with the heart man believeth unto righteousness; and with the mouth confession is made unto salvation."* Romans 10:9,10 (KJV).

Repent of your sin. *"If we confess our sins, He is faithful and just to forgive us our sins, and to cleanse us from all unrighteousness."* I John 1:9 (KJV).

Receive Jesus as Lord and Savior. *"But as many as received Him, to them gave He power to become the children of God, even to them that believe on His name."* John 1:12 (KJV); *"He that believeth on the Son hath everlasting life; and he that believeth not the Son shall not see life, but the wrath of God abideth on him."* John 3:36 (KJV), and *"How shall we escape, if we neglect so great salvation, which at the first began to be spoken by the Lord, and was confirmed unto us by them that heard Him."* Hebrews 2:3 (KJV).

Do you want to receive Jesus? Read the verses above and agree with God who knows your condition. (That's called confession.) Confess it. Ask Him to take control of your life. (That's called Lordship.) Finally, trust that He is able to do what He has promised to do, then you can thank Him for doing it. You are a born-again believer, a baby in Christ Jesus. Seek out a mature Christian to disciple you, and find a church home where you can learn how to serve Him, a church where people are getting born again and praising God.

We can know the will of God in a specific matter as the Holy Spirit speaks to our spirit. How can we know we are born again? Paul wrote, *"For His Holy Spirit speaks to us deep in our hearts, and tells us that we really are God's children."* Romans 8:16. We know of our relationship with Christ by the witness of the Holy Spirit to our spirit. So it is with knowing the will of God. With that assurance from the Spirit, we can make our request to the Father with full confidence and assurance in His Word.

We need to read the Bible for our spiritual growth. If we fail this requirement, our spiritual growth will be stunted.

The Apostle Paul says, "*I pray that you will begin to understand how incredibly great His power is to help those who believe Him. There is nothing God cannot do for us.*" In Proverbs we read, "*Blessings chase the righteous.*" Proverbs 13:21b.

The righteousness of God is ours. Authority over the devil is ours. We truly have a very rich inheritance in Christ Jesus. Charles Allen wrote, "God is our source of supply and His blessings are not limited by human resources that are available."

Walking and Talking with Jesus

Because I have seen miracles and tragedies in my life, I have confidence God is able to sustain me through it all. My second book published in 1993 by Full Court Press is entitled, "<u>Walking and Talking with Jesus</u>." I subtitled the work, "Building Faith before Tragedy" and was finishing that work when I fell and in effect, broke my body.

God never ceases to amaze me. When the child of God is willing to trust Him, He measures out exactly what is needed so our life can prove him faithful to His word. If you have ever had trouble maintaining a lively and vital prayer life, I believe "Walking and Talking with Jesus" will inspire you. The tragedy of my situation has taught me about a faith in God that trusts God to provide everything. Some people can trust God for great things. The birds of the air rely on Him for basic life. Both are miracles. Neither diminishes the importance of the other. He is a miracle working God. No miracle is small! Neither is the importance of the recipient determined by the "size" of the miracle.

If you are having difficulty coping with life, God's word promises that Jesus Christ will stick "closer than a brother." He can be a friend, companion, and lover literally walking and talking with you in a relationship that will endure. You can grow through the circumstances that have made you prisoner. I believe you will be challenged to become the Savior's companion as well.

In John 13:34, 35 and I Thessalonians 4:9, 5:11, the Bible instructs Christians to live reciprocally within the family of Christ. That means that I love you and you love me. I encourage you and you encourage me. I pray for you and you pray for me. I am certain that those prayer warriors are responsible for the victories I experience every day. Let's pray for each other and set heavenly forces into action.

Prayer is the foremost tool to move heaven into this life. Jesus prayed, *"Thy kingdom come. Thy will be done in earth as it is in heaven."* Matthew 6:10 (KJV). God has promised He will answer and never forsake us if we trust and seek Him. Psalms 9:10 (KJV). The Bible is filled with examples of God's answers to prayer for those who sought Him.

God answers prayer. Count on it! Whatever God has promised in His word, He will do. If you are abiding in God and His Word, He will give you your heart's desire according to His will. Just be sure you are praying in accordance with His will, and that you are abiding close to the master. God says we are to be filled with the knowledge of His will; therefore, we can expect God to reveal His will to us. God will answer no matter how dark your situation, God's word remains true. The failure to believe God is the oldest sin of all, dating all the way back to the Garden of Eden. Do you believe God? Do you spend time with Him in the Garden, walking and talking with Him? If you want to get close to God, spend time with Him. Begin courting his presence. In this kind of relationship you will feel secure. God says we are to renew the spirit of our mind. Our mind is our soul. It is where God regenerates and leads us into His rest. A friend told me a long time ago, *"And now just as you trusted Christ to save you, trust Him, too, for each day's problems; live in vital union with Him."* Colossians 2:6 (LB).

You must open your heart to the moving of the Spirit of God. Sow a seed. When you sow a seed, you must wrap your faith around it. Be attached to it like glue. Expect great things from God. God is spirit and He gave man a spirit so that He could come to Him and mingle his own life with man's life. Your only activity should be to yield yourself completely to the inner workings of the spirit. Jesus Christ comes into your inner being the day you ask Christ into your life; yield to His workings.

A Recap of Fresh Miracles

The path of the Christian is strewn with God's daily miracles. My life is evidence of that fact. In April, 1996, my life was spared. It had become impossible for my body to hold food; I was mal-nutritioned and dehydrated. The doctor put me on Total Nutritional Feeding (TPN) by IV drip, fourteen hours daily. I am kept alive by the TPN. I cannot eat food nor drink fluids. God feeds the sparrows, and He feeds me one drip at a time.

In January, 1997, I entered the hospital with pneumonia, an infected bladder and infection in my Hickman line. Infection in the Hickman line can quickly become a life and death situation. I hallucinated for days because my electrolytes were low. I was given blood, and gradually pulled through by the grace of God.

December, 1997, was when I had the multiplication of mouth ulcers. My blood count was very low. For a week I did not realize I was in the hospital. They gave me blood, but I was very sick and my body didn't respond to the treatment. Days later the doctor told Acie, "Marolyn will not be able to survive this. You need to prepare for her burial. If by chance she does survive, she will be in a nursing home for the rest of her life." I did survive! God raised me up from death's bed and I praise the Lord everyday that I am not in a nursing home!

Acie still cannot believe I am able to live on "nutritional feeding." He thought the body would not be able to survive without the intake of food. With each day that passes, he feels I am one day closer to my heavenly home. Food is vitally important to sustain life. Since I cannot eat or drink, Acie thinks I am an angel because I am alive. To him I am more in heaven than I am on earth.

On the evening of February 10, 1998, a telephone call came for me from a long distance caller, a lady who said she felt heavily burdened for me. She told me that she had been trying to reach me all day without success. I listened as she began to tell me she had heard my testimony several years earlier and has had a burden to pray for me. She said a friend had been keeping her apprised of my deteriorating condition and she knew of my near death experience in January and December, 1997. She said, "I feel so strongly that I need to pray with you. I can't get you off my heart. I have a missionary friend here with me and I wonder if you would mind if I ask her to pray for you right here over the telephone?" I replied, "Sure, I would love for you to pray with me. I need all the prayer I can get." She began to voice a fervent prayer taking authority over the devil and praying for every part of my body, for total healing of my digestive system and autonomic disorder. She prayed a hedge of protection around me. After we prayed, I thanked her and asked her to continue to remember me in prayer as I would for her.

The next day I went to the Lab for my weekly blood test. One of the great dangers of having a Hickman central line is that blood clots can form in the tubing. If that happens the blockage could move directly into my heart and become a matter life and death. I have my blood drawn and tested weekly. The nurse always draws saline into the syringe, then inserts it into the tubing before drawing out my blood supply.

This particular day, February 11, 1998, the nurse had a problem inserting the saline. She could not push it through the tubing. It was blocked. She tried again and again. Since she couldn't push the saline into the tubing, she pulled back on the syringe and when she did a large clot of blood broke loose and came into the syringe. "That's a huge clot," the nurse said. "If that had been pushed through, it would have gone directly into your heart. You know what that would have meant! Let me check to see if there are any more clots in the tubing. She pulled back on another syringe and drew out a couple small pieces from the line.

I love the way God had a Christian surgeon in Michigan who specialized in the Hickman line surgery on duty the night of July 24, 1998. We were visiting my family and had gone to dinner when my Hickman line (my nutritional feeding tube) caught on something, snapped, and broke. The doctor had to replace my Hickman line. God is watching over and caring for me in so many ways. I praise Him for it all.

Do you believe in miracles? I do! I can't live without them! When the Lord brought that clot out of my tubing instead of allowing it to go into my heart, that was a miracle! People are praying for me. They rally around the throne praying for me. *"Thanks be unto God who causes us to triumph in Christ Jesus."* 2 Corinthians 2:14. Our Lord knows the way through the wilderness. He knows the way that I take.

Complete in Him

Be aware that our big sin as believers is not believing God to do what He says He will do. That has to grieve the heart of God very deeply. When sin and disbelief are present in our lives, we cannot claim the promises of God. This is scary. Without the ability to claim the promises of God, we are powerless. We must assume the responsibility to deal with sin. This is of maximum importance if we are to keep a right relationship with God. When our relationship with Him is right, we can expect Him to keep His promises to us; and He will! God will bring glory to Himself in meeting our needs as we hold a firm faith and trust in Him. Paul said, *"And my God shall supply all your need according to his riches in glory by Christ Jesus."* Philippians 4:19 (KJV).

No one can live a life of "sinless perfection." That's why God made a way for us to confess our sins daily. Neither is "sinless perfection" a prerequisite for God's marvelous healing grace manifested in the life of a child of God. *"Is any one sick? He should call for the elders of the church and they should pray over him and pour a little oil upon him, calling on the Lord to heal him. And their prayer, if offered in faith, will heal him, for the Lord will make him well; and if his sickness was caused by some sin, the Lord will forgive him."* James 5:14,15 (LB). The prayer offered in faith is the only requirement for healing. If sin contributes to the sickness, then the Lord will forgive that as well.

"Dear Friends (believers), God the Father chose you long ago and knew you would become one of His children. The Holy Spirit has been at work in your hearts, cleansing you with the blood of Jesus Christ and making you to please Him. May God bless you richly and grant you increasing freedom from all anxiety and fear. All honor to God, the God and Father of our Lord Jesus Christ; for it is His boundless mercy that has given us the privilege of being born again, so we are now members of God's own family." I Peter 1:2-3a (LB).

"And God has reserved for his children the priceless gift of eternal life; it is kept in heaven for you, pure and undefiled, beyond the reach of change and decay. And God, in His mighty power, will make sure you get there safely to receive it, because you are trusting in Him. It will be yours in that coming last day for all to see. So be truly glad! There is wonderful joy ahead, even though the going is rough for a while down here. These trials are only to test your faith to see whether or not it is

strong and pure." I Peter 1:4-7a (LB) *"so if your faith remains strong after being tried in the test tube of fiery trial, it will bring much praise, glory and honor on the day His return."* I Peter 1:7b (LB)

My! That makes my heart leap for joy. We belong to Christ, and He is the one who is directing our steps. He knows the steps we take from here to Glory, and may he find us faithful. Let this be a comfort to those of you who are going through great trials. The devil wants to heap guilt upon those who are sick by making them feel they have committed a sin and that the trial they are going through is due to something they have done. Always remember it's the devil who lays heavy guilt upon people. The Holy Spirit brings conviction, not guilt, and His burden is always light.

If you have been hiding from God because you have a sin that is not dealt with, Genesis tells us of the fall of man and how man turned his back on God and chose to live independently. *"Then the man and his wife heard the sound of the Lord God as He was walking in the garden in the cool of the day, and they hid from the Lord God among the trees of the garden."* But the Lord God called to the man, *"Where are you?"* He (Adam) answered, *"I heard you in the garden, and I was afraid because I was naked; so I hid."* Genesis 3:8,9 (NIV). Go to God . . . He's looking for you. Sin has to be dealt with on a regular basis.

Listen to David as he writes with joy and excitement. *"Come and hear, all of you who reverence the Lord, and I will tell you what He did for me. For I cried to Him for help, with praises ready on my tongue. He would not have listened if I had not confessed my sins. But He listened! He heard my prayer! He paid attention to it! Blessed be God who didn't turn away when I was praying, and didn't refuse me His kindness and love."* Psalm 66:16-20. David was conscious of the need to confess sin before he brought his requests into the presence of the Lord. Harbored sin in the life hinders the Lord from hearing our prayers.

It is normal for Christians, born of the Spirit of God, to covet spiritual development and to forsake worldliness and sin. The Christian lays aside his self life. It is abnormal for him not to do this because he is now born of the Holy Spirit and cannot enjoy the things of the world anymore.

Christians experience a full salvation - salvation unto eternal life, as well as daily salvation. This is true due to our position in Christ. The Holy Spirit has released us from the power of the old nature. Our "desires" and "want-to's" have changed. Things once loved are no longer desired.

God's people must develop a deep sense of those things that displease the Lord. Each one of us is personally responsible for sin in our lives. Sin must be exposed, denounced, confessed and forsaken. We must hate sin, recognizing that it offends Holy God.

Personal faith in Christ demands holy living. Paul wrote to Titus, *"For the free gift of eternal salvation is now being offered to everyone; and along with this gift comes the realization that God wants us to turn from godless living and sinful pleasures and to live good, God-fearing lives day after day."* Titus 2:11-12. It is our responsibility to progress in holiness and in a disciplined life. We are not to seek ways to satisfy our evil, fleshly desires.

Paul said, *"So, dear brothers, you have no obligations whatever to your old sinful nature to do what it begs you to do. For if you keep on following it you are lost and will perish, but if through the power of the Holy Spirit you crush it and its evil deeds, you shall live. For all who are led by the Spirit of God are sons of God."* Romans 8:12-14.

Watchman Nee said, "Just asking for the Spirit to take complete authority over our soul is a wrong assumption, for unless 'we' deliver to death our natural life, its power and self-will; unless we wholly desire in our mind and will to obey and rely wholly upon the Holy Spirit, we will not see Him actually performing.

We must be ready to have His life so fill our Spirit that the soul life is immobilized. The Lord uses His Word to separate Soul and Spirit. Be willing to obey every 'word' as God has commanded."

We are not to live in bondage to the flesh but are to actively co-operate with God as He works in our lives. Neither the devil nor Christ can do anything in our lives without our consent. Our strength to overcome sin and wrong comes through the resurrection power of Jesus Christ within us. If God is going to deliver us, then we must allow Him to do it. This is accomplished as the deeds of the body are put to death by the Holy Spirit, and by the act of our will. It is futile to try to reform or to change. Rather, we must declare ourselves dead to sin. Paul wrote, "*So look upon your old sin nature as dead and unresponsive to sin, and instead be alive to God, alert to Him, through Jesus Christ our Lord.*" Romans 6:11. As Christians, we need to be sold out to Jesus Christ with a heart that yearns to live a holy life. Solomon wisely said, "*Winking at sin leads to sorrow; bold reproof leads to peace.*" Proverbs 10:10.

Pray Even When it is Difficult

Sometimes when we go to God in prayer and call out to Him from the innermost chamber of our being, we feel like we're talking to Him from a dark, cold room. All of God's children should desire to feel and experience the presence of the Holy Spirit every time they pray, but sometimes that just doesn't happen. Sometimes when in prayer we feel cold and weak. The Lord seems to be far off. Remember what the Lord says: "Stand silent! Know that I am God!" (Psalm 46:10a). Even in these times, God is working in our spirit. Our minds may not comprehend this encounter with God since we do not feel His power or have the ability to exercise faith to believe Him. Trust His promise, ". . . I will never, never fail you nor forsake you" (Hebrews 13:5b). Remember God is the one who gave you the desire to pray. He is drawing you by His Spirit.

Grace to Endure

When we have a difficult time in prayer, we must continue to pursue after God. When we do this, we will grow spiritually as we focus the full attention of our innermost spirit upon Him Who is within us. We must not allow restlessness or anxiety to creep in. Remember that the Holy Spirit is within you all the time.

David had hope in God! He said, *"I shall yet praise him again. Yes, I shall again praise him for his help. Yet I am standing here depressed and gloomy, but I will meditate upon your kindness. But 0 my soul, don't be discouraged. Don't be upset. Expect God to act! For I know that I shall again have plenty of reason to praise him for all that he will do. He is my help! He is my God!"* (Psalm 42:4-6a; 11).

David also prayed, *"I am poor and weak, yet the Lord is thinking about me right now! 0 my God, you are my helper. You are my Savior; come quickly, and save me. Please don't delay!"* Psalm 40:17 (LB). In Psalm 66 we read, *"Come and hear, all of you who reverence the Lord, and I will tell you what he did for me: For I cried to him for help, with praises ready on my tongue. He would not have listened if I had not confessed my sins. But he listened! He heard my prayer! He paid attention to it! Blessed be God who didn't turn away when I was praying, and didn't refuse me his kindness and love."* Psalm 66:16-20 (LB).

When we feel cold and far from God as we seek His face in prayer, we need to do as David did. Sin gives the feeling of coldness and darkness. We must confess our sin. With unconfessed sin in our lives, we cannot force God to listen to our prayers for He will not hear, no matter how hard and earnestly we pray.

David confessed his sins and rested in the assurance that God would answer his prayers. His gloom and discouragement were replaced with joy and encouragement. He said, *"O my soul, why be so gloomy and discouraged? Trust in God! I shall again praise him for his wondrous help; he will make me smile again, for he is my God."* Psalm 43:5.

We need to keep in mind the admonition of James, ". . . *The earnest prayer of a righteous man has great power and wonderful results.*" James 5:16b.

As children of God, sometimes our hearts are so uncertain and we feel God is so far away from us. Our confidence and assurance sometimes fluctuate. We must learn to develop a spirit of complete trust in Him, not based on our feelings.

God has provided a oneness in Christ for us. Our trust in God by faith is based upon our position in Christ. We can come boldly to the throne of Grace, anytime and anywhere. All who have been born again, cleansed by the blood of Christ and resurrected in Him, have the right and authority to come into the presence of Almighty God fearlessly and with boldness. Always remember a clean conscience is necessary for great faith. Ours is a high and holy calling of God in His Son, Jesus Christ. However, if your heart condemns you, then it is likely that you have sinned. On the other hand, the devil sometimes accuses God's children unjustly.

When we know we have confessed and turned from all known sin, and yet we feel depressed, or lack assurance and confidence in God, we need to be aware that Satan tries to cut off our communication with our heavenly Father. Satan sends these feelings to us to hinder our prayers and make them ineffective. We must guard against his attacks. He takes away our desire to pray, makes us feel unworthy of God's provisions and causes us not to trust God to answer. Satan is working against us all of the time. He makes us feel restless, unhappy and out of sorts. He robs us of our joy and peace. Paul had to resist Satan and thus the evil spirit left him. Satan is overcome by the blood of the Lamb. Permit the Holy Spirit to take control of your life! Don't be hesitant or defeated when you don't feel God's power. It's not how you feel that counts. Believe God and accept Him by faith.

The blood Jesus shed on Calvary's cross will never lose its power. God's forgiveness is always there for us, anytime we ask Him for it. God does not want us guilt-ridden. The blood covers us from all unrighteousness. When we suffer with a prolonged illness, Satan tries to imprison our spirit. When we are bound in spirit, we tend to withdraw. It's a "weight of oppression" upon us. It comes over our spirit to deprive us of our light joyful happiness. It renders us powerless to live life in all its fullness. At sometime in life, everyone experiences a feeling of withdrawal that weighs them down. One may think that is normal, and therefore, disregard it. But if we are aware that a spirit of oppression has come upon us, then we will know to fight against it. We must set our will against it and resist the "spirit of opposition" through prayer, praise, and worship.

David knew about days of defeat in his inner spirit. He spoke to himself when he asked, *"Why art thou cast down, O my soul? Why art thou disquieted within me?"* Psalms 42:5 (KJV). He felt hemmed in, and he learned to pray his way out of it by singing praises to God. As he did this, the blockage lifted and his spirit was freed. David said, *"My mouth will praise thee with joyful lips."* Psalms 63:5b (KJV). "I will love thee, O Lord, my strength. The Lord is my rock, my fortress, my deliverer; my God, my strength, in whom I will trust; my buckler, and the horn of my salvation, and my high tower. I will call upon the Lord, who is worthy to be praised; so shall I be saved from my enemies." Psalms 18:1-3 (KJV).

There are times we feel God so near, our soul leaps for joy. Other times we feel sick at heart, even worse when we think we are to blame because of our unfaithfulness and disobedience. That gives us a distressed conscience. To seek forgiveness day after day before the throne of God seems blasphemous. You wonder how a holy God can have anything to do with you in that state. Don't torment yourself! God will take away the weary restlessness. Never lose your confidence before God. He sees you through the blood of Jesus Christ. You stand before Him perfectly righteous; therefore, you are accepted in the Beloved. That gives you the right to come to God and ask for deliverance from the fiery trial that tries your soul.

Why Does A Person Get Sick?

Some people mistreat their bodies with obesity, drugs, smoking, alcohol, and lack of exercise and sleep. If we get sick in those situations, we can't blame anyone but ourselves. It is not God's fault. Others contract germs, disease or suffer from the effects of aging. But, in any case, the end result is the same. Sickness causes us to realize just how fragile and temporary life is. If illness does anything positive, it causes a Christian to look up. Not by reason that one is bedfast, but to receive strength, patience and endurance from the Lord to be able to keep on going, living with all the pain and anguish.

I have received countless cards and letters from people around the world. They are a joy to me. They are my life-line prayer partners. Most of them say they are praying for me, that God would give me the strength to endure and the patience to wait for God's answer. Some believe that a lack of faith is responsible for my condition. Some also believe that I need to make sure there is no unconfessed sin in my life. If healing doesn't manifest itself then, I should search my heart deeper for a sin problem of which I am not aware. My faith should immediately bring about my healing. The godly Christian is a healthy Christian and anything less demonstrates a lack of faith. However, this places all the responsibility for healing upon the sick and places them under guilt. God does not hold us accountable for sins of which we are not aware. But once He has dealt with us regarding a specific sin, we are responsible and must turn from that sin, or we will pay the price.

Sickness can be caused for three reasons. One is because of sin in the life. Paul addressed this type of sickness in I Corinthians 11:27-30 (NIV),"*Therefore, whoever eats the bread or drinks the cup of the Lord in an unworthy manner will be guilty of sinning against the body and blood of the Lord. A man ought to examine himself before he eats of the bread and drinks of the cup. For anyone who eats and drinks without recognizing the body of the Lord eats and drinks judgment on himself. That is why many among you are weak and sick, and a number of you have fallen asleep.*" Many kings in the old testament were afflicted due to sin in their lives. Some had confessed and were delivered, others didn't confess and died. One is a sickness to the glory of God. This type sickness is referred to in John 9:1-3 (NIV). "*As He went along, He saw a man blind from birth. His disciples asked Him, 'Rabbi, who sinned, this man or his parents, that he was born blind?' Neither this man nor his parents sinned*", said Jesus, but this happened so that the work of God might be displayed in his life." One is sickness unto death. In 2 Kings 5, Elisha was instrumental in the healing of Naaman. Elisha was a Godly man who walked with God and then sickness came upon him and according to 2 Kings 13:14, it was a sickness unto death.

If it is a sickness caused by sin, we must reconcile it with God, turn from that sin, ask God for forgiveness and anyone else involved, and accept God's cleansing and forgiveness. Jeremiah 18:1-6 (KJV) says we are like clay in the potter's hand. "*O house of Israel, can I not do with you as this potter? says the Lord. As the clay is in the potter's hand so are you in my hand, O house of Israel.*" God almighty is remodeling the saints. He puts us on the potter's wheel. All things that happen around you are for reshaping you into a better vessel. He looks and sees the marred vessel; He breaks it, melts it and remakes it all over again. When God starts to remold us, He warns us not to fight with our maker. "*Woe unto him who striveth with his maker.*" Isaiah 45:9(KJV) God has a purpose for everything He does. We are not to say, "Why me, Lord."

Why not me? *"Behold, I have refined you but not as silver, I have tested you in the furnace of affliction. **For my own sake** will I do it."* Isaiah 48:18(KJV). If it is a sickness for the glory of God, He says He will not allow more than we can bear in His strength (I Corinthians 10:13), His grace is sufficient; His strength is made perfect in weakness (2 Corinthians 12:9). Therefore, commit your illness to the Lord. If it is a sickness unto death, God's grace is always sufficient in the hour of need.

Sickness is allowed by God because it is part of the curse that was placed upon mankind as the result of Adam's sin in the Garden of Eden. Galatians 3:13 (KJV) says, *"Christ has redeemed us from the curse of the law."* It says in Isaiah 53:4 *"Surely He has born our grief and carried our sorrows."* He bore our pain and suffering. Oh yes, I pray that God will heal me! I believe in the power of God to touch and heal those who are sick. I claim healing for my body just as I prayed and trusted God to give sight to my blind eyes. God answered that prayer and gave me a wonderful marvelous miracle. God is the same yesterday, today and forever! Praise His Holy Name!

Satan buffets God's people. We must dress for the battle by putting on God's special armor, *"the helmet of salvation and the sword of the spirit"*, which is the "Word" of God. We are to stand against the wiles of Satan by faith. Faith is acting upon the revealed Word of God. His Word is true. It has never failed. You stand by the Word of God and the God of the Word will stand by you! Some sickness is designed to bring glory to God even when the devil may be the one causing it. Miracles took place when Jesus walked on earth for wide spread evangelism. We are living in the latter days. In Joel 2:28-30, the prophet Joel predicted that in the last days God would pour out His spirit upon all flesh and He would pour forth His spirit through signs, wonders and miracles. God is still performing miracles today! I am a strong believer in faith healing. I am totally trusting God for deliverance from this terrible disease that has come upon my body.

The power Jesus had when He walked upon earth as a man was given to God's people at Pentecost when Jesus said, "*I am going to my Father. Now you must carry on my work and greater work than I do ye shall do. Go, lay hands on the sick and they shall be healed.*" All are not healed, but that is God's business. When we witness, all are not saved. That also is God's business. Our work is to do what He tells us to do. God said we are to lay hands on the sick. That is our responsibility. What God does with it is His business. Exodus 33:18-25(NIV) says, "*I will have compassion upon whom I will.*" When God answered Job's anguished questions with a reminder that He was God the creator of the universe, Job responded, "*I know that you can do all things; no plan of yours can be thwarted.*" Job 42:2 (NIV). Job came to God in awe realizing that God was too wonderful to comprehend.

The Word of God says, "*Therefore, there is now no condemnation for those who are in Christ Jesus.*" Romans 8:1(NIV). For thirty years Joseph was a righteous man who chose to obey God. Joseph grew up in a house of rejection, was hated and almost killed by his brothers, sold into slavery, blamed by Potiphar's wife, falsely accused, and thrown into prison. He had walked in obedience to God, and had not violated God's principles. Thirty years later he was moved from slavery to prime minister, second only to the Pharoah of Egypt. He was in charge of Potiphar's household, the jail, and over the land of Egypt. God used Joseph's calamity to deliver His people Israel. In the Old Testament we read about saints who suffered trials, hardships, afflictions, persecutions and death for the sake of the gospel. They were not delivered nor protected from disaster. Jesus himself was crucified at the hands of men. God used that act to redeem the world through His selfless act.

God is concerned with the willingness of His people to obey Him and to live in peace within the boundaries of their lives. God will give us the "desire of our heart" when it is in keeping with His wonderful overall great plan. He births a desire within us, and He fulfills that desire when we pray. God heard the weeping of Sarah, Hannah and Elizabeth without condemning their tears. He reached out to them to meet their needs. He sent a High-Priest to Hannah. He sent an Angel to Abraham and Sarah. He allowed Elizabeth the joy of spending part of her pregnancy with Mary.

God didn't send an angel to me, but He sent Christian friends who bring God's love to me. He sends spontaneous offers of help from people who are sensitive to my situation and rally around to help me. He sends friends who say how much they hurt for me. Some can't get the words out for choking on the tears. Others respond by saying, "You're a very special person," or "You inspire me". People seem to know just the right words to say at the right times. God's people aren't always delivered from the terror of the enemy. Through the ages, the greatest men and women in God's service have been tortured, scourged, chained, imprisoned, stoned and killed. Christians can find themselves in horrible situations and sickness. Being in pain and going through trials and tough times does not mean God has abandoned you. He will never leave you nor forsake you.

God says, *"Fear not; for I have redeemed thee...When thou passest through the waters, I will be with thee; and through the rivers, they shall not overflow thee; when thou walkest through the fire, thou shall not be burned, neither shall the flame kindle upon thee. For I am the Lord thy God, the Holy One of Israel, they Savior;"* Isaiah 43:1-3 (KJV).

Job said he was looking for God but couldn't find Him, but God was there all the time. God knew what Job was doing. Job said, *"But He knows the way that I take; when He has tested me, I will come forth as gold."* Job 23:10 (NIV).

Grace to Endure

The Apostle Paul was stoned at Lystra and left for dead. While laying there he had a vision that he was caught up in the third heaven and was in the presence of God. Shortly after this wonderful experience the apostle describes the thorn in his flesh as a "messenger of Satan to buffet him."

In the Believer's Bible Commentary, William MacDonald wrote, "In one sense this represents an effort on Satan's part to hinder Paul in the work of the Lord. But God is greater than Satan, and He used the thorn to further God's work by keeping Paul humble.

In 2 Corinthians 12:8, Paul pleaded three times with the Lord that the thorn in the flesh might depart from him. In verse 9, Paul's prayer was answered but not in the way he hoped. In effect, God said to Paul, I will not remove the thorn, but I will do something better; I will give you grace to bear it. And just remember Paul, that although I have not forgotten you and what you asked for, I am giving you what you need most deeply. You want my power and strength to accompany your preaching, don't you? Well, the best way to have that happen is to keep you in a place of weakness. This was God's repeated answer to Paul's repeated prayer. And it continues to be God's answer to his suffering people throughout the world. Better than the removal of trial and suffering is the companionship of the Son of God in them and the assurance of His strength and enabling grace.

Notice that God says, '*My grace is sufficient for you.*' We don't have to ask Him to make His grace sufficient, it already is! The apostle is completely satisfied with the Lord's answer, so he says, '*Therefore, most gladly will I rather boast in my infirmities, that the power of Christ may rest upon me.*' When the Lord explained the wisdom of His actions, instead of complaining and grumbling about the thorn, in effect, Paul said he would not want it any other way. He would rather boast in his infirmities.

He would get down on his knees and thank God for them and gladly endure them if only the power of Christ might rest upon him.

J. Oswell Sanders puts it well,

> "The world's philosophy is what can't be cured must be endured." But Paul radiantly testifies, *'What can't be cured can be enjoyed.'* He also said, *'I enjoy weakness, sufferings, privations and difficulties.'* So wonderful did he prove God's grace to be, that he even welcomed fresh occasions of drawing upon its fullness. *'I gladly glory. I even enjoy my thorn.'* The apostle Paul had his calamities. He was God's chosen servant to take the Gospel to the Gentile world. He was chosen to demonstrate the power of God. Remarkably, Paul the apostle laid hands on people and they were healed, but as far as we know, Paul died bearing his own "thorn in the flesh" and he said he bore it to the glory of God."

Ready To Get Those Tickets?

It had been one and one half years since we had seen Sharon, John and the children. Spring and summer were rapidly passing us by. I had this strong desire, a great emotional need, to see my children. If we didn't make the trip soon, the Alaskan winter would be set in and we would not be able to see them for another year. I was hurting to see them. Acie refused to make the trip over and over again because he truly felt that the trip would be too much for me. He feared that it would weaken my body and I would be more susceptible to infections. He truly feared it would cost me my life.

March came and I said, "Acie, we need to make our flight reservations for Alaska 30 days in advance. So if we can work our schedules right, we can go see the children in April." April passed - May, June, July and he kept holding back. He wouldn't consider the trip. I had a couple of mothers at the church try to help me persuade him that this trip had to be taken based on the fact that mothers need to see their children. I was grieving because Acie wouldn't agree to the trip and we'd have to wait another year before we would be able to go if we didn't schedule it for August or September. Who knows what next year may bring - none of us can count our tomorrow's.

Two mothers highly respected by Acie had just talked with Acie about what this trip would mean to me and how necessary it was that I go. Acie was beginning to plot in his mind of trying to make the trip. One week he would be more positive about it, but the next week fear of losing me took over....so back and forth things went. One day he came in and said, "We'll fly into Anchorage, Alaska and take a motel room and let the kids drive over to visit us there." He didn't want me to make that one last flight into Homer, Alaska where they live. I said, "No way, if we can't go to Homer, I don't care about going." I said, "Acie, I need to see the house they live in, their bedrooms, the kitchen, where the telephones are located in the house, the grocery store where they shop, meet their friends and experience going to church with them where they worship. I have this need to see them in their setting and feel their love in the atmosphere of their home. When they telephone us I want to visualize them there. That brings a wonderful feeling of closeness."

July 24th was already upon us and if we made the trip in late August or September, the 30 day advance tickets had to be purchased now or winter would set in and we would not be able to go in 1999. It would be too cold for me. Our daughter, Sharon e-mailed the following letter. As Acie read it he could hardly read between the tears.

Dad,
I was thinking about Mom. She said she isn't doing those classes anymore - therapy. What is she doing? Is she out and about during the day? You know she and John cannot be still for a minute! It truly makes them sick. It is depressing to them. I hope her spirits are still up. I remember when I lived in Dover. The ederly lady across the street had been mowing her own grass. Her chil-

dren said she wasn't capable anymore. She went down fast after that. I am sure you see that a lot with the Senior Adults at the church. There is something about having your freedom and independence. What independence does she have? What, other than sit around the house, is she doing? Is she going shopping - grocery store? Mall? Visiting the hospital? The elderly? The sick? Friends? She needs this stuff ALOT!!! Is she feeling like these old people that have it all then suddenly get old and can't do anything? Does she feel grounded like a teenager without a car? Does she feel helpless? Out of control? If I couldn't do what I needed to do when I needed to do it, I would be out of control, angry, depressed, in bad shape. When I need a break, I jump in the car and go. She can't. I know you do the best you can. But what else can be done? Can you drop her off at the mall for an hour or two in her scooter? There are lots of people around the mall to help if she gets to feeling bad. Of course, there is always your beeper....

I know seeing the grandkids would do so much good! Even if it is too much on her, I think emotional health is as important as physical health. What does she have to look forward to? What goals? What is planned that she can revolve her thoughts around? You have plans - You go to work, to the hospital, to the park, to eat with friends, to do the funerals, the weddings, out for a day with Steve, to prayer time with the staff, to Wed. night dinner, to eat with the staff, to deacon's meetings, to visitation - You get the idea!!! Mom looks forward to.... church on Sunday, a speaking engagement a month from now and NOTHING ELSE!!!

I'm not preaching at you. I know you do a lot!!! More than a little. You do the BEST you can do. I just feel like something is missing in her life right now. One more thing, Dad - there is a need God instills in every woman. It is the God given desire to please her husband. We want to cook you the best dinners you ever had, keep a clean house for you, keep your shirts ironed for when you need them. Do you see how our lives revolve around our husbands? A man gets a scoop of ice cream for he and his wife. He gives her the smaller piece. A woman always gives her husband the biggest and the best. When all the guests are over for dinner and she serves the salad, I guarantee from my own experience, if you like Mandarin oranges, your salad will have more Mandarin oranges than anyone else's because it is a way she can show her love for you. I clean John's toes, rub his back, all sorts of things to show my love to him. What can Mom do for you? Can she make your bed pretty? Can she vacuum your floors, can she fix you a dinner at 6:00 p.m.? Can she please you in bed? Can she iron your shirts for you? She needs to fulfill your needs!! She can't. That must hurt her! It would me. I'm not telling you to have her make the bed even though her hands, arms and legs can't manage it. I am just letting you know what I have been thinking about all the way up here in Alaska. You know how I always talked to you about her feelings when we were in the living room. Well, we're in the living room and I'm just giving you some things to think about.

By the way, I need to get the tickets purchased. September 17-27. How does that do? I don't want to wait till later - for Mom's sake. It is important that she get here soon. She needs it emotionally. I don't want to push it too close to her speaking engagement. We can't afford it before the engagement because I need 30 day notice and so it must be in September. The 17-27th seems to be the absolute best time for her. John and I have talked about coming to see you, but it wouldn't be as nice for you guys. Plus, we CANNOT afford it for many years. $4,200 plus tax, plus hidden flight charges, plus meals - $5,000 in transportation alone if we were to come see you. The longer we put it off, the worse Mom gets. It would make her crazy to wait till next year, plus, her health will be worse unless God intervenes with a full fledged miracle. Winter is coming soon, so we can't wait till fall for her sake. It is her deepest wish and even if it were the last flight she ever took, I couldn't imagine depriving her of this important request. I do know how bad she is. Grandma Brink tells me, Prayer Tower keeps me informed and she and I talk about twice a week. Of course, I hear it in her trembling voice every time we talk.

I know you've got Steve, but you can talk to me too. I know it is most difficult to see the love of your life go down so painfully and so slowly for son long, such a strong woman, too. You must cry a lot and grieve for the parts of her you've already lost. I'm so sorry. I want you to know this is not a judgmental letter, just some things to think on, okay. I love you, Daddy!!!

Your Baby,

Sharon

P.S. Wanna play checkers at the foot of the bed? You get the BIG bowl of popcorn and put a few kernels on my paper towel, so I would just get them out of your bowl. I wanted to be sure to get as much as you. I loved it when you crunched ice for me to eat. I do that for Jess now. Happy memories - Archie Bunker, Starsky & Hutch, the program with Maude in it. Three's Company AFTER I went to bed. (-:}

Sharon had hit the nail on the head. Her wisdom and deep understanding is from the Lord. Three days later, Acie came to me in the bedroom where I was laying connected to my Parenteral Nutritional Feeding and said, "You better go ahead and purchase those air line tickets to Alaska." I was excited as I asked, "What changed your mind?" He replied, "That letter from Sharon." Thank you, Jesus! Praise the Lord! We were going to see our children! I was so happy!

Acie was yet a bit fearful and greatly concerned. He shared his heart with the ministers attending the pastor's luncheon on Monday, and asked for prayer over my health and the trip. Afterwards, someone gave him a check saying, "Go and have a good time with your family." His eyes filled with tears as he realized that this was confirmation from God he had made the right decision and God's blessing was upon it. Each time Acie began to question his decision, someone else would give toward the trip saying, "We'll be praying that all goes well, Acie. Have a good time."

Two weeks before departure I was getting nervous - not because of my health as much as making sure I didn't leave home without some of my medical supplies. There is the tubing, syringes, medications, etc., etc., not only for the TPN bags and supplies, but the bladder needs as well. This was an awesome undertaking. Although I am a detailed person, blessed with the gift of organization, I knew all the bases had to be covered. Not only did I need to pack the supplies for use at Sharon's house, but I needed bags of nutritional feeding packed on ice for use on the plane so I could connect my feeding while on board the flight. This meant a separate supply of everything. It was nerve racking, but I was determined I could handle it - somehow, I would do it.

As we boarded the plane, I explained to the flight attendant what I had to do while in flight, and showed her a letter of medical necessity from my doctor stating the drugs, needles, etc. are my life substance and cannot be withheld from me. She thanked me for having the letter available and showed it to the pilot and someone inside the terminal before take-off. When she gave it back to me she asked what she could do to help. She felt the big 14 x 8" cold bag of liquid nutrient and said, "Oh, I'd hate to put that cold stuff into my veins." I explained to her that it would drip for 14 hours. She said, "When you get ready to hook up, if you would push the call button, I'll warm the bag for you by wrapping it in warm towels." She was so thoughtful. I didn't know how I was going to warm it up. It cannot be placed in a microwave and even at room temperature it is much too cold for me.

This trip was very profitable. I gained a real education as to how to travel with all my necessary medical supplies as well as my electric scooter. The airline personnel were wonderful to assist us through the airports. They called a mechanic to attach wires on the scooter which had been disconnected to avoid battery connections from throwing off sparks in the luggage department. They helped us with every little emergency.

Our last flight from Anchorage into Homer was scheduled to be "on time" when we arrived at the gate. Shortly thereafter, the sign was changed to "delayed flight." When the gate assistant was no longer busy, I asked about the delay. The attendant said,

"The plane had been running a little behind all day causing the departure planes a little delay." Meanwhile, Sharon and John were waiting for us at the Homer Airport (a 30 minute flight) when she asked the gate attendant why the plane from Anchorage was being delayed. He said, "There's a lady getting on with an electric scooter and we couldn't get it through the luggage door of the plane so they had to swap planes in Anchorage for her." Sharon replied, "Thanks, that's my mom."

Oh, what a joy to see them and all of our five grandchildren. Hugs and kisses, hugs and kisses! We were all so very excited to be together. We all went to bed and the first morning, John said, "Guys, if we want to go out fishing on the boats, we may need to go out today because the forecast is rain for the rest of the week with possible snow on Friday. It has been raining early this morning, but I believe it is going to lift and fair off. So this may be the only day we'll be able to take the boat out." My thoughts were, "Oh, today, already, so soon?" But I said, "Yes, we don't want to miss it, let's go!"

We spent the day fishing, eating lunch on the boat and had a great time! I was totally exhausted, but the boat had not only a kitchen, but also sleeping quarters if I needed to lay down. Just knowing I was with my children was enough for me. My heart was thrilled with unspeakable joy!

The week passed too quickly. It was a long painful trip home, but I knew I could recuperate at home. God was so good to grant me my desire! I praise Him for the strength He gave me and His Grace to Endure!

Thanks be to God

Jesus is worthy of our Praise! Not only did He open my blind eyes, but He has also demonstrated His glory in many ways throughout the earth. His Word says, *"Praise him for the growing fields, for they display his greatness. Let the trees of the forest rustle* with praise." Psalms 96:12 (LB), (NIV), "*He makes the clouds His chariots and rides upon the wings of the wind. He makes winds His messengers, flames of fire His servants.*" Psalms 104:3-4 (NIV). "*The mighty ocean thunders His praise.*" Psalms 93:3 (LB). He is the one and only true God! The Psalmist also says, "*Let the sea in all its vastness roar with praise! Let the earth and all those living on it shout, 'Glory to the Lord'*" (Psalm 98:7-8).

Paul said, "*I will therefore that men pray every where, lifting up holy hands, without wrath and doubting.*" I Timothy 2:8 (KJV). Believers should be the happiest people on planet earth and should express that happiness in exuberant praise to the Lord. So clap your hands!

I believe that the ultimate praise to God is to be found in the clapping and lifting up of holy hands. In Psalms we read, "*O clap your hands, all ye people; shout unto God with the voice of triumph.*" Psalm 47:1 (KJV). Isaiah tells us, "*For ye shall go out with joy, and be led forth with peace: the mountains and the hills shall break forth before you into singing, and all the trees of the field shall clap their hands.*" Isaiah 55:12(KJV). Certainly if the trees of the fields are pictured as applauding God with their leaves and branches, should we do less? "*Lift up your hands in the sanctuary and bless the Lord.*" Psalms 134:2(KJV). I sincerely believe that these words should be taken literally.

God desires that we live our lives in constant glory, praise and honor, both to Him and for Him. Psalms 50:14-15 (LB) says, "*What I want from you is your true thanks; I want your promises fulfilled. I want you to trust me in your times of trouble, so I can rescue you, and you can give me glory.*"

Psalm 96:1-2 says, "*Sing a new song to the Lord! Sing it everywhere around the world! Sing out his praises! Bless his name! Each day tell someone that he saves.*" If we enjoy lifting our voices in praise to the Lord now, what will it be like when we're at home in heaven with Him? It is beyond our comprehension.

It is important for us to learn how to bless (praise) the Lord by bringing into remembrance the glorious things He has done for us. Many Psalms contain lists of praise items. Look at some of the things David listed in Psalm 103.

> *"I bless the holy name of God with all my heart. Yes, I will bless the Lord and not forget the glorious things he does for me.*
>
> *He forgives all my sins. He heals me. He ransoms me from hell. He surrounds me with lovingkindness and tender mercies! He fills my life with good things! My youth is renewed like the eagle's! He gives justice to all who are treated unfairly. He revealed his will and nature to Moses and the people of Israel.*
>
> *He is merciful and tender toward those who don't deserve it; he is slow to get angry and full of kindness and love. He never bears a grudge, nor remains angry forever. He has not punished us as we deserve for all our sins, for his mercy toward those who fear and honor him is as great as the height of the heavens above the earth. He has removed our sins as far away from us as the east is from the west. He is like a father to us, tender and sympathetic to those who reverence him."* Psalms 103:1-13 (LB).

This Psalm of David provides a pattern for us to use when we express our praise to the Lord for all He has done for us.

Our confidence must be in our relationship with Jesus Christ our Lord. We read in Jeremiah, *"But blessed is the man who trusts in the Lord and has made the Lord his hope and confidence."* Jeremiah 17:7.

Paul prayed for the Ephesians, *"That He would grant you, according to the riches of His glory, to be strengthened with power through His Spirit in the inner man: so that Christ may dwell in your hearts through faith: and that you, being rooted and grounded in love, may be able to comprehend with all the saints what is the breadth and length and height and depth, and to know the love of Christ which surpasses knowledge, that you may be filled up to all the fullness of God."* Ephesians 3:16-19 (NAS).

Begin each day saying, "Oh Jesus, I love You, I love You, I love You." Rejoice in the God of your salvation. Allow His warm, tender presence to flood your soul. Pray with the Psalmist, *"How I love your laws! How I enjoy your commands! Come, come to me. I call to them, for I love them and will let them fill my life. Never forget your promises to me your servant, for they are my only hope. They give me strength in all my troubles; how they refresh and revive me."* Psalm 119:47-50. *"Stand ready to help me because I have chosen to follow your will."* Psalm 119:173 Quote scripture to God. He will honor His Word.

Worship God

Worship is essential to prayer. The Psalmist says, *"O magnify the Lord with me, and let us exalt his name together."* Psalm 34:3 (KJV). Intimate fellowship with God comes to us when we magnify Him for Who He is, as well as for all He has done, is doing and will do for us. The Christian is richly blessed who meditates especially on the wonder of it all that "Jesus loves me!"

We should be delighted with the Lord and find our pleasure in obeying Him.

When we are not operating in the Spirit, we know it. But when the soul of man (will, mind and emotion) becomes involved, prayer becomes filled with anxiety, frustration and difficulties on every hand. When prayer is of the Spirit, it is not forced, but is rather very joyous, free and unhindered.

The Spirit of God within us is very powerful. We must keep drawing back to His Spirit, keeping the sweet fellowship with God flowing in and through us as we are before Him in prayer throughout the day.

Lord, perfect us. Let us rejoice in your word. Make it quick and powerful, sharper than any two-edged sword, piercing to the dividing asunder of soul and spirit. And Lord, make it a discerner of the thoughts and intents of the heart. May we be so inspired by your word that we joy in it until we see you, until you come and pour righteousness upon us, until you transform us from spiritual dwarfs to giants in the faith. Even the aged will be fruitful. Clothe each one with the authority of Calvary, the power of Pentecost, and the might of Jesus.

God, may you be glorified through the affliction of your children. You have a purpose in the suffering and you have a purpose in our trials. You allow them to enter our lives for a reason. (Satan has to get God's approval.) May we run after you with our whole heart until we see your power change our lives. May we see your purpose and fulfill it. Amen.

God's Boxes of Love

I have in my hands two boxes
Which God gave me to hold.
He said, "Put all your sorrows in the black,
And all your joys in the Gold."

I heeded His words, and in the two boxes
Both my joys and sorrows I stored.
But though the gold became heavier each day
The black was as light as before.

With curiosity, I opened the black
I wanted to find out why,
And I saw, in the base of the box, a hole
Which my sorrows had fallen out by.

I showed the hole to God, and mused aloud,
"I wonder where my sorrows could be."
He smiled a gentle smile at me,
"My child, they are all here with me."

I asked, "God, why give me the boxes
Why the gold, and the black with the hole?
"My child, the gold is for you to count your blessings,
And the black is for you to let go."

Much of my pain and distress over the past years has been chronic and will continue until God, in His ultimate wisdom, says it is time to do another miracle. I am asking God not to wait another thirteen years to bring about this miracle. I have received my healing by Faith. I am trusting God for the manifestation of my healing. Until that day, I'll serve Him joyfully with a song in my heart and a spring in my step because Jesus is Lord! He is my Rapha, my healer and my deliverer. Blessed be the name of the Lord!

Jesus says, *"My son, attend to my Words, incline thine ear unto my sayings. Let them not depart from thine eyes, keep them in the midst of thine heart. For they (God's words) are life unto those that find them, and "health" to all their flesh."* Proverbs 4:20-22 (KJV). Let the scripture minister to your spirit.

Bibliography

Prayer Changes Things by Charles Allen
Spire Press, 1974.

All Things Are Possible Through Prayer by Charles Allen
Fleming H. Revell, Publisher,6030 Fulton St., Grand Rapids,
MI 49301

The Spiritual Man by Watchman Nee, 1977
Christian Fellowship Publishers, 11515 Allecingie Pkwy.,
Richmond, VA 23235

Something To Live By by Dorothea S. Kopplin, 1945
Doubleday and Company, Inc.,1540 Broadway, New York, NY
10036

Practical Religion by John Charles Ryle, D.D., Reprinted 1977
Baker Book House, P. O. Box 6287, Grand Rapids, MI 49516

Don't Waste Your Sorrows by Paul E. Billheimer, (c) 1977,
Christian Literature Crusade, Box 1449, Ft. Washington, PA
19034-8449

Grace Grows Best in Winter by Margaret Clarkson, (c) 1984,
W. B. Erdman Publishing Co., 255 Jefferson S.E., Grand
Rapids, MI 49503-4570

Making Sense out of Suffering by Jack Wintz, (c) 1996,
Abby Press, 1 Hill Drive, St. Meinrad, IN 47577

Believer's Bible Commentary by William MacDonald, (c) 1917
Thomas Nelson Publisher, Nashville, Tennessee 37201
Pages 1865-1866. Used by permission

The Ministry Of Intercession by Andrew Murray
Whitaker House, 1982

The Prayer Life by Andrew Murray
Moody Press, 820 N. La Salle, Chicago, IL 68610

PERMISSION FOR SONGS

(1)   Nothing but the Blood, by Robert Lowrey (c) 1826-1899

(2)   In the Garden, by C. Austin Miles (c) 1912, 1940 Rodeheaver Co.

(3)   Only Believe, by Paul Radar (c) 1950, The Rodeheaver, Hallmark Co.,   Winona Lake, Indiana

(4)   You are my Sunshine by Jimmy Davis

(5)   Beautiful, Beautiful Brown Eyes

(6)   Turn Your Eyes Upon Jesus by Helen H. Lemmel

           (c) 1972, Benson Music Group

(7)   Every Moment of Every Day by Norman Clayton (c) 1967, Word, Inc.

(8)   Cleanse Me by Maor: Melody (c) 1958 New Songs of Inspiration #3

(9)   His Eye Is On The Sparrow by Charles H. Gabriel

           (c) 1934 Homer A. Rodeheaver

(10)   Until Then by Stuart Hamblen (c) 1958 Hamblen Music Co.

(11)   Rock of Ages, Cleft For Me - Psalms 94:22 Words Augustus M. Toplady 1775, 1776. Tune Toplady, Thomas Hastings, 1832

(12)   Satisfied by Clara Tear Williams, 1858-1937; Ralph E. Hudson 1848-1901

(13)   Learning To Lean by John Stallings, 1976, 1983 by Heart Warming Music Co. of Benson Co., Nashville, Tennessee used by permission

(14)   O For A Thousand Tongues, by Charles Wesley (c) 1739

(15)   Every Promise In The Book Is Mine, by Pearl Spencer Smith (c) 1937, Singspiration

How to contact the Author

Marolyn Ford

P.O. Box 341571

Memphis, Tn 38134

www.marolynford.com

E-Mail: marolyn@marolynford.com